BULLO

THE NEXT GENERATION

MARLEE RANACHER

BULLO

THE NEXT GENERATION

RANDOM HOUSE AUSTRALIA

Random House Australia Pty Ltd
20 Alfred Street, Milsons Point, NSW 2061
http://www.randomhouse.com.au

Sydney New York Toronto
London Auckland Johannesburg

First published by Random House Australia 2003

National Library of Australia
Cataloguing-in-Publication Entry

Ranacher, Marlee
Bullo : the next generation

ISBN 1 74051 155 7.

1. Ranacher, Marlee. 2. Henderson family. 3. Women
ranchers – Northern Territory – Bullo River Station –
Biography. 4. Bullo River Station (N.T.). I. Title.

636.0092

Cover photography by David Hancock, SkyScans
Jacket and text design by Gayna Murphy, Greendot Design
Typeset by Midland Typesetters, Maryborough, Victoria
Printed and bound by Griffin Press, Netley, South Australia

To Franz

If a wish were mine
In this life we will be together until I dream no more
In eternity that you will find me again
That I shall always love you so.

PROLOGUE

I HAVE ALWAYS BEEN AN OPTIMISTIC PERSON. There have been many challenges in my life but I've always met them head on. That's the way I was raised by my father, for better or worse.

However, I was finding it hard to stay positive one steamy January morning in 2000 as I made my way through Darwin airport. As I reached the gate where my plane was waiting the automatic doors opened and the thick, humid air of the northern wet season hit me. Within moments I was covered with perspiration.

I resigned myself to an uncomfortable walk across the tarmac and then, sweating and puffing, climbed slowly up the stairs to board the flight. I was five months' pregnant and my little baby did not feel so little any more. I squeezed past flight attendants and passengers struggling with their bags at overhead lockers. Everyone looked as hot and bothered as I did. I took my seat at the rear of the cabin, wriggling around to make myself as comfortable as possible. I gazed out the window and tried to think of nothing in particular, but tears soon welled in my eyes.

Hardly a day had passed since I'd found out about my mother's intention to sell Bullo River Station, our family property in the Northern Territory, that I had not burst into uncontrollable sobbing. Dark sunglasses almost permanently covered my red, swollen eyes. In my entire life I had never been overcome by so many dark emotions.

My husband Franz was worried. In our nine years of marriage he had never seen me less than strong. Franz and Ben, our three-year-old son, came into my disordered thoughts, which had the immediate effect of turning my tears into torrents. I was grateful for the privacy of a window seat and turned my head away so people couldn't see my distress. Franz had organised this trip for me to see Monty Roberts, the horse-whispering guru who was in Brisbane for one day only to give a talk. He hoped that if I got my mind off our worries for a little while, perhaps I would snap out of this miserable state.

I kept asking myself, 'How did everything become such a mess?' I had always been close to my mother, and our business partnership over the past 15 years had been successful beyond our dreams. I had worked for almost my whole life of 38 years on Bullo, and had invested everything, on a practical and an emotional level, into it. My mother and I always had an understanding that the property was part of our future. I would raise my family there and, in time, it would pass to my children.

Now my whole life as I'd known it seemed to be at an end. My mother had become someone I no longer recognised. She had decided to sell Bullo, our home. She had not consulted me about her decision and I had only found out by chance about her intention and the steps she had already taken towards making the sale. By the time I sat on the plane waiting to go to Brisbane she was refusing to even speak to Franz and me. When we had still been speaking, she had made it clear that she was not interested in working out a deal with us and refused to acknowledge that I had any interest, financial or otherwise, in the property. It was true I had nothing in writing about my stake in Bullo and I had no money to speak of that I could use to buy it. The only time I had ever been paid for my work on Bullo was during the five years after my mother's books became successful and even then my salary was just $20,000 a year – not much for what I did. My payment was my home and my future security.

To add to my grief about my mother, and my fears about losing my beloved Bullo and my very way of life, I had also developed complications with my pregnancy. A preliminary test had shown that I was probably developing gestational diabetes which, unmanaged, could be potentially life-threatening to myself and my baby.

About 20 minutes into the flight, as breakfast was being served, the hair on the back of my neck suddenly prickled as my brain registered the smell of burning. I looked up at the same time that we *all* looked up! The cabin was rapidly filling with thick smoke. It caught in the back of my throat. I put my coat to my face and breathed through the cloth. There was an eerie silence. Everyone was remarkably calm but in their eyes I saw the fear that was also surging through me.

I had been in four forced landings with my father – when you fly light planes on a property like ours they are part of everyday life. Now, in a large commercial passenger plane, there was nothing that I could do. My life was in the hands of other people and fate would decide the outcome. I had been more or less in control all my life and now I wasn't. So I let go.

This was a life-changing moment for me. I saw the truth with absolute blinding clarity. I had been mourning the loss of things that were not important. I already had what was important in life. My only thoughts were of Franz and Ben and my unborn child. As I sat waiting for the plane to crash there was nothing I would not have given to be with them. To have our second child and all be together again. Now that I knew the worth of what I had, I started to pray these were not my final moments.

The captain spun the jet around abruptly and shut down one of the engines, and the smoke slowly began to clear from the cabin. Our wounded jet limped back to Darwin. I, too, had found my direction. I knew what I had to do. I would try everything I could to save the land I loved. If I lost it, then at least I would know I had done everything possible to keep it.

I had been reminded how fleeting and precarious life really is. From now on I would live every day as if it were my last. I would stop feeling sorry for myself, and be grateful for the good things in my life. I would not be afraid any more.

1

I WAS LUCKY TO HAVE BEEN BORN AT ALL. A month after their wedding, my parents set sail for a belated honeymoon on my father's 57-foot yacht – and had a nearly fatal encounter with a cyclone in the South China Sea. Father and his Filipino boat boy sailed through the eye of the monster with no engine, much skill, and even more raw luck. My father lashed my mother to the mast so she wouldn't be washed overboard, reassuring her that if they went down, at least they would all go down together. Unbeknown to her at the time, she was already pregnant with me.

I don't recall ever having family holidays as a child, and my mother's terrifying experience in the cyclone may well have been the reason. I know for sure that my father would never have considered having gentle seaside holidays like those enjoyed by most people. If only my mother had known that avoiding family holidays wouldn't be nearly enough to protect her from my father's enthusiasms. As it turned out, much of her life with him would be spent in the eye of one storm or another.

My father was Charles English Henderson III. A southern born gentleman from an old Maryland family, he cut a striking appearance. He had piercing, dark blue eyes, a tall, athletic build and an aura of complete confidence. A man of great intelligence and a true character, Father was witty, charming and charismatic. He was also an extremely manipulative and chauvinistic man who liked to get his own way and to control those around him. He was the sort of person who could either drain the energy from you, or energise and inspire you, depending on your temperament. I really think he missed his era. He would have made a brilliant explorer on one of the great sailing ships of centuries past.

Father was studying engineering at university when World War II broke out. To his family's horror he immediately joined the US Navy and underwent 90 days' training to become a naval bomber pilot. For his bravery and many combat victories as Lieutenant Commander of the Torpedo Ten Night Bomber Squadron on the *Enterprise*, he was to become a highly decorated war hero.

My father did not like the peacetime military and left as soon as the war was over. He started up a shipping business in the Philippines, transporting mainly timber and copra. He married Barbara Childers and they had six sons, two of whom died tragically. The eldest, at the age of nine, backed into the blades of a wind generator on my father's yacht *The Lady Barbara*, and the second died of pneumonia. Decades later, Father still could not talk about them. He and Barbara divorced when David, the youngest, was still a toddler.

My mother, Sara Jane Barton, was born and raised in Sydney, the youngest of six siblings. She had red hair, a temperament to match, and a strong athletic build she had inherited from her father. The family lived very comfortably. Early on, she followed her passion in life and became a talented and successful tennis player. She would undoubtedly have gone on to great things in the world of sport but for a near-fatal car accident at the age of 18. It took her two years to recover and learn to walk again. Her injuries put an end to her dreams of reaching the top of the professional tennis circuit.

In 1959, at the age of 25, Mother was doing office work in a pioneering computer company when she met my father, who was in Sydney on a business trip. She had lived a sheltered, ordered and normal life up to that point, and was not at all wise in the ways of the world. She fell totally and passionately in love with the handsome and exciting American who was 15 years her senior.

My father was quick to assess my mother's family dynamics and, recognising where the strength lay, set about charming my grandmother. He had one-on-one afternoon teas and long chats with her, and completely charmed her. He was very persuasive when he chose to be; neither Nan nor my mother had a chance. Within six months Mother was willingly whisked off to a lavish wedding in Hong Kong and then to live a life of luxury in Manila, in the Philippines, where my father's shipping business was based.

My father had entered my mother's life, swept her off her feet and taken control of everything. She didn't really find her feet or herself again until he passed away 26 years later.

——————

Having survived my father's whirlwind courtship, the wedding and the honeymoon cyclone, my mother discovered she was pregnant. She had not mastered the birth controls available at the time and had fallen pregnant with me virtually straight after the wedding. As my father, mother and father's boat boy, Ernesto, made their way to Hong Kong in my father's badly damaged yacht, my mother was weak from days of throwing up. She had put it down to sea sickness. In fact, it was a combination of sea sickness, morning sickness and amoebic dysentery. She ended up in hospital, living on rice water, for weeks. Once she had recovered from her initial violent bout of sickness she then endured many more months of standard morning sickness. Later, she told me she craved Coca-Cola and toasted tomato sandwiches throughout her entire pregnancy as they were the only things she could keep down. To this day I hate Coke and am allergic to tomatoes.

My mother gave birth to me in a Catholic hospital in Manila where all the white and wealthy went for medical treatment. The labour dragged on for what seemed to her like an eternity in hell. In those days the father didn't attend the birth, so she was alone and frightened.

I was a skinny seven pounds at birth – I had never quite caught up after my mother's illness and morning sickness. I had a full head of dark brown hair just like my father. But my mother has always thought I am a carbon copy of her only sister and eldest sibling, my Aunty Sue. I was christened Murray Lee, though for as long as I can remember, everyone has used my nickname, Marlee.

Father had made it clear to Mother he wanted a son. He saw my birth as only a temporary setback to his plans, and was sure the next one would be a boy. My mother was quick to set him straight: 'There won't be a next one!'

Mother settled into her mothering role, determined that I would be the only child she would raise. One year later, she found herself pregnant again. Years later, she told me that if she had mastered the limited birth control methods of the time she wouldn't have had any children.

To add to her despair, it was about this time that she realised – or perhaps faced and accepted the truth – that my father had been unfaithful to her on more than one occasion. In his usual charming fashion, my father promised it would not happen again. My mother was young, pregnant and naïve. She believed him.

My sister Bonnie's birth was even more difficult than mine. She weighed over nine pounds and came into the world after an aggressive forceps delivery. Mother said she thought she was going to split in half. My father was expecting a boy. I suspect that mother, despite having two healthy children, was made to feel a failure for not having produced a male the second time round.

My early life in the Philippines was happy and carefree. We lived a privileged life with an army of servants to cook, clean and do the laundry. Bonnie and I each had a personal ya ya, or nanny, to look after us. I have only good memories of my ya ya; she made me feel like the most important, loved child on earth. My mother said that our ya yas loved my sister and I as if we were their own. We were very spoilt with the attention of not only our parents but our ya yas as well.

My love of horses and riding was first kindled at the Manila Polo Club, where I took riding lessons from the age of three from a very loud and proper British instructor. My pony Blaze was so fat and round I practically had to do the splits to sit on him. I would bounce around the arena to my ex-military instructor's bellow of 'Sit up straight, heels down, toes up, shorten your reins.' I loved every minute of it and would gladly have suffered most things just to be astride a horse. I have always felt at one with these noble creatures.

———◦•◦•◦———

My father was well connected with the political party of the day; in the Philippines it was essential to be if your business was to succeed. In 1965 a general election was called. At the same time, my father's ships, and all his cargo, were stuck in several ports due to wharf strikes. It was costing his relatively young business tens of thousands of dollars a day. When the political party he had supported lost the election, he lost the connections he needed to be able to borrow the money to save his business.

We left the Philippines with nothing, apart from the clothes my mother packed in our bags. My father even had to borrow money for our airfares to Australia.

Up until this point I had lived in the oblivious bliss of childhood, happy and secure. Now, at the age of four, I felt the impact and influence of other people's actions and events upon my life. As we were leaving the Philippines it dawned on me that all was not well between my parents. The reason why was lost to me, but I know I felt apprehensive.

We were heading to my father's only remaining major asset: a property he had bought just before I was born, in the late 1950s. Bullo River Station, in the northwest corner of the Northern Territory, was in the outback of the outback. It was more than isolated, and completely undeveloped.

For many years, Father had discussed with his cousin Gus, who had been involved in his shipping business, the possibility of live cattle shipments to Asia from Darwin, where Gus had an office. At that time, cattle were shipped only out of Queensland and southern ports. My father reasoned, correctly, that to ship from Darwin would reduce the distance by as much as three quarters. The Northern Territory cattle were also cheaper, because back then, generally speaking, they were of a lesser quality than their southern counterparts.

On a business trip to Darwin, Father had taken the time to look around at available land. He was particularly interested in properties that had sea access, his idea being to ship cattle directly off the property. Bullo River Station caught his eye. Bullo River Valley, between the Western Australian border and the mighty Victoria River, is bounded by impassable ranges of 1,000-foot table-top mountains and cliffs. The Bullo River starts and finishes on Bullo, running right through the middle of the property into the Victoria River, which forms the eastern boundary of the station. It has abundant permanent springs, and huge natural lakes and billabongs dot the property. At that time, large herds of wild scrub cattle roamed freely on the well-grassed, unfenced land. It met all of his criteria, and he purchased the million acres of Australian wilderness that was to irrevocably change all of our lives in wonderful and tragic ways.

My mother was initially overjoyed by the prospect of going home to Australia. Although we lived well in Manila I believe she deeply missed her family and all that was familiar to her. She did not speak the local language and had few, if any, of her own friends.

When we arrived in Australia by plane – it was a long, slow trip in comparison to air travel today – my father went ahead to the property while we briefly visited my mother's family in Sydney. I can't recall my grandparents visiting us in Manila, but I instinctively warmed to them both now. Nan was a tall, elegant, slender woman with beautiful silver-grey hair. She was never still for long, always doing something for someone, and was involved in the Red Cross and other charities all her life. Poppa was a quiet man of solid build, with very little hair on his round, shiny head. He wasn't a great conversationalist but made up for it by making funny faces and wiggling his ears at Bonnie and I. We thought it was great, and I spent a good deal of my time trying to get my own ears to wiggle.

There were shocks in store, though. For the first time ever I was cold – it didn't get cold in the Philippines. And as I wandered through my grandparents' large, draughty house in Lakemba, in the outer suburbs of Sydney, I couldn't even find the servants' quarters. Where was my ya ya? My mother explained to me in language a four-year-old could understand that I no longer had someone to care for me exclusively and cater to all my needs. I wandered off digesting this shocking piece of information and all the questions it raised. Who was going to dress me? Who was going to read to me, do my hair and play with me? You asked your ya ya to do these things. When I addressed my concerns to my mother she told me that I would have to learn to do them myself. This was not something I wanted to hear.

I found our changed circumstances difficult to understand; this Australian lifestyle was so unfamiliar to me. However, my mother was happy amongst her family and friends. She was more relaxed and contented than I had seen her in my short life.

Father called Mother with our flight details. We were to fly to Darwin, from where we were to catch the mail plane to Bullo. Father would be out getting supplies and would drive back, ready to meet us on our arrival.

He hadn't quite filled my mother in on what to expect in her new home; I am sure she never would have gone if she had any idea of the truth. As a child she had visited her uncle's sheep property and enjoyed all the comforts of the large, sprawling homestead. My mother later told me that she expected a cattle station to be much the same, although perhaps a little more isolated because of its size. Coming from a comfortable middle-class upbringing in Sydney and then the luxury of the Philippines expat lifestyle, my mother could never have imagined there was such a place as Bullo was in 1965.

I vividly remember the first time we set foot on the parched winter soil of Bullo River Station. We had flown in on a big DC3 that did a fortnightly flight to Perth, stopping at some of the remote properties along the way with mail and supplies. The plane left us in a cloud of fine bull dust on the airstrip at Bullo with our luggage. There was no one in sight. We were all dressed to the nines in hand-tailored clothes from our former life. We stood for a while waiting. Nothing happened. No one came. We had been travelling all day and were tired and hungry.

My mother was looking a bit uneasy and began cursing my father under her breath as we tramped through deep, pale-brown bull dust towards the only visible manmade structure, a dusty, three-sided tin shed. The powder-fine dust mushroomed up with each step we took and our legs were filthy by the time we reached our destination.

'We will wait for your father here,' Mother announced quite confidently.

She was trying to put on a brave face for my sister and me. It must have been very hard for her. She had left Sydney in good spirits, sure there would be an established homestead with all the creature comforts one might expect of a million-acre property. Frankly, I think she looked forward to being the mistress of such an expanse.

I really needed to go to the toilet; there was a toilet in the shed but it wasn't connected to any plumbing. All Mother could find for me to go in was an empty paint tin. I was mortified. Go to the toilet in that? Memories of my smiling ya ya reading to me while I sat on my personal, private toilet came to mind. This was just too much. First I lose my ya ya and now I'm expected to go to the toilet in a paint tin? Legs crossed, I flatly refused.

Mother threw the paint tin down and said 'Fine. Go in your pants. I don't care!' Then she dissolved into tears.

I did use the paint tin after that. Bonnie was also crying by now. She wasn't quite three years old; she was tired and hungry and didn't understand why Mother and I were so upset.

A further search of the tin shed revealed a lot of empty rum bottles and rubbish, but no water to drink or food to eat. We sat for the afternoon in our bleak surroundings – my poor mother trying to keep a brave face and two little children looking for comfort she couldn't offer. Such was the scene that greeted my father when he turned up just before dark. He drove up to the shed with some very rough and unkempt-looking men in an old truck that was loaded with everything from axes to mattresses – all covered in a thick layer of dust. My sister and I were excited to see our father. He looked tired and was also covered in dust, but was cheerful and positive. My mother gave a sigh of relief.

'Charles, we are hungry and tired and it is very late. I want to go straight to the homestead and put the children to bed.'

This sounded like an excellent idea to me. We all looked towards my father expectantly.

'Charles?' my mother repeated, with just a hint of rising panic.

My father looked uncomfortable.

'This is the homestead,' he said quietly.

My mother's face said it all. Disbelief, shock, complete horror, fear, fury and then tears. My father patted her on

the back and tried to point out the bright side of things –
a difficult task under the circumstances, but he was rarely
daunted. It was a bit like his 'At least if we go down, we
all go down together' reassurance. Feeling the tension
between our parents, my sister and I had dissolved into
tears again. We were not off to a great start. As much as
it would be romantic to say so, the pioneering thing did
not immediately capture our imaginations.

That night, murky brown water from an unknown
source was brought to us in rusty flour drums so we could
wash. We slept on the new but dusty mattresses my father
had brought on the back of the truck. He had neglected
to bring beds or sheets. Attention to detail was never one
of my father's strong points. My mother was in a state of
shock and burst into tears every time she looked at my
father.

If there had been some way Mother could have left in
the first weeks I am certain you would not have seen her
for dust, but by the time the mail plane did come back
again Father had convinced her to give it a go. They would
build a grand homestead and become the cattle king and
queen of the north. This must have been a much more
inspiring vision for my mother to cling to than her only
alternative: fleeing penniless back to her family with two
children and no prospects for the future. My mother still
loved my father, and I suppose wanted to believe him when
he said that everything would turn out rosy in the end.

He hired men and set to work to try and turn the shed
into a grand homestead. They felled huge bloodwood trees
as uprights and crossbeams, and started to lay the sandstone
floors. Unfortunately, that was as far as they got and the
shed was to remain half-finished for many years to come.

My mother wavered between the excitement of carving
a home out of the wilderness like a true pioneer, and the
sheer terror of being isolated in such primitive conditions
with two small children and an unpredictable husband.

For my sister and I, on the other hand, things were

turning out rather well. I quickly came to terms with losing my ya ya and using the paint-tin toilet. The men were digging a well out the back of the shed so we would soon have running water and a real toilet but why would I care about such a triviality when I learned that there were few restrictions on my movements here in the outback? There was a real sense of freedom about the place. We ran around half-naked most of the day and no one minded at all.

The Aboriginal stockmen and their families who lived on Bullo numbered around 50, depending on how many were walkabout. They had moved from the adjoining Auvergne station after Bullo had been split off as a new lease, and set up a camp about half a kilometre from our homestead. I had never seen black-skinned people like the Aborigines before moving to Bullo and I admit I was a bit frightened at first. When they smiled, though, their faces lit up, and I soon became used to their tobacco-stained teeth and initiation scars. I knew they were friendly and that they really liked children. I couldn't understand a word they said to each other, but I managed to communicate with them in the round-about way children do.

There were only a few white stockmen, and they were very rough looking. They always had many days' growth on their faces and hand-rolled cigarettes hanging from their dry, sunburnt lips. I can't say that I understood much of what they said either. When and if they did speak to you they looked at the ground, their faces hidden under their wide-brimmed felt hats. The communication between them seemed to be a series of grunts accompanied by occasional hand movements to indicate direction.

All the stockmen smelt terrible to me. It was a blend of sweat, dust, dry blood, horse, cow, stale clothes worn for more than a week at a time, tobacco, both the rolled and chewing varieties, rum and poor to nonexistent dental hygiene. I am certain that this is one of the reasons bush people like a bit of space between one another. I came to learn early that all conversations should be held upwind.

Apart from our homestead the only structures were the Aborigines' huts. In those days everyone had a swag and home was where you rolled it out. The white stockmen either found an out-of-the-way corner in the homestead or a spot under a tree, depending on how social they were. In any case, they were out bush mustering most of the time.

I soon fell into the daily pattern of life on Bullo. The days started early and were long. All the work was focused on the cattle operation: mustering, drafting, branding, weaning, culling and selling cattle, breaking in horses, fencing and building yards to handle the stock.

On a needs basis the stockmen would take the station's old .308 rifle out, and shoot and slaughter a beast for meat rations. This regular event was called 'getting a killer'. The stockmen would bone out the carcass and lay the meat on a bed of gum leaves on the back of the four-wheel drive then bring the killer back, accompanied by lots of Aborigines from the local tribe, camp dogs, flies and big, red meat ants. Getting a killer was a happy event as it meant fresh meat. My sister and I, who were really getting into the spirit of this exciting new life, picked up on the festive vibes and hopped right into helping unload the hot, bloody chunks of meat. To our amazement, the meat moved as though it was alive (some of the nerves remained active for a while after the beast was dead).

I remember my mother emerging from the homestead on one such occasion to see her daughters half-naked amongst the Aborigines, covered in blood, with large pieces of still-moving meat in their eager possession, surrounded by a swarm of blowflies. We were rather proud of our efforts and greeted her with broad smiles: 'Look at us, Mummy, we're helping.' She responded by bursting into tears and making a hasty retreat. My father went to calm her down and we, a little perplexed by her response, went back to unloading the killer. Hey, wasn't this fun?

As we only had a couple of small, decrepit, old kerosene-fuelled fridges most of the meat was salted and unceremoniously dumped on old wire bed frames that served as drying racks. There the meat sat until the salt had sapped all the moisture out. In the end it didn't look like meat at all but more like badly misshapen pieces of old leather. It was as unappetising as it looked, which is why fresh meat was such a treat. On 'killer night' we had a barbecue on an open fire. The men would cook all the bits that wouldn't keep, such as the liver, kidneys, sweetbreads, tripe and our favourite, rib bones. They were tough but so, so tasty. It must have been like a scene from the *Flintstones* – all of us sitting around the fire gnawing on three-foot long rib bones. My mother was in despair.

Everything was wild out there in our first year at Bullo. The horses were no exception. None of them were quiet enough for me to ride. I had to be content to watch them gallop by, spellbound by the mobs of 100 or more. To a four-year-old – or a forty-year-old – it was a breathtaking sight. Occasionally, to my mother's horror, the horses would go right through the shed. After one such occasion she demanded that my father erect a fence immediately. She felt it was just too dangerous for us children. She was undoubtedly right. He did agree but, as usual, put my mother's request at the end of a big list of jobs.

It was not long after she had made her feelings known about the fence that we were all asleep one night on the floor in our one room when my mother woke to see the large silhouette of a stockhorse standing over us. The horse had wandered in looking for the horse feed that was stacked in bags not far from where we slept. My mother threw her mattress over Bonnie and I to protect us, but this startled the horse, which then slipped on the concrete floor. As he was thrashing about trying to regain his footing he kicked my mother in the head. It was very dramatic. Pitch black, the horse thrashing about, Bonnie and I yelling because we didn't know why someone was trying to smother us with a mattress, my mother yelling at my father, and my father trying to get the horse out. The Flying Doctor was called and at first light they took my mother to hospital with concussion.

The fence went up immediately thereafter and we moved into a caravan that was parked in the middle of the shed. Bonnie and I had a tough time while Mother was away recovering. Father was not at all domestic; meals were whatever came out of the tin he opened.

We were very glad to have our mother back, but she arrived with a heavy heart. Her sadness was evident to two little girls who were trying to do their best. I am sure Mother didn't think she would survive this country her husband had brought her to.

As the 'Missus', the official title given to the head white woman of the station, my mother was expected to attend to minor medical problems. When one of the Aboriginal men came up with a cough and a sore throat my mother did what her mother had always done and mixed up a hot rum-and-milk toddy. At this time the Aborigines were not considered citizens and were not allowed to drink. The stockman's face lit up with delight when he saw what my mother was offering him. After sculling the toddy he took off at speed.

My mother was well pleased she had been able to handle the medical situation but was not prepared for the 40 coughing Aborigines standing outside the kitchen area a short time later. Rising to the occasion, she started brewing bulk rum toddies for this apparent flu epidemic sweeping the local tribe. When my father and our station manager John turned up, the queue disappeared instantly. My mother was left standing, bewildered, with her pot of flu cure. John was horrified that she had used his rum. My father thought the whole incident was very amusing and laughed loudly at my mother, who was not at all pleased that she was the source of his merriment.

Of my mother's many worries the redback spiders were of particular concern. She knew they were deadly to children under five and our homestead was full of them. She took us aside soon after we arrived and showed us what they looked like, and what their sticky web felt like. Then she delivered a very serious lecture on the dangers – namely death – to us if we were bitten. She left us with strict instructions to come and get her immediately if we came across any of these deadly creatures. It was not long before we found some and dutifully went to our mother. The reaction we got from her was unprecedented. Never before had we captured her attention completely and so instantaneously, or been so lavishly praised for our actions. What more could a child want? We became dedicated redback hunters and soon showed her that there were hundreds of them. My poor mother. With each new discovery she came closer and closer to a nervous breakdown.

With the approach of the 1965 wet season Bonnie and I suffered uncomfortable outbreaks of prickly heat, an excruciating, itchy rash brought on by the intense heat during the build-up to the wet season. My mother covered us from head to toe in calamine lotion, but as the temperature climbed above 40 degrees Celsius, and the humidity crept above 80 per cent, our rashes spread. To keep us cool my mother requested that a small sandstone paddle pool be built for Bonnie and I, and once it was operational we practically lived in it. That solved our prickly heat problem. My mother was not without initiative in circumstances that would have stopped many less determined people.

In all, our first year in the outback turned out to be rather idyllic for us children. We swam, hunted redbacks, played with the Aboriginal children and generally thrived in this free and easy lifestyle. My father was happy because he was being what he wanted to be – an eccentric pioneer. For my mother, however, it was everything that she hated and feared.

2

As our first year in the bush drew to a close my father came to the realisation that no quick wealth would be made on Bullo, and his initial thrill at being a pioneer began to wane. His mother back in the USA was not well and his brother Edmund was pushing to put her in a home and take over the family properties. My father was against any such course of action, adamant that my grandmother was healthy and sharp as a tack. (He was more right than he knew – she was to outlive both my father and Uncle Edmund.) Father, no doubt having hatched plans to make a fortune in the US, decided at the end of 1965 to uproot the family again. Before leaving for America, my father went into partnership with our station manager, John, who would keep Bullo running while we were away.

While both Mother and Father seemed very pleased about the prospect of going to the States, my own feelings were rather neutral. I had never been to America so had no idea what to expect. My parents had told me about snow, and that did sound like it had a lot of possibilities.

On one of our final days at Bullo, Bonnie and I were playing at jumping back and forth between two 44-gallon drums laid on their sides. Bonnie slipped and hit her arm on the steel drum as she fell. She crashed to the ground screaming in agony. One look at her arm was enough for me. It was bent at an impossible angle. I tried to sit Bonnie in a comfortable position but there wasn't one. I hurried to get Mother.

She was in the middle of the daily radio transmission that was our only means of communicating with the outside world in those days. I tugged urgently on her sleeve to get her attention.

'Not now,' she said without looking at me. I kept at it. '*Not now*!'

I went back to Bonnie who was sobbing in a pathetic little heap on the ground. It was clear she was in a lot of pain. I helped her up and led her to the radio room, where I again tugged on my mother's sleeve. She spun around in a fury, and then saw Bonnie's arm. She dropped the radio mike and let out a wail of deep horror, tears in her eyes. Medical emergencies involving her daughters were never one of her strengths. Soon it was off to the hospital to get Bonnie's arm set in a cast.

———•◦•••◦•———

My mother wasted no time packing our bags for America. She did it with blinding speed and we left Bullo without a backward glance. We flew to Darwin in our little plane, which was then put up for sale, and caught a commercial flight to Sydney to visit Mother's family.

Being civilised again was a bit of a trial for Bonnie and me. We had to wear shoes and clothes, and we didn't remember them being so uncomfortable. Sydney was a shock after Bullo – so many people, cars, buildings and roads.

Bonnie loved dogs and within minutes of arriving at our grandparents' house she threw herself onto their old dog, which was fast asleep on the sofa. The dog bit Bonnie on the face in fright and we were soon off to the hospital again, this time for a tetanus injection and stitches.

My mother had her family spellbound with stories of her

year in the outback and enjoyed almost a celebrity status for having survived the ordeal. The end of our visit came all too soon for her. It had always been her wish to settle in Sydney, but she couldn't persuade my father. He was far too independent and adventurous to settle in Sydney suburbia. She once again said her tearful goodbyes to her family, and we boarded the first of many connecting flights that would take us to America and our new life.

———•·••·•———

Easton, my father's home town, on the eastern shore of Chesapeake Bay in Maryland, was very different from the wilds of north Australia. The country was flat and soft-looking, with rolling fields of corn and soya beans broken up by tall pine forests and swamps.

The people seemed nice enough, but not at all laid back like the Australians we'd come to love. There was definitely no sense of freedom. This was a restrictive and conservative society, which is why my father had never fitted in, although he loved his home, family and the traditions that went with Eastern Shore life. People lived in real houses that had been built at least 100 years ago, and went to church every Sunday. We were expected to wear clothes and shoes at all times, and go to school. The killers and rib bones from our previous year in the outback may as well have existed on a different planet.

My paternal grandmother did not strike me as a warm person. Short, stout and matronly, she always seemed to have an expression of disapproval on her face. If there was a warm, cuddly grandmother underneath that austere exterior she kept it well hidden. She dedicated her life to upholding the family name and maintaining their country estate, Lloyds Landing, which had been in the family for many generations. Situated in the prime real estate belt alongside the Choptank River, it comprised 1,200-odd acres of farming and pine forests.

She made hams according to a time-honoured family recipe, to be eaten on special occasions with Maryland beaten biscuits. She planted and tended her garden, and went to her Episcopalian church every Sunday. She read the Bible for answers to her problems. She had been brought up with ideas that were current 100 years ago; she still believed that you were born into your place and that was where you stayed.

Her husband had died before I was born, and since then, she had lived in the 17th Century house on Lloyds Landing with only her black cook and housekeeper, Nora. Nora was a warm-hearted woman who had been presented to my grandmother as a wedding present. True to her upbringing, my grandmother would sit at the big dining room table alone and Nora would sit at the kitchen table alone, and they would converse through the open door. In my grandmother's era, no person of colour would sleep 'above boards'. Accordingly, Nora slept in the cellar. Despite the fact that they were great lifelong friends, they never ate together and Nora never slept upstairs. It just was not done. Nora cooked for my grandmother for her whole life, until she passed away in her 70s.

We had arrived at Lloyds Landing travel weary from our long flight. We had barely set foot in the house when Bonnie spied my grandmother's old beagle fast asleep and tackled the dog head on. Munch, a very kind but simple-minded dog, immediately bit my poor sister on the face. She was really battle scarred now, with her arm still in a cast and two lots of stitches from two separate dog bites.

Initially we stayed with our grandmother at Lloyds Landing. My father enjoyed it, as Nora and my grandmother adored him and spoilt him to excess. I think it was a mystery to my grandmother how she had produced such an eccentric rebel for a son. The qualities that she so admired in him she also simultaneously condemned. She was raised to be conservative, frugal and dutiful. My father was none of these things. Nevertheless, she showered him with attention, which he expected and loved.

It was evident even to me at my tender age that my mother was not welcomed warmly into the fold of my father's family. My grandmother was civil but no more than she had to be. She had never considered my mother a suitable match for her son.

Living amongst all my grandmother's antiques was nerve-racking for Mother, Bonnie and I. Even being outside the house was a trial because my grandmother entered her award-winning garden in the prestigious annual *House and Garden* competition. We soon learned that the nearby pine forests were the only safe place to play. Several months later we moved into a rambling old farmhouse on Rigby's Marsh Farm, part of my grandmother's property. The farmhouse wasn't large but it was comfortable, and we were glad to have our own space. Rigby's Marsh Farm was set amongst pine forest and cornfields, and to my great delight had a small paddock and stables.

My father put his engineering studies to use by securing an aircraft design job in Washington. This, plus the many other business ideas he was always trying to get off the ground, meant he was away most of the time. He would drive to Washington before we woke and would usually get back when we had already gone to bed.

My first school experience was not great. At five, I was enrolled in the first grade at The Country School, 'the' private school to go to. My parents couldn't afford it but my grandmother picked up the fees, insisting that this was the school her grandchildren must attend. There was no messing around with toys or singing songs at this school. I soon found that the other first graders had already attended two years of schooling and could count to 100, do basic maths and write cursive. I hadn't done any of this, and with the help of my teacher felt like a complete dunce. All my teacher was missing was the broomstick. She would drag me up in front of the class and humiliate me in front of all the other children. I just wanted to crawl away and die. I hated her and didn't want to go to school. I started wetting my bed and became very troubled.

I was not the only child suffering at her hands. Another girl who had come into first grade cold was also having all sorts of problems. Our mothers took the school to task but their complaints were to no avail. I was soon taken out of The Country School and would later be much happier at a public school called Idawile.

Meanwhile, my mother was doing her best to fit in with stiff Maryland society and live up to the expectations of my father's family. She had come from an easy-going middle-class family where you were who you were. In Maryland, what your great-grandfather did, which side of the civil war he fought on, how old your family was and what families you were connected to were all important factors in your social standing. Old money and an old landed family on the southern side were the right credentials to have in order to get invited to 'the' parties and join 'the' clubs. Mother's efforts to be accepted were largely in vain.

One thing my mother did have going for her in polite southern society was that she was an excellent tennis player. As soon as the word got around about how good she was and what a fun couple she and my father were, my parents had invitations to tennis afternoons at some of the very best homes in the district. Our favourite by far was Senator Morton's home. Next to the stables was a paddock full of strawberries. The first time we visited, Bonnie and I were given a bowl of sugar each and let loose while the adults partied and played tennis. We had a glorious afternoon stuffing ourselves with strawberries, followed by an evening of upset stomachs. Mrs Morton's daughter would occasionally hoist me up onto Bold or Tickertape, huge horses bred for fox hunting. I felt more than on top of the world astride one of these gentle giants.

To my delight father purchased a small, black Shetland pony for our empty stable, paying the princely sum of $25. She was virtually at death's door and on the way to the

knackery. I named her Lucky. Bonnie and I started riding
lessons with Mrs Barner, who was originally from Australia
and an excellent instructor. This was Bonnie's first experience of riding and initially she was not as enthusiastic
as I was. She felt the cold badly and didn't like to be
outdoors for too long in the winter. My parents didn't push
her, to their credit.

Jumping was my favourite part of horse riding – the
higher the better. By the time I was eight I was a well-
accomplished rider for my age, so Mrs Barner entered me
in the jumping competition at her annual horse show. The
judge came out from England, and as we lived in an area
populated with wealthy, horsy people there was quite a turn
out. Lucky flatly refused to jump anything so I borrowed
one of Mrs Barner's ponies, Limelight, for the occasion. He
did not have the most attractive personality; in fact, he
permanently had his ears back, a really sour look on his
pure white face and a rather malicious glint in his beady
black eyes. But he would jump virtually anything. He was
very difficult to ride – he would kick up his hind legs mid-
jump – but it was worth the effort because of his amazing
jumping ability.

I entered in the open jumping class and was the youngest
by far; some of the competitors were well into their teens.
There were some very rich riders, so immaculately groomed
that you could see your face in their custom-made fine
leather boots. Some had their own grooms tending their
string of expensive show horses.

By contrast, I was wearing a jumper, winter track pants
and rubber boots, riding on a fat, hairy, borrowed pony.
Poor old Limelight looked a bit like a goat next to some of
those fine horses. I didn't think I had a chance but decided
to go out and just enjoy myself, which I did. As usual,
Limelight burned around the course with no faults and
no refusals.

Standing in line waiting for the judge to announce the
winner, I was thinking of something else and I didn't hear

my number called. The girl standing next to me gave me a sharp dig in the ribs and said 'That's you.' She had a rather annoyed look on her face, as if to say 'How on earth could you win?' She was right of course. I was equally shocked – then delighted. My mother and father were there to see my triumph and I was very proud.

Every Sunday without fail we got into our best clothes and headed off to church. I was certain there had to be better things to do on a Sunday, like riding. I never did enjoy Sunday school – the Bible stories just didn't make any sense to me. The grown ups who gathered outside the church after the service smiled sweetly at each other but as I wandered through the crowd I often overheard them make nasty comments about each other.

'She's worn the same dress three times,' said one.

'Well, she does get her clothes at the charity shop. What do you expect?' replied another.

These people obviously left their charitable selves at the church door as they exited each week.

To my young eyes there seemed to be a lot of different religious groups that all believed theirs was the only one. Shirley, who came to help in our house and baby-sit us occasionally, was a devout Seventh Day Adventist. She told us in no uncertain terms that if we didn't convert to her religion we would all be burned when the big fireball came. I wanted to know when the fire was coming and how it knew to go around one person and not another. She didn't really ever have a satisfactory answer.

Just how much I disliked the whole church caper came home to me one Sunday morning when Lucky stomped on my big toe with her hard little hoof. My toe started to swell at an alarming rate. Even through the escalating pain my one thought was that I wouldn't have to go to church. To further confirm my scepticism my parents argued over who would take me to the hospital – they didn't want to go to church either. Mother eventually won with 'They're your family. If it's so important to you why don't you go?'

For that Sunday at least my mother and I got out of going.

In the New Year of 1969 our little sister was born. She was the first baby of the year in Easton, and she and my mother made the front page of the local paper. My parents had not decided firmly on a name when my grandmother suggested Janet Frockle Henderson. She immediately justified this beauty by explaining that it was the name of one of our ancestors, who had royal connections. It was my mother's opinion that she would need all the connections she could get with a name like that. My parents had been expecting a Daniel, so they changed it to Danielle. She was christened Danielle Manadeir – an old family surname, I was told – Henderson, a beautiful name for our gorgeous baby sister. Bonnie and I were glad to have Danielle as a little sister. To us she was the chubbiest, cutest baby, and she rarely cried without good reason.

It was clear to me around this time that things between my parents were bad. The arrival of Danielle probably only made things more difficult. Although I didn't know it at the time my father was constantly having affairs, both with local women and in Washington. He more and more frequently stayed in Washington overnight, supposedly on business. Mother would find out what he'd really been up to and Father would smooth things over and promise to never do it again. But of course he did.

I vividly remember an argument during which my father had hold of my mother's shoulders and was shaking her roughly; she was sobbing and hysterical. I had a feeling that he was about to hit her, although I cannot say that I had ever seen him do so. I felt that I must protect her, so I stepped in and told my father to stop. He ordered me to leave and I refused. It was the first time I had openly defied him and I was frightened because I knew he was not the sort of person to cross. He was furious but I stood my ground. For the first time I understood the power of the truth. He knew I was right.

He stormed out of the house and drove off in a fury. I

did what I could to comfort Mother, which would not have amounted to much given I was only eight and did not grasp the complexities of adult relationships. I didn't really understand what it was all about, and felt powerless and guilty, as though it were my fault this had happened.

From that time on, my father was a lot harder on me. In his opinion, I was trouble and difficult to control, and needed a firmer hand.

One day I went to ask my mother for something; I don't recall what. She was frequently at the end of her tether these days and this was one of those moments. She broke down in tears and started yelling about how unhappy she was. Her words were devastating because I thought they meant it was somehow my fault that she was so unhappy. With a heavy heart, I took my bike and set off across the cornfields. I eventually came to a farm that belonged to my grandmother but had been share-farmed by another family for two generations. I came to a large barn full of happy-looking animals, including two beautiful chestnut ponies. This was my kind of place. I was hungry and tried to eat some of the corn meant for the livestock. It was hard and tasted dreadful. I wondered how the animals could be so enthusiastic about eating this stuff; it certainly wasn't anything like the succulent corn on the cob I was used to. After my dismal meal I climbed into the hay loft and fell asleep. That is where the farmer, Mr Marvel, found me. He phoned around to find out who was missing a child, with quick results. My mother and father came to pick me up. My mother was sobbing quietly by the car. My father looked serious but hugged me and told me that I was very loved and must never run away again.

Out of bad sometimes comes good. After that, Mr Marvel often brought his ponies over to Rigby's Marsh for Bonnie and I to ride on. He and I became friends, and even after our family moved away we wrote to each other, until he died some 30 years later.

3

WHEN I WAS NEARLY NINE MY FATHER decided we were
going to move back to Australia. None of his business
ventures – such as designing a surveillance aircraft you
could assemble and launch in the Vietnam jungle, or trying
to turn the abandoned New York wharves into a helicopter
airport – had succeeded and he seemed to think there were
more opportunities in Australia.

Yet again we packed our belongings. My parents could
not afford to have everything shipped over to Australia
so we were allowed to take only what we could fit in our
luggage. Now that I was older, leaving my treasured possessions behind was harder. To placate me, Father promised
me my own horse when we got to Bullo.

I had only good memories of the outback and was
looking forward to returning. Mother was happier than I
had seen her in a long time at the prospect of returning to
Australia and seeing her family again. However, the thought
of continuing on to Bullo did not bring her any joy. My
mother tried again to persuade my father to settle in Sydney,
with absolutely no success. After stopping briefly in Sydney
to do his duty of visiting Mother's family, Father left to sort
out problems at the station, and my mother and my sisters
and I settled back for an extended visit.

It was more peaceful with Father away, and Mother was more relaxed. She enrolled Bonnie and I into Meriden, a small private school in the inner west of Sydney. Our daily trips on the school bus were like journeys in hell. Students from the nearby boys school also caught our bus; they inhabited the back of the bus while the girls cowered in the front. The boys carried thick elastic bands, which they wielded with great skill and accuracy upon us girls. On one particular nightmare journey a boy flicked Bonnie on her arm, leaving a large, red welt and bringing tears to her eyes. He then grabbed her hat and took off to the boys' half of the bus.

That was it. I had had enough. I stood up and marched into enemy territory. I went up to the offender, who was quite a bit bigger than me, and demanded my sister's hat back. He looked down and laughed at me – a mistake, he was to find out. I grabbed him by the shirt collar, pulled him off balance and decked him. Sitting on the bus floor with blood all over his face he didn't look nearly so smug. I grabbed Bonnie's hat and walked back to the girls' half of the bus with a confident air I didn't particularly feel. I fully expected a retaliatory rear attack, but it never came. I had learned something new about myself and the world around me. After that day, although the chaos still raged around us, we Henderson girls were in an invisible safety bubble.

We had spent about three months in Sydney when my father returned from the station. He had purchased a six-seater aircraft, which he was going to fly us all back to Bullo in. Bonnie and I didn't think it was the least bit unusual that our father would buy a plane and fly us across Australia to a remote million-acre property.

As we piled into our plane for the journey to Bullo, I felt a rising sense of anticipation. Father seemed to have come back into his own, after having been rather downcast because of his business failures in America. I think he thrived on the freedom of the Australian lifestyle and his enthusiasm, for me anyway, was infectious. I was obsessed by the tantalising promise of my own horse. I had only ever ridden ponies and to own a horse was just about the pinnacle of my dreams at that point in my life.

After a couple of days' flying, in the softening light of the setting sun I saw the Bullo River Valley again. The beauty of this wild land took my breath away. As soon as I set foot on the dusty airstrip I felt strangely at home. My mother sighed in sad resignation.

In the four years we had been away John, my father's partner and station manager, had been busy building yards and fences, but the 'homestead' was still basically a three-sided tin shed, albeit slightly extended. Knowing what she did of life on Bullo, in Sydney Mother had bought a truckload of necessities. She had purchased everything from a tractor to 1,000 candles at auction. When the truck bearing these trappings of comfort arrived she set about trying to make a home out of our shed.

The only electricity we had came from an old low-voltage generator. It was situated only two steps away from the back door – no doubt thanks to a practical male concern that it be close for ease of turning on and off. It was deafeningly loud, making conversation completely impossible when it was running. And for all the discomfort it brought, it could only power a few feeble, pale-yellow lights. Candlelight was actually brighter. The thousand candles were to be our main providers of light for nearly a year, until a 240-volt generator was installed.

We would sit around the dinner table at night, each of us with our candle. A gust of wind would come through and blow them all out. There would be the sound of people searching about in the darkness, the rattle of multiple matchboxes and then the simultaneous lighting of matches. Dinner would continue until the next gust of wind.

We still had the dreaded kero fridges; on cold winter nights it was actually colder outside than it was inside the fridges. As a consequence, most of our food was tinned or dried. Anything fresh was eaten with great reverence. We would only get fresh vegetables and fruit when father went to town, or other people came out to Bullo – it was an unwritten rule that anyone coming out from town brought supplies for the isolated cattle stations in the far north.

Cooking was done on a state-of-the-art wood stove. My mother, who didn't like cooking anyway, hated this fire-breathing dragon. During the hotter wet season months everyone was permanently saturated in sweat. The temperature would be around 40 degrees Celsius, with high humidity, and it made cooking on the wood stove like tending the fires of hell.

Recreational activities were limited on Bullo but fortunately Bonnie now loved riding as much as I did. We had been promised a colt each, but until they were broken in we rode two old, retired stockhorses. My father no doubt allowed us to ride them so he could get some peace, as I badgered him at every opportunity about my long-promised horse. My temporary horse, Stockman, was a tall, bony bay with a lovely nature. There were no spare saddles so we rode bareback, and to this day I clearly remember exactly how uncomfortable his bony back was.

As a nine-year-old who was on the short side, getting up onto Stockman from ground level was a challenge. It took many failed attempts before I mastered a winning technique. Grabbing two large chunks of mane in my hands, I would leap up as high as I could, simultaneously getting my left elbow over his neck and the big toe of my left foot into the indent above the knee of Stockman's front left leg. From there I would fling my right leg over his back and, if I got the timing and coordination right, I would just get the heel of my bare foot hooked over his backbone. Then I'd put my left knee in the indent above his left shoulder, and heave and wiggle my way on. It was quite a workout; I needed a moment to catch my breath afterwards. My success was of course entirely dependent on old Stockman standing still throughout all of this, which he ever so patiently did for me – most of the time.

Bonnie and I went on our first muster with our father, John, our station manager, and half a dozen stockmen to tiny Billabong Paddock, at the end of our airstrip. We were so excited as we rode through stands of huge ghost gums. We thought we were in the deepest bush; in actual fact we were only a kilometre from the homestead. We were told to stay on our horses and wait next to a mangrove tree near the paddock gate, which the men intended to push cattle through. From there we watched them ride out wide to encircle a small mob of bush cattle feeding on the open flat in the distance. The cattle saw them and took off. They thundered past us, the stockmen close on their heels, working as a team to bring them under control. The cattle passed so close I could hear their laboured breathing. They headed towards thick tea-tree scrub in the distance. We heard the mob crashing through the trees and the men cursing as they battled to wheel the cattle round. The noise grew louder and louder as they chased the mob back towards us. They galloped past, the cattle still leading. They disappeared into more scrub – more crashing, more cursing. This time, when the cattle emerged they were wide-eyed, foaming and drooling, and trying to get the stockmen with their horns. Gone was the cohesive teamwork; the men were going in all directions, and the cattle were chasing them.

Bonnie and I sat on our horses rooted to the spot, spell-bound by the excitement and drama of this spectacle. Entertainment just didn't get better than this. The men did not share our enthusiasm. The fact that they had lost the cattle didn't dampen my spirits, though, and I couldn't wait to have a go at mustering myself; it was the most exciting thing I had ever seen.

Our next adventure with my father was not nearly so enjoyable. It was late in the season and my father wanted to check the water level in Nutwood Creek, a good hour-and-a-half's ride away. It was very hot, and the heat waves snaked over the big, open plains we rode across. When we got there the water was undrinkable. Bonnie and I were devastated. My mouth was too parched to swallow and we were both sunburnt. Bonnie broke into tears she was so thirsty. Father told her to stop crying, but she didn't. So he then called her over in a sweet voice. She went to him thinking she would get some sympathy; instead, he angrily stuffed his hanky into her mouth and again told her to stop crying. She became more hysterical than ever. That was enough for me.

I urged old Stockman into a canter and took off home. My mother, seeing the state I was in, wanted to know what happened and where Bonnie was. She got a very scary look in her eyes, her anger bubbling up as I recounted the whole tale of woe in dramatic detail to her. She stormed out of the house. I knew I had just got my father into an awful lot of trouble, but he deserved it. Mother was waiting for them at the back gate when they returned, and boy did he cop it.

Aside from that horrible day, this was a period of relative peace on the home front. Relations between my parents were more positive than I could remember them being for years. For the first time they were working together in the same direction. Mother had taken up the challenge of making the shed into a house. Not much had changed to the original design but with the arrival of the supply truck we had chairs and tables, and materials to put ceilings in the rooms that existed – Bonnie and I slept in one room next to our parents' room and the radio room, where John slept, and Danielle was in with my parents. Father was doing his pioneering thing. There were no other women around to tempt Father, so Mother was relaxed.

There were, as always, problems on the horizon. The cattle market collapsed virtually overnight. By the time Father had mustered the cattle and delivered them to the abattoirs the bills outweighed the payment. The cattle were worth nothing.

Despite the fact that trouble seemed to find my family, Father remained an admirable optimist. He often said to me that if you look hard enough you can nearly always turn a negative into a positive. Given his rocky personal and business past he had had a lot of practice, and was really getting rather good at it. He set about finding a way to add value to our worthless stock.

Beef was still fetching reasonable prices in butcher shops, so he decided the way forward was to cut out the middleman. He put a proposal to the local graziers that they get together to build their own abattoir and market their own meat. They thought he was crazy. He was an American, and as far as they were concerned, Americans and wild, fanatical schemes were synonymous. They wanted no part. My father was not daunted, only annoyed by their short-sightedness. He had had many good ideas throughout his life that were ahead of their time, and I think he had become immune to people's negative reactions. In the 60s, when Australia had no live cattle exports to speak of, he said that our greatest market would be the Far East. Everyone thought he was insane. Thirty-five years later, Asia is our primary market and more than a million cattle are exported from the north of Australia annually.

Undeterred by the negativism of the other graziers he went ahead with his plan on his own, and the Bullo River abattoir was born. While his ideas were usually good my father did not have the patient nature or practical talent to bring them to fruition, and these shortcomings were often his undoing. Fortunately, the Bullo River abattoir was to be an exception, relatively speaking that is.

After much work by many dubious and unskilled labourers the abattoir was completed. It looked just as you would expect – like it had been built by dubious and unskilled labourers. It was situated about a quarter of a kilometre from the house, far enough away so that the distinctive smell didn't reach the homestead. My mother was horrified by the thought of having an abattoir on the property and, apart from the grand opening that my father convinced her to attend, she would never go near it.

I think the inspectors looked at the makeshift operation and cringed, but the thought of having my father driving them up the wall was worse; it was easier to let him go ahead. My father employed several extra men to slaughter and quarter the beasts. Cubicles were cordoned off at the back of the homestead for the new staff and later my father also bought a caravan for some of them to live in.

My father started supplying the local Aboriginal mission butcher shops with full quarters of meat on the bone. He managed to win these contracts because he could guarantee delivery all year round. The other companies delivered by truck and every wet season the roads closed for months, often leaving the communities with no meat. My father planned to deliver by plane so the only delay would be a week or so if a cyclone brought bad weather. Once again that mad American was doing things nobody else had done. But he was proven right and the abattoir did see us through the 70s cattle depression. Without it the property would not have survived.

———————

At the tender age of nine, I was sure that John, our station manager, had to be the toughest man on earth. A man of few words, he had a wiry build, chiselled features, and bowed legs from a lifetime in the saddle. He was an exceptionally good horseman, bushman and cattleman, all skills I greatly admired. And, unlike many of the characters we came across in the outback he was very well spoken and educated; he came from a good Perth family.

John didn't mind a drink. One of my first memories of John is of him emerging early one morning from the radio room where he slept. He'd had a hard night. He swayed – you couldn't really call it walking – all the way to the store-room, and took a bottle of Worcestershire sauce and a tin of possibly the hottest chillies on earth from a shelf. He threw his head back and ate the chillies in one gulp. His face went red and he broke out in a sweat immediately. Then he sculled some Worcestershire sauce. Coughing, he wiped the dribbles from his mouth on his sleeve and mumbled 'Ahhgg, no kick.' He walked with a newfound steadiness to a horse that was being patiently held by an Aboriginal stockman. He swung on and had barely eased into the saddle when the horse dropped his head and hopped a couple of times. John growled in annoyance, pulled the horse's head up, settled him into a fast walk and rode off into the bush.

John chose and broke in my first colt, a strong, grey gelding I named Holy Smoke. I have always liked horses with a bit of fire and Holy Smoke had plenty of that. He was a lot for me to handle, and at times I didn't. I came to terms with the fact that I was in control only part of the time; in-between I'd just hang on for dear life.

Father would take me along on musters close to the homestead. Having learned the hard way I made sure that I had water and a roll of toilet paper whenever we headed off. Gum leaves were not an option as far as I was concerned. One day when we were near Nutwood Creek, Holy Smoke took fright and bolted. He clamped the bit hard between his teeth and I was fighting to bring him under control. Suddenly my toilet paper started to unravel. Holy Smoke glanced back, saw a 10-foot-long paper monster chasing him, and went supersonic. All I could do was try to offload the offending toilet roll as we careered at breakneck speed through the scrub.

We were heading straight for a thick stand of a fluffy-looking, dark green bush. In the few seconds I had left I thought that the bushes didn't look too bad a place to crash. Was I ever wrong. The fluffy-looking bush was Parkinsonia and under the fluff were long, sharp thorns. I came out the other side covered in scratches and blood, with my shirt torn. Having met my first Parkinsonia bush I knew that in future I'd rather bail out before going through. It was a nasty way to learn never to judge a book by its cover.

I had seen very little of my four half-brothers, the children from my father's first marriage, up to now. They had visited us in the Philippines in my early childhood, but I didn't remember much. I guess my father felt guilty that he had spent so little time with them and perhaps wanted to make up for his absence while they were growing up. Whatever the reasons, he invited the boys to come up to Bullo from Sydney where they lived with their mother, Barbara, and their step-father, Sam. They were to each come and go many times over the years.

David, the youngest, came up to live with us at the age of 13. He was a tall, thin, serious young man with blue eyes and dark blondish hair. It was clear, even to me as a child, that he wanted desperately to please our father.

Being only a few years apart in age, Bonnie, David and I did virtually everything together. In the mornings we fed the chickens and collected the eggs, and then started correspondence school for the day, except on the occasions we were allowed to go on musters.

In those early days my father came up with lots of schemes to increase profits. He decided it would be a good idea to supply pork to the missions as well as beef, so he purchased about 20 sows to start off a breeding herd. With the addition of the pigs to my father's business empire Bonnie, David and I now also had the task of feeding and caring for them. Feeding these smart but smelly animals was the worst of jobs and took up a good deal of our time after school. We fed them on the offal from the cattle slaughtered in the abattoir and sorghum cooked into a swill. Initially, the abattoir only slaughtered stock about once every ten days, and the offal was kept in 44-gallon drums outside for at least a week between kills. By the second day it was alive with maggots – the smell defies description. Having dragged the offal out of the drums we had to put it into wood-fired boilers with the sorghum. Then we had to scoop the cooked swill into buckets and put it into the feeding troughs.

Having witnessed pigs eat I know how insulting it is to be called one. As we struggled out with the buckets of swill the pigs would rush at us. Tired of their complete lack of manners I carried a whip and used it to keep them away from us until all the food was in the troughs. If any of them put their hooves in the trough or bullied their neighbours they got a sharp crack on the ear from my whip. Intelligent animals, they learned with impressive speed. They were the models of good behaviour as long as they knew I could reach them with the whip.

No matter how much we scrubbed ourselves we always smelt of the pigs and nobody would sit near us at meals. I can clearly remember that as we walked into the kitchen conversation ceased momentarily as everyone looked for the source of that terrible smell.

———•◦•◦•———

The closest town to Bullo was Timber Creek, 200 kilometres away, 76 kilometres of which was a rough dirt road that was closed for four months or more a year due to the wet season. It was a collection of buildings so small in number that if you sneezed while driving past, you'd miss it. Katherine was just under 500 kilometres away by road but was also very small with only the most basic shops – supplying the most basic supplies. Going into town really meant going to Darwin, 850 kilometres away. This happened rarely; it was normal for me not to leave the property for a year. I even recall not leaving the station for a two-year stretch, from the age of 13 to nearly 15. Father flew to Darwin regularly but most of the time once the meat was loaded onto the plane there wasn't enough room for all of us; besides, with school, the chickens, the pigs and mustering, our days were long and full. Nonetheless my father did recognise the necessity of an occasional trip to town, mainly to maintain my mother's sanity.

My mother hated flying. She would break out in a sweat and get diarrhoea as soon as she knew she had to fly. There was some substance to her fear. My father was a notorious aviator and was often making forced landings, but fortunately he walked away from every one without a scratch.

The first forced landing I can remember took place when we were flying into the Katherine airfield to drop John off – we were on our way to Darwin. There was a loud bang – a con rod put a hole in the engine block, oil went everywhere and the oil pressure started to drop rapidly. My father radioed a distress call to the tower. Suddenly I had my own emergency – a very urgent call of nature. I was still recovering from a bad stomach bug. Our aircraft continued to lose oil, which began to cover the windscreen. Once the oil pressure dropped beyond a certain point the engine would stop. John, who was sitting in the front passenger seat, was calling out the oil pressure as it dropped, while Father concentrated all his efforts on landing our stricken plane. The windscreen was now covered in oil, except for one small patch on the bottom left-hand corner that my father was peering through. He had hoped to make it to the airstrip but we were quickly losing height and it was now obvious that there was no way we were going to clear the high security fence surrounding the airfield. His only option was to land in an adjacent paddock. This he did expertly. He cleared a barbed-wire fence and put her down gently in long grass generously dotted with brick-red anthills.

Remarkably he didn't hit anything. How he achieved this no one knows.

As soon as we touched down the airport fire engine made a most spectacular arrival, crashing straight through the high security fence. Sirens blaring and lights flashing, it screeched to a halt by our plane at the same time as a large number of other emergency vehicles converged on us. It was impressive but a bit of an anticlimax as we were all fine; the plane wasn't even damaged.

Mother was shaken. John was pale and limp, leaning up against the plane's propeller, trying unsuccessfully to light a cigarette. His hands were visibly shaking when one of the rescue team caught sight of him, gave him a stern warning about smoking next to an aircraft and led him away in a daze. I was sobbing mournfully because I had lost the battle to control my bowels. The rescue team were very nice and tried to comfort me. They thought I was distressed because of the forced landing. I was too ashamed to tell them why I was really crying.

On the trips to town that did not include a forced landing we booked into a hotel for at least a few days. My sisters and I lost ourselves in the bliss of television, fresh fruit, ice creams, milkshakes and the saddle shop. The owner of the saddle shop was an engaging, softly spoken American man who had made several offers to buy my plaits. They were so long that I could sit on them. He wanted to cut them off and hang them over his door and tell everyone they had belonged to a genuine American Indian. Every time I went in there he tried, but I couldn't bring myself to part with my hair. Mother spent her time visiting hairdressers, beauticians and dress shops. According to her their selections were very limited, although the longer you were up in the bush the better they looked.

We nearly always made a trip to the book store, where my mother would spend quite a bit of money buying all of us, including herself, books. This ritual instilled in me a great respect and love of books that will be with me forever. My father spent most of the time doing business on the phone, drinking beer, and eating cheese, crackers and salami. When he wasn't pursuing these activities he was arguing with Gus, his cousin and business partner of many years.

Neither my mother nor my father drove much. Mother had driven in America but hated it and was not at all confident. Father was a better driver but thought it was a waste of his time and preferred to be driven. At huge cost he would hire a taxi for the day and have the driver take him all over Darwin to buy the many and varied requisitions needed at the station.

My sisters and I enjoyed the luxuries that went with a town trip, but by the end of a week we were itching to go home. We missed our horses, our dogs and our freedom.

Only a few years after our return to Bullo John was increasingly at loggerheads with my father. John's knowledge and experience of cattle were superior to Father's. He was cautious in business, careful with money, and liked to take the time to do things properly – just about the opposite of my father in every aspect. I think John had envisaged a partnership in which he and my father would work together. The truth was, with Father, you worked *for* him not *with* him. Father always got his way and John became more and more frustrated. He wanted to end the partnership. Father and his cousin, Gus, agreed to buy out John's share of the company. To cut a long story short they really did him over in the deal. I suspect that John came to resent my father for what they had done to him.

John left the property not long after that. Once they had finalised their business they never spoke again. I was sad to see him go. Apart from the fact that he was a character who indelibly coloured my childhood, I had great respect for his horse, cattle and bush skills. I doubted that we would ever find anyone who could fill his shoes, and thought that without his stock knowledge the cattle side of the business would suffer. It turned out I was right on both counts.

4

BY THE TIME I WAS 13 SCHOOLING was becoming a problem. It was difficult to find good teachers who were willing to come out and stay in this very isolated part of the north. We had had a few governesses of varying success, but the isolation was too much for all of them in the end. In-between, my mother supervised us, but it was increasingly difficult for her to find the time to help me with my school work, which was becoming harder and harder. If she was too busy, we just did the best we could. We had no strict routine of set school days and designated holidays, as in a normal school. We fitted in correspondence school between our work and spent most of what should have been our school breaks catching up on assignments because we had been working during the term. My parents decided to send Bonnie and I to a boarding school in Adelaide.

My half-brother, Frazer, had been staying with us at Bullo for some time while he decided what to do now that he had finished school, which he had excelled at. David had already returned to Sydney to finish school with the intention of going on to agricultural college. Now Frazer had decided to leave and study medicine in the USA. I am certain that he saw no future in Bullo, only a lifetime of back-breaking work while putting up with my impossible father, who expected far too much from everyone, especially his sons. Father, Frazer, Bonnie and I climbed into the plane with a small load of frozen meat in cartons and took off for Darwin to catch our respective flights – Bonnie and I to Adelaide, Frazer to America.

Frazer and my father sat in the front seat talking – or rather my father was lecturing and Frazer was listening, as was normally the case. Bonnie and I sat in the row of seats behind them. Bonnie seemed more affected by Frazer's departure than I did, as she had been quite close to him. My thoughts were consumed by how much I did not want to leave home and go to boarding school. Mother and Father had attempted to convince me how much fun it would be and how lucky I was to be going to such a good school. It was to no avail; I did not feel excited or lucky. By now I was in love with Bullo and wanted to stay there doing all the exciting things I'd been allowed to do for the past four years. I had never been to Adelaide and the idea of leaving my family to go to a strange school and live in a strange city with people I didn't know did not sit well with me.

My mother both did and didn't want us to go. She knew that with all the interruptions of daily work we were not getting the sort of education she would like us to have. She was struggling under the weight of dealing with Father, her general dissatisfaction with her life, and all the cares and worries of running the homestead. To add to all this, Danielle was now five and ready to start school as well. Mother was floundering. Father could see the writing on the wall and agreed that we should go to boarding school, despite his archaic opinion that women didn't need to be as well educated as men as their primary role in life was to marry, have children and be there for their husbands.

We were flying over the huge flood plains to the west of the Daly River when the plane's engine stopped with no warning. Father tried to restart the engine without success. 'Here we go again,' I thought. I was not afraid as I pulled my seat belt tight and checked Bonnie's. We leant forward and braced for the impact. We came to rest in a swamp between two huge ghost gums, with a ten-feet-high ant hill right in front of us. I was certain that no one else had a father who crashed quite as well as mine.

The load of meat had ended up on top of Bonnie and me. Frazer pushed the heavy cartons off and we all got out as quickly as possible in case of fire. The plane had come to rest in about two feet of water, the undercarriage was ripped off, the propellor was all bent, and the radio was not working. By law my father had filed a flight plan complete with a nominated search and rescue time. We were due to arrive in 40 minutes, and when we failed to show up, emergency services would start a search. However, as the plane was parked perfectly under two trees it would be very difficult for any rescuers to spot us. Bonnie and I waded to a drier piece of ground to make a camp; it was a real possibility that we may be spending the night out here. I hoped not as there were thick swarms of mozzies already. Meanwhile Father and Frazer got the radio operational.

Then, in the far distance we heard the drone of a search-and-rescue aircraft. My father guided the rescuers to us over the radio but the foliage our plane was under was so thick that they couldn't see us even when they were right overhead. We found an old blanket in the plane, soaked it in aviation fuel, put it in the top of a pandanus bush and lit it. A huge burst of flames, and the smoke from the burning of the green pandanus leaves, clearly marked our position for the rescue plane. They couldn't land in the terrain so they flew back and gave our coordinates to a military helicopter, which arrived a few hours later to pick us up. Even the helicopter had trouble finding a spot to land. Soggy but all in good order we climbed in and made it to Darwin before dark. Well, it had taken my mind off boarding school for a little while.

Bonnie and I went from the wilderness to The Wilderness School. When it was established some 90 years before it was in the wilderness, but by the time we arrived there it had been engulfed by the outer suburbs of Adelaide. It was an alien landscape compared to the outback. The routine was a shock for us too. There were three bells for everything: one to warn us it was about to happen; one to let us know we should be there; one to say it was now over and we should be gone. I was a bit out of step with the other girls because I wasn't up with all the latest music or fashions. I dreamed of the latest Syd Hill saddle instead.

We sent a pitiful letter back to our parents about how much we were suffering. The food was awful; we were cold; it was like living in a prison; there were 40 bells a day that regulated our every move and nearly drove us insane. The litany of complaint was long. My parents sent sympathetic replies and my mother, in pity, sent us a package of biltong, which is like beef jerky. The other girls were suitably horrified to see us chewing these unappetising bits of dry meat.

My parents, as was so often the case, had their own problems. My father more and more often stayed away overnight in Darwin, ostensibly on business. Or so he said. He was playing up with other women again. He had totally lost my respect. Of all the difficulties we had in our father–daughter relationship our disagreement over his treatment of my mother was to prove the biggest.

We had been in boarding school less than a year when Mother packed her bags and came down to Adelaide with Danielle and her dog, Hottentot. To our great delight she rented a house and took us out of boarding school. We finished the year as day students, while Danielle attended the kindergarten at Wilderness.

My mother had read a book written by an American woman from the city who had married a chicken farmer. It was called *The Egg and I* and had sold a million copies. My mother reasoned that her life was equally interesting and decided that she was going to write a book, make enough money to leave Father and live in the comfort she craved. Her book would be called *Through the Saltbush Backwards*, an appropriate description of life with my father. Each day we caught the bus to school and left her labouring over the book that would set her free. Proud of her efforts, she was totally devastated when the one publishing house she approached knocked her back. She did not have a lot of confidence and did not persevere.

Down and beaten, my mother resigned herself to her fate. Cattle prices were abysmal and the business was struggling; there was no money for her to continue to live in Adelaide or for us to stay in boarding school. She packed her book away, packed our bags, and we all went back to Bullo for Christmas.

We were overjoyed to hear that we would not be returning to boarding school and that we were home for good. Mother did not share our enthusiasm. Father set about finding another tutor for us and we fell back into the same routine of no routine. As a result our education did suffer.

My father was always extremely attentive to my mother when she returned from one of her spells away. He convinced her, as usual, that he would pull off the big deal soon and that she would have all the money and comforts she deserved. Briefly, we all lived in peace. Father would invariably get caught out again, though, and the whole scenario would repeat itself. Mother would explode and leave, usually going to Sydney to stay with her sister or mother. How long she stayed away depended on how mad she was with my father, what the financial situation was, and how she felt about living with her relatives. She never felt comfortable having to depend upon her family and my father knew this. At the appropriate time he would start working on her; eventually he would bring her around to his way of thinking, and she would once again return.

Bullo offers some of the best fishing in the north. Being keen fisher people our parents bought Bonnie and I our first fishing rods for our 11th and 13th birthdays respectively. Up to this point in our angling careers, we had only used old hand reels. With our new equipment we could now go and fish in the river for the premium game fish of the north, the barramundi. This presented a dilemma for my mother: the river was full of saltwater crocs. After we drove her up the wall with our pleading she agreed to come with us. We set off, my mother carrying an old branding iron for protection. Bonnie and I thought it a rather odd weapon; a gun perhaps, but what self-respecting bush person carries a branding iron around? My mother would not be swayed and we set off on the one-kilometre walk up the airstrip to the river.

Shad, my black Labrador, and I went ahead while Mother, Bonnie, Danielle and the other dogs followed at a more sedate pace. Shad was a born hunter; she weaved back and forth in front of me trying to pick up a scent. As we neared the river she ran ahead and jumped into the brown water to cool off. I called for her to get out. Crocs love to eat dogs; they're a handy snack size. As I slid down the river bank my blood froze. Shad was in the middle of the river swimming towards me, with a good-sized saltwater croc closing in at an alarming speed. My 'come' command came out as a frantic screech as I ran to the river's edge. Shad was swimming flat out now; she had seen the croc behind her. As her front paws touched the bank I grabbed her by the scruff of the neck and almost simultaneously the croc grabbed her back legs.

My mother had heard my hysterical screaming and envisaged her worst nightmare – one of her children in the jaws of a crocodile. Covered in sweat and out of breath she came sliding down the muddy bank. Only slightly relieved to see it was my dog and not me that the croc had hold of she gave the croc her best tennis stroke on its snout with the old branding iron that we had so teased her about. The croc had never encountered prey such as us and thought it was all too much. It let go of Shad and retreated, disappearing silently beneath the water. Mother, Shad and I struggled up the slippery, steep bank and collapsed at the top, covered in mud and quite out of breath. Danielle, whom Mother had stowed in the prickly branches of a Parkinsonia tree for safety, was howling loudly. We gathered ourselves and went home. The next day one of the men went down to the river and shot the croc, which was about eight feet long. Not the biggest, but certainly big enough to eat a dog or one of us.

This incident did nothing to dampen our enthusiasm for fishing. Crocodiles are just one of the hazards you put up with to catch barramundi. Our mother, however, declined all future invitations and lived in fear each time we set off with our rods. As we became more skilled we caught many impressive-sized barra. To catch a ten-kilo fish was not unusual, but it was rather a heavy load to carry over a kilometre home. I decided to remedy this problem by taking Danielle's donkey, Honky Tonk, as our pack animal.

Danielle had been given Honky Tonk to ride when she was four years old because all the horses were too big and wild for her. There were few donkeys on Bullo but across the river on Bradshaw Station there were thousands of them, so my parents arranged to have one sent over. The donkey arrived one day unannounced, tied up in a mustering plane that had come from Bradshaw; he was young, and the most adorable, fluffy, grey thing you could imagine. He looked like the cherub of the donkey world and we all fell in love with him instantly. Who would have thought he would grow up into such a sour old thing? We named him Honky Tonk after the noise he made.

The first time we decided to use him we had instructions from our mother to be home by 4.00 pm. I didn't have a watch so I set an old-fashioned alarm clock and put it in Honky Tonk's pack. He was opposed to any kind of work and was not at all impressed by his new appointment as fish donkey. We had a great afternoon of fishing and caught two 25 lb barra, which I gutted and scaled on the river bank. The Aborigines simply threw the entire fish, guts and all, onto the coals, but Mother didn't appreciate us turning up in the kitchen with unprepared fish. We always had to bring back our catch looking as though we had just bought it from a supermarket, or she got upset.

It was nearly 4.00 pm when we decided to start out for home. I was heaving the two big fish over Honky's back when he swung around and let fly with both hind legs. I saw it coming and tried to duck but wasn't quick enough. One of his hooves collected me on the right side of my face, driving my teeth right through my cheek. Stunned and flat on my back in the dirt I heard the alarm go off and saw Honky take off with the two fish flapping furiously at his sides. Bonnie helped me to my feet and got me back home.

I had a long, painful night at Bullo because it was too late to fly out. My father flew me into the Darwin hospital the next morning. Luckily my jaw was in one piece and it was just a matter of waiting for the swelling to go down and keeping any infection at bay. I could only see out of one eye and could only eat through a straw. The men didn't find Honky until the next day; he was in good health, minus the fish and the alarm clock.

The wet season of 1974 set in and we headed to Darwin for a week of Christmas shopping. My sisters and I didn't have any money of our own, so we trailed along while my mother made the Christmas purchases. She enjoyed shopping and was good at choosing gifts. If we had our heart set on buying something in particular for Father we would ask her to include it in the shopping. If we wanted to buy something for her then we had to approach our father, but he preferred us to make our own cards and gifts. On the occasions he lashed out and bought Mother gifts he usually got it completely wrong. He would buy eight books that he wanted to read but that my mother didn't (at least not in this lifetime), or a cookbook so she could cook for him (she hated cooking) or a beer-making kit so she could make beer for him. In later years he finally got the message and would ask us what to get her.

With the plane packed up with all sorts of festive food and gifts we zigzagged our way home through the heavy monsoon weather; it certainly looked as though we were in for some rain. On Christmas Eve we decorated our bush Christmas tree, which was a type of tropical pine tree with pine needles rather than leaves, and put our gifts under it, excited by the prospect of opening them the next morning.

Early on Christmas Day we woke to the sobering news that Darwin had been hit by Cyclone Tracy overnight. She had literally wiped our outback town off the map. Despite the fact that Darwin airport was closed to all but military and evacuation aircraft, my father flew in a few days after the cyclone with a load of fresh meat and to help in any way he could. He wasn't given permission to land but, in typical style, he did anyway. He checked up on his cousin, Gus, and his friends. None of them had homes any more but at least they were all in one piece. There was no food, drinking water or power. Everything was rotting and disease was a real threat, particularly in the hot, humid conditions of the wet season. The trees were stripped of their foliage and the streets looked like an abandoned ghost town.

It was not long after Cyclone Tracy that Poppa, my mother's father passed away unexpectedly. Mother had adored him and was grief stricken. My father obtained permission and flew her into the still restricted Darwin airport, where she caught a flight south for Poppa's funeral and then stayed on to help my grandmother sort out her affairs.

Life was much harder for us with her gone because Father didn't really have any idea about children, particularly the female of the species. He only understood the deployment of troops. Bonnie and I checked fences, brought cattle in from the holding paddocks for the abattoir to slaughter, and looked after about 100 chickens. I also baked bread for around 30 people daily on our old wood stove. Each morning before school I set the yeast to rise before adding it to a huge bowl of flour. While it was rising I chopped the wood and fired up the stove so there would be plenty of hot coals to bake the bread later. In my morning school break I knocked down and kneaded the dough, and put it into bread tins for the final rise, and then put the tins in the wood stove so we would have fresh bread by lunch. In addition, while Mother was away I often had to cook all the meals for 30 people, as we were regularly in between cooks who came and went.

The staff had one day off a week, and on that day things were even worse for Bonnie and I. At 5.00 am Father would wake us up to cook breakfast and carry out his long list of requirements for the day, ranging from cleaning the grease off the plane's undercarriage to mowing lawns, typing and answering the phone. The only solution was to pack supplies the night before and have our horses in the yard so we could ride out quietly at 4.00 am before he rose to haunt us.

———•••••———

Several of my father's friends who had lost their homes in Cyclone Tracy had managed to save their pets, but had nowhere to keep them and no food to feed them. There was no room on the evacuation planes to take them along and the military were destroying strays to control the spread of disease. My father's friends begged him to bring their pets to the safety of our home, and he agreed.

Early in 1975 we still had some of the Cyclone Tracy pets boarding. One in particular, a black Labrador, was a real city slicker. He had no idea about horses and cattle but must have had a deep-seated wish to be a farm dog because he chased everything at every opportunity. I had just saddled Holy Smoke and was waiting in the homestead yard for my father. Holy Smoke was standing peacefully under a tree when the dog came up behind him and bit one of his legs. He took off like a bullet with the dog hot on his heels, barking. My father's big piebald horse, Peter, also took fright, and galloped off in the opposite direction. Bonnie's mare, Chablis, was standing under a flame tree at the front fence. Holy and Peter wheeled around when they came to the fence and now galloped straight at each other, towards Bonnie's mare. She looked nervously both ways; she saw them coming straight for her. The dog was still barking ferociously at Holy Smoke's heels. I watched in horror as the mare, at the last possible moment of escape, jumped over the fence and the other two horses collided at a flat-out gallop. They fell to the ground. Peter was thrashing about but Holy Smoke lay very still, barely breathing. Peter struggled to his feet – he had a broken shoulder. One of the Aboriginal stockmen looked at Holy Smoke and shook his head gravely, without uttering a word. I knew what it meant. Holy Smoke only lived a moment more. I was devastated; I had truly loved that horse. I crumpled beside his still warm body in a sobbing heap. The Aboriginal stockmen kindly buried him for me under a bottle tree that had stood on the banks of the Bullo River for a thousand years. I felt lost and numb. My parents gave me another horse, as we had hundreds, but none was ever as special as Holy had been.

By the time I was 14, Father had not been well for quite a while. He had contracted pneumonia a few years earlier and had never quite recovered. He went to the doctor and after a few tests was diagnosed as having the early stages of emphysema. When I was a young child my father had smoked a pipe and cigars, generally with cocktails at sunset. He occasionally lit up a cigar when we were in the plane, but after I threw up a few times he refrained. To this day the smell of tobacco smoke makes me ill. My mother hated him smoking and convinced him to stop in his mid-40s, but by then the damage had been done.

The doctor recommended he change his lifestyle and do lung-strengthening exercises to control his condition. He stubbornly refused. My mother initially pushed him to take the doctor's advice but eventually gave up in frustration. He thought he could beat anything, including emphysema, on his own terms. He was wrong, and so began the slow and painful decline of his health. Along with his health went his cheerful optimism, visions and ideas, which had scared – and inspired – us all for so long.

5

WHENEVER WE COULD FIT IT IN, BONNIE and I liked to go out mustering with the Aboriginal stockmen. Uncanny bushmen and accomplished cattlemen, they were patient with us and generous with their knowledge. Our head stockman was Peter Frazer, a well-built Irish–Aboriginal man with a broad, kind face and the best smile. He was a man of few words, but when he did choose to speak it was well worth listening. He carried himself with the quiet confidence of a good leader and had the respect of those who worked for him. Of all the people who have passed through my life Peter taught me the most about cattle, horses, good humour and leadership, all by example.

Peter oversaw a stock camp of about ten Aboriginal stockmen, who would camp out for several weeks at a time, depending on how far away the muster site was.

Our first job with them was horse tailing. We had to get up hours before everyone else, saddle up the night horses – quiet horses kept in a small pen overnight – and head off into a large holding paddock to bring back horses for the stockmen to ride that day. Cattle mustering is very demanding so each stockman needed at least four horses so they could rest those that were tired or injured. This meant we needed to get a minimum of 40 horses rounded up and corralled in an enclosure.

We also had to get about half a dozen pack mules to carry all the gear. They could bear more for longer and further than horses, and were considerably tougher. They were also terribly cunning. All night the clanging of their bells rang through the clear winter air – until about 4.00 am, when silence fell because they knew we would be coming to get them soon. They would stand in the deepest, thickest scrub. Every morning they hid and every morning we found them – eventually.

Our other unenviable job as horse tailers was to pack and unpack the mules. With the exception of one small, white mule called Snowy, who was quite sweet, they had devil-possessed natures. The very sight of them glaring at me struck fear in my heart. Fear is good sometimes; it has saved my neck more than once and it certainly wasn't misplaced with these beasts.

One morning Bonnie walked too close to a packed and tethered mule when I was off at a distance saddling my horse. The mule lunged forward, locked his huge jaws over her shoulder, picked her up off the ground and shook her. She looked like a rag doll hanging out of the mule's mouth. One of the stockmen, yelling blasphemous Aboriginal dialect, walloped the mule across the head with a lump of wood. The mule rolled his eyes, let Bonnie go and ran backwards to avoid the stick-wielding stockman. Bonnie was shaken and had some impressive imprints of the mule's teeth on her shoulder but had come through the ordeal remarkably well. The mule never caught her off guard again – nor did he learn. All the mules were the same; until their dying day we had to pack them with a lump of wood handy.

By late in the cattle season in 1976, when I was nearly 15 years old, Bonnie and I had graduated from horse tailers to stockwomen. We were camped with the stockmen at Lesley Lake, home to thousands of birds, which swim among the sweetest-smelling water lilies. In the still of the

Nan and my mother at her childhood home in Lakemba.

My father, Charles E Henderson III, in naval uniform.

My father and mother and Nan and Pop (Mother's parents) in Manila.

My mother and me in Manila.

Above: Me aged 2 in Manila.

Left: My ya ya and me in Manila.

Bonnie's christening, 1963.

Bullo homestead from a distance. A far cry from our life in Manila.

Cutting up 'a killer'. The meat was then salted and put on an old wire bed frame that served as a drying rack.

Bonnie and me helping Mother care for a baby emu.

Bonnie and me in front of our little Tri-pacer plane with Len Robinson, the station mechanic.

Bullo 1965: my father roping Mother in front of the shed. Jack, my eldest half brother, is in the foreground and Hugh, my second half brother, is in the background.

Lloyd's Landing, my grandmother's house in Maryland, USA.

Bonnie and me building a snowman at Lloyd's Landing.

Family photo taken in 1970 just before we left the USA to come home to Bullo.

Back at Bullo: Danielle, Bonnie and me outside the homestead that now had screens and a front door.

The developing Bullo homestead.

My favourite photo of my father taken in 1973 during an exercise to demonstrate Aboriginal tracking skills.

A Hercules taking off after one of the many army exercises on Bullo.

Above: A rare photo of almost all the family at Bullo (only Hugh is missing). Clockwise from left: Jack, David, Bonnie, my mother and father, me, Danielle and Frazer sitting.

Left: The back of the homestead. The windmill pumped the homestead water supply from a hand-dug well.

Mustering with a helicopter.

Left: Danielle, my mother and Bleep, our pet brolga.

Below: My half brother Hugh in Philadelphia.

Charles and Sara sitting in the now expanded homestead.

My father entertaining at Bullo one of the many times my mother left.

Above: Charlie and me at our engagement party – the last time the family was together.

Left: Charlie and me on our wedding day.

Charlie on our block of land in Queensland.

evening its mirror-like waters reflect ancient cycads and red sandstone cliffs. I have often thought it must be one of the most beautiful places on earth. Our camp was by a deep billabong a few hundred metres back from the lake. Each day we would set off at daylight with coacher – or quiet, tamed – cattle and spare horses to muster wild cattle for branding and sale. This old style of mustering was hard on everyone; the days were long and at times the work of handling wild scrub cattle was dangerous.

Today was special. It was Peter's 65th birthday, and it was to be his last season as head stockman as he intended to retire. There was no doubt that it was well deserved, but the thought saddened me. On this clear, cold morning Peter was up first; within minutes he had a welcoming fire going. We huddled around it to keep warm, a nod a well-accepted substitute for 'Good morning'. Breakfast was simple: tea in your large chipped and dented tin cup, bread or damper with jam, or leftover stew for the brave.

In the early quiet, there was time to reflect, something we all do too little of in our modern world. Nearby, the horses milled about, their warm breath visible on the dawn air. There is a particular smell of the Australian bush on cold, dewy mornings, and it mingled with the smoke of the bloodwood campfire and the fine dust rising up from the horses' hooves.

Without a word Peter headed for the horse enclosure, bridle over his arm, and so began the day. The horses were just as savvy as the mules; they knew exactly which horses were to be ridden first. The ones we wanted were always right at the back of the bunch, their mates in front looking at us innocently, as if they happened to be there by chance. After considerable time and effort, and with thick dust now hanging on the still, morning air, we all had our horses.

For those riding younger horses saddling up was not always straightforward. Just as one of the stockmen, named Hector, was about to mount, his fresh colt tucked his tail in and arched his back. Hector's brother, one-eyed Anzac,

moved his quiet horse in front of the young gelding to
steady him. We sat silently on our horses, waiting. It is one
of the worst feelings to have everyone watching when you
know your horse is like a bomb waiting to go off. Hector
gingerly slipped his worn boot into the stirrup. His horse
had broken into a sweat and was rolling his eyes and
moving sideways. Hector put weight in the stirrup, hopping
sideways to stay with the horse. Then in one swift, perfectly
fluid motion he swung up, eased into the saddle as light
as a feather, and slipped his boot into the other stirrup. For
a moment the horse stood rooted to the spot – then the
peace of the morning was well and truly shattered. The
horse dropped his head violently between his front legs and
humped his back up so much he looked like a prawn. Off
he went, grunting and leaping impressively in an effort to
dislodge his rider. But it was not to be one for the horse
this morning; Hector held tight.

Peter smiled – good, that meant we wouldn't have to
spend the next hour bringing back a loose horse. We set
off at a brisk walk. Hector's colt took some time to settle;
he kept dropping his head and humping up as we walked
along. It took us about an hour to get the mob of coacher
cattle together and settled down, then we left the Lesley
Lake Paddock and headed into unfenced bush.

No one talked as we pushed the coachers along; your
voice might carry for great distances and spook the wild
cattle. Every now and then Peter would motion that a few
of us were to head off to pick up and bring back a fresh
mob of wild cattle. The coacher mob would continue along
at a steady pace as we slipped away quietly into the bush.
When we came upon a mob of bush cattle, usually number-
ing five to 15 head, we would stealthily skirt around behind
them, preferably downwind. Once behind the mob we
would stop briefly to check and tighten our saddles, and
then move in quietly. As soon as the cattle spotted us they
would be off as fast as their legs could carry them.

The old stockhorses knew what to do. Without being

asked they'd break into a gallop, bearing down on the fleeing cattle enthusiastically. One rider on each flank and one at the rear, we guided the cattle in the direction of the coacher mob. Peter somehow seemed to know when we were coming in with the bush cattle and would pull up the coachers before anyone else could see or hear them. As soon as the bush cattle came into view the men around the coachers would open ranks and move aside so we could bring the two mobs of cattle together. Once the wild cattle mixed in with the quiet coacher cattle they generally settled down quickly, with the exception of the odd rogue beast. Sometimes the big, sharp-horned bulls wouldn't stop at all, but would go right through the mob and out the other side.

This day, a big red-and-white shorthorn bull was giving us no end of trouble. We had managed to get him back several times, but with increasing difficulty, as he was losing his fear of us. It was too dangerous to get close to him on a horse as he might gore it. The bull broke from the mob again. He had a wild, high-headed look about him as he struck off into the bush at a fast, stiff-legged trot. When cattle get this look about them, they will usually stop for nothing. One of the stockmen rode along behind the bull until the animal had lost his wind, jumped off his horse, and ran with the grace of a gazelle up behind the aggravated beast and grabbed his tail. The bull responded instantly by swinging around to try and hook the stockman with his horns. As the beast turned, for just a moment he was off balance; this was what the stockman was waiting for. He pulled the bull sideways and the beast hit the ground with a thud, an expression of fury and puzzlement on his face. Before the bull had time to gather himself, the stockman grabbed one of his hind legs and lifted it up. Cattle get up off the ground back feet first only, so if you hold one of their hind legs up, regardless of size or strength, they are quite helpless.

Peter pulled his horn saw out and went over to help while we brought the coachers up close to the rogue beast.

It took a few minutes of vigorous sawing to remove the bull's deadly horns, while he struggled and bellowed in fury. The next thing Peter did was to get an old piece of timber and give the bull a good hiding. The first time I saw this done I thought 'How terrible. Why would anyone do this?' I have learned that in the bush things are always done for a reason. When two bulls fight for dominance, the winner gives the loser a thorough beating. The bull would now be submissive – that was the theory anyway. The shaken beast pawed the ground, snorting and glaring at us, then his wild-eyed gaze locked onto my horse. He came towards me with deadly purpose in his eyes. My horse, Stratus, was a kicker. This bull had no idea what he was in for. I spun Stratus around and waited. As soon as the bull was in range Stratus let fly with both hind legs, knocking the bull right off his feet. That was it for the bull, he had had enough. He made a hasty retreat to the safety of the coacher cattle.

As the sun set behind the ranges we wearily brought the mob back to the paddock at the lake and unsaddled our horses. Bonnie and I had talked about doing something special for Peter's birthday. We had no gift for him but thought a cake might be a nice gesture. Before we became too comfortable out of the saddle, we caught our spare horses and saddled them for the ride back to the homestead. I told Peter that we needed to go home but would definitely be back that night. I could see that he was curious as to why we were leaving, but he was too polite to ask. We headed off into the darkness. It would be a 23-kilometre ride there and back.

As we made our way past the lake the magpie geese and ducks stirred and the full moon rose to light the way for us. Our horses knew where we were going and settled down into a fast walk, single file, along a well-used cattle pad – a track formed by cattle following the same route to and from feed and water each day. Once we left the lake behind us we rode through several miles of thick scrub. We didn't talk much; we were too tired.

The scrub stopped abruptly and we came out onto a treeless, black-soil plain. Bright moonlight was shining on Brolga Swamp in front of us. No theatre could surpass this spectacle. The ceiling was a billion stars shining sharp and bright, as they can only in outback skies. The luminous moon lit a watery stage framed by water lilies, as the graceful brolgas did their elaborate and joyful dance. We watched, mesmerised for a time, and then, reminding ourselves of our journey's purpose, set off across the plain to the Bullo River.

We stopped on the bank and looked carefully for any crocs. It looked clear and the tide was low, so we wouldn't have to swim. The horses waded into the muddy water; it only came to their chests. We lifted our feet up onto our saddles to keep dry. It was only a short way now, through the River Paddock, and we were home.

Bonnie whipped up a chocolate cake in no time while I made some icing. Transporting the cake back iced could be a problem so we decided to ice it when we got to the camp. We packed a bottle of champagne as a finishing touch. It was about two hours after our first crossing that we came back to the Bullo again. The big king tide was coming in and the water level was rising fast. With the cake and icing held high we urged our horses into the river. They plunged into the murky, swirling water, swimming strongly for the other side. The water was warm, but we were awfully cold as soon as we came out. At least the birthday cake made it across dry. We walked into the stock camp about an hour later, damp and cold. After attending to our horses we hastily iced the cake and lit the candles – we didn't quite have 65 but the thought was there.

Peter was sitting at the fire with the other men. Bonnie and I crept up from behind to surprise him with his birthday cake. Not in a million years had he guessed what we had been up to. His expression went from surprise to embarrassment and then deep emotion. His eyes were watering as he said 'No one has ever done this for me. Thank you.' He was lost for further words, but in his awkward silence his gratitude was obvious. I quickly pulled out the bottle of champagne and poured some for everyone while Bonnie cut up the cake.

We sat around the fire sipping champagne in our battered tin cups, eating chocolate cake and chatting. I told Peter that we didn't know how we would manage when he left. He smiled and said that I knew enough now to take over, and that he had told my father this. I was deeply touched, but definitely didn't feel as confident as Peter did. I bid everyone goodnight, crawled wearily into my swag and fell instantly asleep. The next cattle season, in my 15th year, I took over the stock camp.

On an average we did a muster every two or three weeks on Bullo. Each could take anything from one hour to several weeks. There were no set time frames and no set area; we tried to cover as much country as possible but each day was different. Generally we stayed out until we had picked up 200 head of bush cattle with the coachers then we walked them back to the homestead yards where we drafted them, sorting them into categories of age, sex, those to be branded and those to be sold. The sale cattle were put in a holding paddock until we had stockpiled a mob of cattle from 4 to 800 head, then we would arrange a sale.

We were lucky to experience the old way of mustering. Times were changing and aerial mustering with helicopters looked to be the way of the future. Father was very enthusiastic about pursuing the new way and gradually introduced the technique, until eventually we were using as many as four choppers in unison, with stockmen on the ground, to bring thousands of cattle together and into a yard in just one day, when it would have taken stockmen alone months to achieve the same. Mustering with helicopters is exciting, dangerous and loud and requires a high level of skill from the pilots; I would rate it right up there with war. The pilots push their machines to the limit, flying close to the ground between trees, and in some cases under them. I still get an adrenaline rush mustering in choppers, even after all these years.

6

WHEN I WAS GROWING UP WE DIDN'T have TV at Bullo. Our big entertainment for the week was the Saturday night movie. This meant an old 16 mm film hired from an outlet in Darwin and screened after dinner in the living room of the homestead. Everyone came, and made an effort to dress with more care than usual. Even the roughest sorts sat quietly on their very best behaviour, patiently waiting for the old projector to spring to life and the movie to appear on the sheet on the wall that served as our screen.

Westerns were always popular with the stockmen, my father liked war movies, the male abattoir workers liked movies that we couldn't show, and my mother liked romantic comedies that no one else wanted to watch. To keep the majority happy a range of movies were shown, from *The Good, the Bad and the Ugly*, to *The Eagle has Landed* and *Alien*.

We marvelled at how movie horses could gallop for hours without sweating or getting tired, never needed food and were always saddled. How could anyone get passionate in a haystack? Hay is prickly, itchy stuff. And how could two men have a fight without losing their hats or getting a smudge of dirt on their perfectly pressed shirts? Hollywood!

It was not until I was well into my 20s that we got a

satellite dish and joined the rest of the world. The truth is, apart from the daily news – which is quite depressing at times – I don't think I missed out on much. I probably saw more at an early age than most people ever see. I was viewing the real thing.

I was surrounded by people living, eating and working together in close quarters. For many years the back of our sprawling homestead was a collection of small, temporary rooms hastily cordoned off to cater for the growing numbers of staff. Our homestead's facilities were stretched to the limit, with only one bathroom and toilet between as many as 30 people at one stage. It was like a live show of all of life's scenarios, played out with good and bad endings.

Being so remote, Bullo attracted an unusual mix of people, and we certainly employed our fair share who marched to the beat of their own drums. Cooks came and went with alarming regularity. After a run of complete fruit-cakes we eventually found out that the employment agency we used was situated close to a mental institution. Discharged patients would wander down the street and apply for our cook's position – which was almost permanently advertised – and then come up north as apparently stable people, only to run out of their medication and lose the plot quite suddenly.

It didn't take us long to realise that Alice wasn't a cook at all, so my mother enlisted her to simply help with some of the preparation in the kitchen. After my mother had issued instructions, Alice appeared at her office door.

'There aren't any knives in the kitchen. I *need* knives to cut up the vegetables,' she announced in a short, annoyed tone.

My mother responded with 'Don't be ridiculous; there must be a dozen knives.'

But upon marching out to the kitchen she discovered that there really were no knives. Not even a bread and butter knife.

'I told you so,' said Alice triumphantly.

Everyone got involved in a search of the house – only to discover that the knives were all under Alice's mattress. Needless to say she was sacked, but it was a couple of days before she could get transport out of Bullo. She sneaked into the kitchen and turned off the stove every time my mother turned her back on the cooking, and regularly turned up at the door, a flat, sandstone rock in her hand.

'Can I have this rock?' she would ask my mother each time.

My mother would respond with a short and dismissive 'yes' and Alice would head towards a huge bottle tree about half a kilometre from the house. When I finally asked her what she was doing she said, 'Building a house.'

The next cook, Mrs Edwards, initially seemed perfect. She could actually cook. She and her husband were retired and seemed like the nicest country grandparents – honest, hard-working folk. The first hint of trouble came when the staff started to complain that there wasn't enough food. Then one of the female staff came and said that Mr Edwards was amusing himself at night by shining a torch in the windows of the girls' rooms, perving at them when they were sleeping or partaking in other night-time activities with their partners. The missing food was found stockpiled in the Edwards caravan, and they left hastily in the middle of that night without telling anyone. Shortly after their departure Mother had a call from a debt collector. Dear Mr and Mrs Edwards had put one down payment on their new four-wheel drive and caravan and then done a runner.

One of the biggest characters ever to live at Bullo was Richard Peter Wicks, known to us all as Uncle Dick. Before my half-brother Frazer had left to study in America his last job had been to employ a mechanic; he found Uncle Dick in a Darwin bar. He was a very talented and clever man, and had he not been a hopeless alcoholic he could have had his pick of jobs anywhere. He was a small, thin, wiry man with just the barest padding of flesh on his frame, but he made up for it with a king-sized character. He had a charming manner, a warm smile filled with false teeth, and was softly spoken. An insomniac, he spent most nights reading.

My parents tried in vain for many years to help him beat his alcohol problem. Over the years we saw him drink brake fluid (it used to have an alcoholic base), aftershave, methylated spirits (when the manufacturers added a poisonous purple dye he found a way to remove it), and some personally brewed concoctions that made brake fluid look like a very mild drink indeed. Everyone learned to work around it, although not always successfully.

Perhaps one of the most hair-raising times Dick ever put us through was on a flight to Darwin. I had badly injured my leg mustering and had to fly to Darwin for physiotherapy for months on end. On one such trip the whole family came along. Uncle Dick had been on one of his drinking binges in town, so on our return to Bullo we gave him a lift back. We loaded up our plane with supplies for the station, including a case of Bundaberg Rum intended for my father's nightly grapefruit juice and rum cocktails. While we were standing on the other side of the plane Dick sculled a bottle of the rum. People can die ingesting that much alcohol all at once, so I guess it was a testimony to his capacity. Unaware of what he had done, we finished loading the plane and got in. It was always a tight squeeze because everyone took advantage of a trip to town. On the two-hour flight out of the station you sat on cartons of frozen meat and coming back you sat on supplies for the station, which was better – at least your bum wasn't numb.

Father was lined up on the runway and had received his takeoff clearance. He applied full throttle to the engine and it roared into life. We reached takeoff speed and the plane lifted off the tarmac. Dick had been sitting quietly next to my father – (everyone else refused to sit next to Dick because he smelt too bad) – but suddenly he launched himself at Father, trying to strangle him. He had picked the worst possible time. The plane was heavily loaded, we were at a low altitude and airspeed, and it was hot – all the elements to bring on a stall and crash.

'Get the bastard off me,' my father yelled at Mother as the plane wallowed dangerously in the air. She grabbed Dick around the throat and literally dragged him, gagging and blue-faced, back over the seat. Bonnie climbed into Dick's seat while mother threatened to end his days if he so much as moved again. Father brought the plane under control, and Dick was as quiet as a lamb for the remainder of the trip.

Uncle Dick was occasionally assisted by Diesel Don, a Yugoslavian in his late 40s who came to Bullo as an acquaintance of Mad Max, the stone mason who did a lot of work on our homestead over the years. Diesel Don had pretty poor English – he barely spoke any, and his comprehension was about the same. Old Dick did not like working with what he called 'bloody wogs' who rarely understood what he said. The truth was that even native English speakers often walked away from a conversation with Uncle Dick none the wiser. He liked to use rhyming slang: 'Jack halt' was salt, 'Piccadilly' – chilly, 'pigs ear' – beer. Exceptions to the rhyming rule were 'kip'– a sleep, and 'crib' – something to eat. Poor old Diesel Don really didn't have a hope.

One day Uncle Dick had his head down in one of our decrepit pieces of machinery, mumbling away to himself about the fact that the fuel truck had not turned up yet and the generator was just about out of diesel. There was a full 44-gallon drum at the Two Mile gate – unsurprisingly, two miles from the homestead – that would bridge the gap until the truck arrived.

'Don,' Uncle Dick called to get his attention. 'You go Two Mile gate. You know Two Mile?' Don nodded enthusiastically, which is what he did when he really did understand. 'You go Two Mile gate, diesel drum at gate, bring back.'

'Ya ya!' Don was highly animated and Uncle Dick was

sure that he had it all clear. To further add to his optimism Don headed off down the road in the right direction.

A short time later Diesel Don turned up at his side. With a big grin on his face he asked 'Where I putting?'

'Where do you think? In the powerhouse,' Uncle Dick said grumpily.

Don looked puzzled. He'd missed most of what Dick had said but he did understand 'powerhouse'.

He asked with a confused expression on his face: 'Putting in powerhouse?'

'Yes!' Dick responded emphatically.

Don got the message and took off to the powerhouse. Uncle Dick finished the job he was working on and ambled over to the powerhouse to pump the diesel into the tank that supplied the generator. Standing neatly in the shed was the Two Mile gate. You could hear Uncle Dick even over the noise of the generator; none of what he said is printable. Diesel Don, along with the gate, made a hasty retreat back to Two Mile.

***

At 16 I had little in common with other girls my age. There wasn't any of the lighthearted frivolity of a regular teenage life – no parties, no friends my age – just work that stretched from dark to dark some days. I had entered the rather awkward age where you are neither a child nor an adult. It was difficult, as I had the heavy responsibilities of an adult – I was running a stock camp of about eight Aboriginal men – but not the privileges.

Mother had fought long and hard to educate me, but was losing the battle. Many things were against her. For a start, I didn't like school, tutors were more than difficult to find, and my father was unsupportive, believing that girls didn't need an education. Every time he was short-handed on the station he would send Bonnie and I out, and we would willingly go. In the end my mother just gave up.

Despite his archaic attitude to women and education Father didn't mind us conquering some of the most male-dominated fields – he lived and ruled by many contradictory ideas. He taught Bonnie and I to fly, and while he was a rather unorthodox teacher, he was nonetheless a very effective one.

He also organised for me to have my first shooting lessons from a good friend from his military days, Admiral Bob Crutchfield, who was visiting from the USA. For my 16th birthday my father had bought me a double-barrelled 20-gauge shotgun. Most 16-year-olds swoon over their pop idols but for me it was my own gun.

Once I had completed my firearms lessons with the Admiral I headed off hunting regularly. My father loved wild duck so that was generally my quarry. Despite our isolation, my father still managed to invite large numbers of people to our bush home. On one occasion he had a group of American friends coming. In the States wild duck was a big thing because there were strict limits on hunting them. People from the cities would often pay – and this was 30 years ago – $1,000 for a weekend of duck shooting and only come home with one or two ducks. These were eaten with reverence, shared between three or four people who got a sliver each. To impress his guests my father wanted me to go out and get them a whole duck each.

I set off on foot with my new gun, an instruction from my father to bring back 14 ducks and my very best hunting partner, Bleep, our pet brolga. The owners of the Timber Creek pub had rescued him as an orphaned chick and looked after him until he developed two rather expensive habits. He would stare into the rear-vision mirrors of patrons' cars and peck enthusiastically at the strange bird he saw there, breaking mirrors on a daily basis. And he would pick bugs from the cars' radiators with his beak, making holes in them. Since none of our cars had rear-vision mirrors and weren't capable of driving fast enough to plaster insects to the radiator, we offered to give him a new home. We named him Bleep because that was the noise he made when he first arrived, a half-grown, awkward bird. He grew into an impressive specimen of a brogla, over five feet tall, and his bleep turned into a rich trumpeting sound.

To get 14 ducks I would have to stalk the flock and very unsportingly shoot them on the water. Wild ducks are very savvy; if they so much as got wind of me they would fly off to one of the many other billabongs on the property, not returning for days. I approached a flock of several hundred on the water, got down in the grass and crawled along on my belly, Bleep walking beside me. As I neared the ducks they momentarily fell silent and looked my way. They knew something was up, but all they could see was a big brolga walking along in the grass. Everything must be all right. With Bleep and the long grass as my cover I was able to get very close to the unsuspecting birds and shoot as many as I needed.

Bleep was bothered neither by the sound of the gunshot nor the sight of the dead birds. As I waded into the water to retrieve them he walked along beside me, watching curiously. I don't think he thought he was a bird at all. I made several trips, laying the ducks in a row in the grass at the edge of the billabong. As I made my way back with the last load I looked up to see a duck leap up out of the grass and dive into the water. I was mortified. A hunter must never leave wounded prey – it was a cruel and irresponsible thing to do. I picked up my gun and went after the duck. It dived frequently, hiding amongst the water-lily roots. I followed the trail of bubbles and the movement of the lily tops. I spent over an hour wading through water as deep as my chest, chasing the duck around and around lilies, mangrove trees and reeds before I gave up. With a heavy heart, sopping wet, and quite exhausted, I sloshed out of the water and went back to where I had left the ducks. My game were all there in a neat row – and I mean all of them. I groaned. I had been chasing a perfectly healthy duck – no wonder I couldn't get near it.

I flopped down in the grass, lit a fire, boiled up an old flour drum of water and set about the task of gutting and plucking.

My mother always said it was beyond her how she had ever produced such daughters.

———

Once we had mustered all the areas around the homestead we set our sights on the outer areas of the station, where the cattle were much wilder. In some cases they had never seen people before. Bull Creek, over the mountain range that runs south of the homestead, was one such area. The mighty Victoria River runs through the Bull Creek country and is edged by miles of sparkling white tidal salt flats. Then the country gives way to broken black soil plains for a few miles before it abruptly turns to red, sandy soil at the foot of rough sandstone hills that go on for another 40 miles. The cattle that inhabited the area were notoriously mad and had for the most part successfully resisted attempts to capture or quiet them. One of the major problems was access. The ranges that separated the Bullo River Valley and Bull Creek were all but impassable even for four-wheel drive vehicles, but my father thought it might be possible to muster the cattle towards the Victoria River and around the ranges, along the salt flats. He sent Bonnie and I off to check the route.

We knew it would be a long ride so we left at 4.00 am on our fittest horses. We took some sandwiches and a canvas water bag. By lunch we had made it over the range to the creek, where we had expected to find water. It was bone dry. Our water bag was nearly empty and the weather was extremely hot. After a brief stop to eat our lunch we headed towards the Victoria River. Some hours later we came to the end of the mountain range, which gave way to the salt-flat banks of the river. It was seriously hot and our horses were getting sluggish, but we had gone too far to turn around.

As we tried to make our way back home we continually hit deep, tidal saltwater arms of the Victoria River and Bullo River, which were uncrossable where they joined the rivers – the horses would have gone down and stayed down. The only option was to ride around them by going all the way up to their heads in the rough sandstone hills. Heat waves shimmered across the glaringly white salt flats, conjuring tantalising illusions of water. My tongue felt as if it were two sizes too big for my mouth and my head was foggy from dehydration; the only thing that was clear to me was just how horrific it would be to die of thirst.

Fourteen hours after setting out, we rode into the Nutwood Paddock. The hot, salty bore water in the green-slime-filled troughs was unimaginably sweet to me. Our horses sunk their faces deep into the water alongside of us. We all drank and drank and drank for a long time before lifting our heads and sighing deeply. Bonnie and I sat there for some time, completely drained, then hauled ourselves back into our saddles and urged our weary horses the last four kilometres home.

When we arrived we handed in our report to Father. As a rule, when moving cattle, particularly cows with calves, more than 15 kilometres a day is not practical. We told him that trying to muster the Bull Creek cattle along the 65-kilometre route we had just ridden in one day was both mad and impossible. The distance alone was prohibitive, let alone the extremely difficult terrain and complete lack of drinkable water. My father nodded. 'Good work,' he said, dismissing us. That was it. He obviously didn't think it was of particular note that his teenage daughters had ridden 65-odd kilometres and nearly perished. I knew by then that not much would ever please my father.

I headed to our one bathroom – thankfully I was still early enough to beat the evening rush. As the water ran over my dehydrated body I felt like the parched earth when the rain comes after a long dry season. Every cell in my body soaked up the moisture; it was blissful. I had learned a whole new respect for water, which is now indelibly stamped in my consciousness.

Just when I thought that Father didn't care he would catch me off guard and do something very generous. One part of me would be relieved that he was finally rewarding my hard work – another part of me would be nervous about what it was he was really up to.

My half-brother Hugh had lived in the States for some time now and had become engaged to a young woman named Anne, who had visited us briefly at Bullo. It was the whole family's opinion that Hugh would be very fortunate indeed to have Anne as his wife. Hugh was rather good looking and had always been successful with finding lady friends in the past. In Anne he had met his match. She was attractive, intelligent and no pushover.

Anne asked me to be a bridesmaid at their wedding in Philadelphia. Not in a million years did I think my father would let me go, but in his characteristically unpredictable manner he said yes. My social life consisted of the Saturday night movie when the projector was working, so the prospect of travelling to America to a wedding blew me away. My mother was not happy about sending her 16-year-old daughter alone to the States but her protest fell on deaf ears. I really wanted to go and Father had made his decision. In the end most things happened the way my father wanted them to.

I flew to Sydney first and stayed with my mother's sister, Aunty Sue. She had a small frame, a beautiful figure and rich, red hair, and was always dressed to the nines. The owner of several dress shops, she was an astute, hard-working businesswoman with definite opinions on all issues. She had a wonderful sense of humour and was extremely generous to all of us. She had chosen not to have children of her own and spoilt my sisters and I, much to our delight. Without Aunty Sue we probably wouldn't have owned any nice clothes at all. Whenever we visited she always dressed us so that we looked more like civilised girls and less like Northern Territory stockmen. The clothes she gave me for Philadelphia were beautiful, and I must admit it was rather nice to indulge in what seemed to a country girl a frivolous pursuit – preening.

With my new wardrobe I headed to the States feeling a mixture of excitement and apprehension. I was well and truly leaving my box and going out into the big wide world, alone for the first time.

Anne's family home was an old, beautiful mansion set on a small farm in picturesque country. Initially, I felt a little at a loss there, as this was the first time in a long while that I was free of work and responsibilities. But with all the wedding preparations buzzing around me I was soon too preoccupied to think about home, and I settled comfortably into the Philadelphia lifestyle. Anne's whole family made me feel very welcome and made my visit one of the most pleasant times of my life. Hugh and Anne's wedding was a joyous occasion. The reception was held at Anne's family home in a large marquee set amongst the stately old trees on the rolling lawns. I proudly represented my branch of the family.

After the wedding, when it was time for me to go home to Bullo, Hugh took me to buy a good camera. He had long been an avid and talented photographer, and I had always admired his many stunning photos. I am so grateful that he talked me into buying it as otherwise I doubt that we would have any decent pictures of our life on Bullo. However, it did mean spending my very last cent.

On the way home I had to change planes in Hawaii, and was told by the man at the counter that I would need to pay for excess baggage. It briefly crossed my mind that this was a bit odd because, apart from my new camera, I didn't have any extra luggage than when I had flown to America.

'I don't have any money,' I said, showing him my wallet. 'Can I write an IOU or something?'

He looked me up and down in a manner that made me feel not entirely comfortable. In the past year I had noticed men looking at me more frequently in that way.

'You will have to come with me,' he said. He checked my baggage through and motioned me to follow him. I honestly thought we were off to an office to sort out payment. He did have payment in mind – just not the kind I did. We walked for some way, until I noticed that we were in a deserted corridor that looked more like a place where a janitor would keep his equipment than an airport terminal. It finally dawned on me what was happening. Panic swept through me.

'What do you think you're doing?' I asked him, showing my disgust on my face.

He didn't say a word, just looked at me. I spun around and walked quickly back to the terminal, mumbling all the way to myself about what a complete idiot I was.

The rest of the trip to Darwin was uneventful, but I landed a much wiser young girl than I had been when I left only a month before. I was to spend the night in Darwin, which no longer seemed like a big town to me; it was positively cosy and countryish compared to the cities I had just travelled through. My father's cousin, Gus, had offered me the use of one of his spare rooms for the night. My father had left word with Gus that he would be coming in with a load of meat in the morning and would pick me up and take me back to Bullo. I eagerly awaited the morning, as I had begun to miss my home and my family.

Down at Bullo, at the crack of dawn the old abattoir ute struggled up the flat with its load, and Bonnie filled in the invoice as the meat was loaded onto the plane. My father climbed into the plane, started up the engine, and waited for it to reach operating temperature. Once all the gauges were in the green he started the engine checks.

Bonnie was on her way out to the plane with the finished invoice and mail to be posted in Darwin when Gill, one of our long-term staff, stopped her.

'I'll take it out,' she said. 'I need to talk to your father.' Bonnie thought nothing of it and handed over the paper work and mail.

Gill was a tall, slender English woman in her 30s with short, businesslike, brown hair. She was a talented equestrian who, in addition to working on the station, was teaching Bonnie and I the basics of dressage. I greatly admired her horsemanship and the knowledge she generously passed on to us.

My sisters and I had been around aircraft for as long as we could remember, and it had been drilled into us that one must '*Never* walk in front of a plane'. Regardless of whether the engine is running or not, one must always approach a plane from behind. We didn't even think about it any more – it was automatic. Gill went out the front gate, head down, deep in thought. She cut across in front of the plane, and walked straight into the propeller.

When I received a message to say that Gill had been killed and my father would not be coming to Darwin in the plane that day I at first went numb with shock – and then my tears ran freely. I had thought the world of Gill. I had looked upon her as a dear friend. We had talked of going to England and she setting up a job for me riding in a steeple-chasing stable. But fate, I was learning, could be swiftly brutal. In just the blink of an eye Gill was gone.

We had Gill's funeral at Bullo. Father flew the minister and nuns over from a nearby Catholic Aboriginal mission to lead the service. I heard the nuns singing beautifully but through my sadness the rest of the service passed me by. I was off in my own world. Gill was buried under the thousand-year-old bottle tree. Max, the mad but talented stonemason, made Gill's tombstone and Uncle Dick built a fence around her grave to keep the stock out. On the other side of the huge bottle tree lay my beloved Holy Smoke. Now two souls that were dear to me were at rest here.

7

I HAVE ALWAYS FOUND WORK TO BE therapeutic in times of sadness. It gives me time to come to terms with my feelings. Fortunately there was plenty of work on Bullo – and I really needed it now.

As the wet approached there was always a last-minute rush to get the holding paddocks stocked with enough cattle to get us through the next four months or so. Mustering at this time of year is very unpleasant, done either in the sweltering heat or in the first storm's freezing cold. I was camped at Lesley Lake with the Aboriginal stockmen, just after the first good rains, and the low-lying tea-tree country had turned into soup it was so boggy. We had a hard day's mustering, each of us going down in bogs at some point. It looked quite comical. One moment men, horses and wild cattle would be thundering along. The next it was like someone had hit the pause button – from a full gallop to a full stop in an instant, everyone up to their guts in mud. Momentarily the chase was forgotten until everyone extracted themselves from the bog and then it was off again – advantage going to the first one out of the bog.

We rode into the camp late afternoon; a violent tropical storm was brewing. Big cumulonimbus thunderheads were billowing on the horizon. The stockmen looked at the approaching storm and conversed in native dialects about the plan of action. All agreed they should pull down the tents. They were no use in the kind of storm that was coming, which would probably bring winds in excess of 100 kilometres an hour. They would be ripped to pieces and blown away.

Over the years Aborigines have taught me many clever things in the bush, and their tropical storm strategy is as good as I've seen anywhere. They lay out one of the canvas flies on the ground and arrange all the saddles and packs in a circle a few feet in from the edge. Then they fold the canvas in over the saddles so that the structure resembles a pie shell. They put their swags and anything else they want to keep dry in the middle and all climb in, put another fly over the top of the pie and secure it before propping up the middle with a stick on the inside.

That afternoon the men kindly offered me a place inside but I declined. The fact was, even after working with the men for years, I still could not quite stomach their distinctive personal aromas in the open, let alone in a confined space. Predictably the storm did hit, and lashed our little camp viciously. I spent the night wet, cold and miserable. The next morning the pie erupted and the stockmen came out dry, well-rested and cheerful. The only thing I had that was dry was my saddle, which I had put in the pie with the men.

———————

While it was convenient for him, Father was happy for me to run the stock camp. In truth, though, I was just a female, and he moved me aside without a thought when my half-brother David, now 20, came back to Bullo. Of Father's four sons from his previous marriage David was the only one who had taken an interest in the land. He had graduated from agricultural college and Father now planned to groom him to run his cattle empire so he could get on with things that interested him more.

I had been running the stock camp for three years, and I thought I was doing a good job. Clearly, though, how successful I was didn't count. I felt very unappreciated by my Father.

Fresh from college, David had many ideas on the way things should be done. Father also had his ideas – and in the end that was how things were done. It was hard enough working for my father without blood ties, but for a son it was almost impossible. At times Father pushed David to the point of breaking down in tears.

David had a great capacity for work, but having grown up in Sydney with only a brief period at Bullo before heading off to college he had a lot of catching up to do. To be successful in this country you need to be a proficient horseman and cattleman, have good knowledge of the bush and master the art of working with Aborigines. All of these skills are hard-earned, with the latter being the most diffi-cult to acquire. If the Aboriginal stockmen know and respect you, better people to work with in the bush you would be hard-pressed to find. The 'getting to know you' part is not too hard, but gaining their respect is. When you are the boss, Aborigines never complain directly to you; if they don't like you they just leave without a word. And that's what they did to David. There were some 1,200 head of cattle that needed to be drafted and branded, but every-one in the stock camp except a couple of old stockmen, who I suspect were left behind because they were too old to walk, picked up their swags and disappeared in the night. David had a spectacular row with my father, loaded up his Toyota and left too. He had been at Bullo less than a year.

The old stockmen and I were left to pick up the pieces. It was slow going because I couldn't push the old fellows too hard, but we persevered and in the end did get the cattle drafted and branded. Father was appreciative of my efforts, but seemed a little sad and quiet. David was the last of his sons with whom he'd tried to form a peaceful working relationship. His other sons had already long gone, and now it was clear that he couldn't work with David either.

Bonnie was upset by David's departure, as she completely adored her older half-brother. I, on the other hand, never did warm to him, nor he to me. I understood and was completely sympathetic to the reasons he left Bullo, but did not agree at all with the way he did it. He was scathing in his criticism of the men who had walked out in the middle of a job, and yet he did that very thing himself.

After taking time to collect himself David called my father on the phone, and they agreed that David would go to Kingston Rest, a property on the Dunham River just across the border in Western Australia, which my father had purchased as part of his cattle empire. The property, with its well-set-up feedlot and established irrigation system, had huge potential, so David eagerly agreed to manage it. It was their mutual hope that some distance between them would improve their relationship.

With David gone I went back to organising the men, who seemed happy enough to have me back. It was satisfying to return too. I was pleased to see many of the old familiar faces I had known since I was ten years old.

About four times a year we had to get 300 to 400 steers out to the highway, our nearest bitumen road, so they could be transported. Getting large numbers of cattle to the highway by truck was not practical on our road. It took ten hours one way to battle through the bull dust, creeks and jump-ups – and that was on a good run. If the truck got bogged it could take days to get out. Instead, we walked the bulk of the cattle 80 kilometres out and loaded them onto trucks there. It took three to four days, walking the cattle an average of 20 kilometres a day. The first day was always the hardest with the cattle being fresh. It took most of the day for them to find an order that suited them and you were kept busy bringing any rogues into line.

The cattle always walk the best in the cool of the early morning and as the stock camp settled down for the night on the eve of our journey I was paranoid about getting an early start in the morning. I set my alarm clock and the alarm on my wrist watch for 4.00 am, neither of which I trusted. After finally managing to get to sleep I woke up constantly to check the time. When I checked it for what felt like the 12th time I gasped in horror. I had been expecting this for years. Neither alarm had gone off. In the moonlight my watch read 6.00 am. My God, what a disaster. The horse tailer should have gone hours ago. We should have had breakfast and be saddling up by now.

Panicked, I flew out of my swag and hollered at the horse tailer to get the horses. I got the fire going and the billy on and woke up the rest of the men. 'They all seem terribly doughy this morning,' I thought. 'Great, just what I need. I'm late and everyone's slow.' I rolled my swag while the water was boiling for the tea. All the men were up and the camp was a hive of activity. We had breakfast, the horse tailer turned up and we started catching and saddling our horses. It was only now that I slowed down long enough to question why it wasn't daylight yet. By the light of the fire I had another look at my watch, which now read 2.30 am. I slumped down on the ground. I must have read 12.30 as 6.00. How small did I feel? Very small. Sheepishly I admitted my error to the men, who for some reason thought it was amusing. We tied up our horses and had several leisurely cups of tea before getting the earliest start to a drove we ever had.

Halfway through the first day the cattle still hadn't settled and were giving us no end of trouble, breaking at every opportunity. Peter had taught me that one of the quickest ways to settle toey cattle is to walk them across a bit of rocky country. You have to get the balance right, though. If you keep them on the rough country too long they go lame and for too little they get more agitated and won't settle at all. I led the mob off the road into the bush;

by going cross-country we could save a few kilometres and take the cattle across a small sandstone spur. The strategy paid off and the mob had settled nicely by the time we came out of the sandstone hills to the holding paddock at Sixteen Mile for the night.

The next day the cattle walked well. On our third day out, halfway to the Turtle Yard holding paddock we would use that night one of our pack mules went lame. We stopped the mob and rearranged the other mules' loads but couldn't quite get everything on them. It was then that old Honky Tonk the donkey meandered up for an ear scratch. Honky liked to come out with us on trips – he had never actually done any work, he just liked to keep us company. To Honky's infinite disgust, I pressed him into service – the first half a day's work he had ever done in his life. We packed all the heavy items on the other mules, leaving the swags for Honky, which were not so much heavy as bulky. By the time we had bodgied up a pack to suit his smaller frame and secured the swags, all that could be seen of Honky Tonk were the tips of his ears, four little legs sticking out and occasionally the tip of his tail, swishing back and forth in annoyance.

The cattle walked well that day and even with our unscheduled stop to repack the mules we came to Turtle Hole by late afternoon. As we had no way of communicating with the homestead Father always flew out on the third day to see if we were on schedule so that he could coordinate the trucks to meet us at the bitumen. We had just settled the cattle down when the roar of the plane's engine filled the little Turtle Hole valley. Father came in low over the trees. He had a bag of fresh meat hanging out the window. Reliving his bomber days he stuck his head out the window to make the perfect drop. The meat came in right on target; fresh meat for dinner would be very welcome indeed.

Instead of going straight home he climbed and circled for some time, before he came down low over us again.

This time he threw out a toilet roll. I knew what this meant. He was dropping a message; he put the note inside the toilet roll, which unravelled as it fell, making it easy to find. It was a very one-sided form of communication as we had no way of responding, and that suited my father right down to the ground. I traipsed through the thick grass to the toilet roll and read the instructions from our commander. The note, in hurried writing, explained that his glasses had blown off when he had stuck his head out the window to drop the meat and instructed us to find them. His plane disappeared over the horizon.

The evening had already cast a shadow across the valley. I thought we had no chance of finding his glasses. The Aborigines did have remarkable eyesight, but this task would test even their remarkable skills. The grass was a metre-and-a-half long for a start. We had a brief discussion as to where we thought the glasses might have fallen, and then spread out in a long line to search through the grass. No more than three minutes into the search one of the men let out a holler and held up my father's glasses. Not surprisingly, the lenses were shattered, but the frames were still in good condition. My father was an exceptional pilot – he could fly better than most people even with a bag on his head – so we weren't that worried about him landing without his glasses.

It was late afternoon on our fourth day when we finally got the cattle to our destination. My father flew out and landed the plane on the bitumen to meet the cattle buyer and the truck drivers. He taxied the plane to the side of the highway and shut down the engine. I watched from a distance as he and the buyer talked under the shade of the plane's wing. I sank down against a yard post to rest a while. I was feeling exhausted, as I always did by the time we got the cattle to the bitumen. Despite being bone tired at the end of each day I rarely got any decent sleep. I was just too paranoid about losing the cattle in the night. Apart from bulls and bullocks that we did truck because they were too difficult to walk, these cattle were our main income for the year and I was well aware that we could not afford the loss. Between worrying that the alarm wouldn't go off and that the cattle would rush in the night I only managed catnaps.

My father called me over and said, 'John has offered us 76 cents. What do you think?'

Luckily I had the good sense not to say that I thought we should get at least 10 cents more per kilogram per head than that. How could a man as intelligent as my father was supposed to be not have the deal done before we walked the cattle? The buyer had us by the short and curlies. We had to accept his price – or walk them all the way back.

'At that price I'd walk them home,' I said, not hiding my disgust. I left quickly before I felt compelled to tell them both what I really thought. My father did make a deal, but I didn't even bother to ask what it was as it would have only made me hopping mad. I had realised some time ago that my father, while brilliant in some regards, seemed to be completely lacking in practical common sense. I often voiced my displeasure, much to my detriment. He didn't like to be criticised or questioned by anyone.

Father's emphysema grew steadily worse. He coughed constantly and suffered increasing shortness of breath. He didn't help matters by refusing to do what the doctors recommended. He was still sure he could beat it and, not knowing much about the disease, we believed him. He usually did beat the odds somehow.

Flying really knocked him about now so he started hiring pilots to fly the meat orders to the missions. There was an endless pool of eager young aviators wanting to build up their flying hours so they could apply for the plum airline jobs. Gerry was one of these pilots. A serious young Dutchman with big plans for his flying career, he was very Dutch by nature – serious, ordered and precise in everything he did.

My father's big faithful Beaver aircraft was in for a major overhaul and check so he hired a Cessna for Gerry to fly. One day Gerry did all the necessary checks and took off with a load of meat into a clear winter sky. Later that afternoon search and rescue were alerted when Gerry's nominated arrival time had passed. The Cessna's engine had quit on him and Gerry had gone down in the worst country on his flight path. Rescue services found him the next day in a critical condition, his head fractured and fluid leaking from his brain. He was covered in meat ants, which were eating him alive. It was the consensus that it was a miracle he had survived at all.

I was contemplating this latest tragedy as we moved a mob of cattle across the Brolga Swamp plains. Mustering was almost peaceful. There was rarely any conversation of any length between us because there was no need. We all knew what we were doing and just went about our business. It gave me a lot of time to think about life, but often I only ended up with more questions than answers.

I wondered if at any point my life would be truly peaceful or easy; even dull seemed attractive at this stage. I both loved and hated my life. I hated the way my father complicated everything and was emotionally manipulative – but on the other hand, I didn't mind the hard work or the danger, and the wild beauty of the land was good for my soul.

8

WHEN I WAS A CHILD DAYS SEEMED to go on and on forever, and it was like a lifetime between birthdays and Christmases. By the time I was 18, though, my life was like a runaway horse; all I could do was hold on and make the best of the situation.

My father, unlike me, seemed to enjoy a hell-bent pace. I would go so far as to say he thrived on it. If things did settle a little he made sure it wasn't that way for long. Quite suddenly, he decided it would be beneficial for Bonnie, Danielle and I to learn French. 'Yes,' I thought, 'French will be a great help to me when I'm out mustering with the tobacco-spitting stockmen.' Father advertised in France for a genuine French teacher, settling on a woman in her late 20s called Simone. She was very French. She had black hair, dark eyes and a swarthy complexion, in contrast to her bright, cheerful and perhaps a little fuzzy-around-the-edges nature.

Keen to experience all that the north had to offer Simone joined us on a short muster of the homestead paddock. Normally the inexperienced people sit on the tail of the mob, honing their skills on the quieter cattle. I hadn't had time to explain the way things were done when Simone took off after a cow that had broken from the mob.

What a sight she was. For a start she couldn't ride at all; she was flopping all over the place like an out-of-control sack of potatoes. But the worst of it was that the eyes of every man in the camp were riveted to the sight of her bosoms bouncing up and down from her chin to her belly button in what looked to me to be a very painful action. She had more than ample breasts and didn't usually bother with a bra, to the delight of all the men on the property. I guess she saw no reason to wear one when she came out riding either.

The main mob was heading off in all directions because the men seemed to have forgotten their purpose on the muster. I let out a roar that brought them all back, and got Simone's attention. She bounced up to me with a happy grin on her face. Obviously deep down there was a cowgirl in her just dying to get out. When she saw the look on my face she said, 'Did I do wrong?' in her beautiful French accent. I rode beside her and explained the situation and told her that in future she would have to wear a bra when riding. She raised her eyebrows.

'But in Europe it is nothing to be without a bra.'

'Yes, that may be so,' I said, 'but we are in Australia, in the bush, and I can assure you the men are not yet ready for sophisticated European customs. It may take a few more decades.'

At that moment another beast broke and the men chorused enthusiastically, 'Bring it back, Simone.'

As well as her tutoring duties, which she carried out well, Simone tried to help out wherever she could. On one particularly stressful day for my mother Simone sensed she was about to crack – not a difficult thing to spot – and breezed in and offered to make lunch. We had a rather large number of staff and visitors to feed at that point and the cook had just thrown in the towel and walked off. My mother accepted gratefully, after all the girl was French and all the French cook, don't they?

After Simone had laboured for hours the kitchen looked

like a category five cyclone had hit it. She proudly served up her masterpiece: large lettuce leaves each containing a generous dollop of raw mincemeat. It was supposed to be steak tartare.

'Blue,' one of the men piped up, 'you haven't cooked the rissoles.' Simone, who did not take criticism well, burst into tears and ran off. My mother came out to see what all the fuss was about. She stormed into the kitchen, pushed aside the clutter created by Simone and threw the meat into a pan, mumbling furiously to herself. Everyone gave her a wide berth – we all knew when it wasn't safe to get too close. Needless to say Simone didn't do any more cooking.

———

Father was all too charming to Simone and this made the situation between my parents even more tense than usual. He diverted my mother's attention by declaring that it was time Bonnie had a trip back to the States to visit all the relatives. It was only fair, he reasoned, as I had gone a couple of years earlier. Now it was Bonnie's turn, and my mother was to take her.

Father thought the trip away might improve my mother's mood. It may well have done so if she hadn't returned to find that Father had decided he needed a secretary and had hired Simone's friend Julie. Both Simone and Julie lived up to their cultural reputation and flirted openly with my father. Mother was not happy. I was actually looking forward to taking the next mob of cattle out to the highway to get away from the unbearable tension in the house.

The mob went well and it was a relatively uneventful trip out to the road. I had peace and quiet in which to think. Relationships certainly were complicated it seemed. So far in my life I'd seen a rather lot of examples, ranging from bad to very bad. I couldn't think of one where both parties were happy for any length of time. I lived in hope that two people really could live together with mutual respect and happiness, but having only what I had seen at Bullo to draw on the future didn't look very bright.

When we got to the bitumen the trucks were waiting and so was Father. I could tell straight away he had things other than the cattle on his mind. He looked uncomfortable and ill at ease.

'I need you at home,' he said rather seriously. 'Problems.'

I immediately thought someone was hurt.

'No, no,' he assured me, impatiently adding, 'I'll explain in the plane.'

Now I was getting suspicious.

'What about the cattle? I have to load them,' I said.

'The men can do it.'

He really was in a hurry. The men were quite capable of loading the cattle but I had always felt that my job wasn't finished until the cattle were on the trucks. Normally, once that was done, a station vehicle would pick us up and we would drive home and the horse tailer would walk the stockhorses home. This time I had decided to bring the horses home myself as an excuse to stay away a little longer. Father put an end to those plans. He wanted me to drop everything and get in the plane right now, but to his great annoyance I went over and spoke to the men first and attended to my horse. If he wasn't going to tell me what this was all about he could wait a bit.

I got into the plane, the engine roared into life and Father took off. Once we had levelled out he turned to me and said that mother had caught him in bed with Simone and Julie. He assured me that they weren't actually doing anything and that Mother had got it all wrong. He was innocent. I just looked at him in disbelief.

'Talk to your mother she'll listen to you,' he said.

'And what exactly am I supposed to tell her? Do you want me to give her some bullshit story that you were in bed with two beautiful French girls and nothing happened? That it was all completely innocent?'

By now my blood was up. I told him none too politely what I thought of his behaviour and his treatment of my mother. I told him that he was disgusting and that he deserved everything he had coming. Wow, did that get a reaction. He started flipping the plane over and flying nose down, straight at the ground, only pulling out of the dive at the last moment.

Shouting at the top of my voice to be heard above the roar of the engine I told him that the only thing he would get if he continued his aerobatics was a lot of vomit all over him. He certainly wouldn't be getting my cooperation. I wasn't the least bit scared by his tactics; he thought far too much of himself to endanger his own life.

The rest of the flight home was very icy. I did speak to my mother when we got home, but only to offer my sympathy and complete support. She had told Father that she didn't care what he did, she was leaving him anyway. Father told me to talk her out of it, but I told him he deserved everything he got – and more. The old bastard knew he was wrong and that we had the upper hand. He didn't like it.

After one of numerous howling rows with Mother he announced that he would shoot himself if she left. It was not the first time he had threatened this – but the difference was that last time Mother had believed him. This time she was well past boiling point and told him to go right ahead. Then she exited the room, slamming the door so hard the whole wall shook. She was at the other end of the homestead when we heard the gunshot. Bonnie and Simone went to his locked office door, screaming hysterically and trying to get it open. At the end of the wall was a blood-wood post upright. It was possible to slide between the old wooden upright and the screen frame outer wall of the house, which my mother now did. There was Father sitting with a rather satisfied expression on his face. It obviously pleased him that at least someone cared about his well-being. Mother let fly with a string of abuse that still makes my blood run cold to think of. She unlocked the door, flung it open and stormed out, telling the hysterical Simone to shut up as she passed by.

That was the end of our French lessons.

--·—··—·--

Mother didn't leave Bullo; instead she milked her advantage over Father for all it was worth. Father knew that the best way to keep Mother occupied and relatively happy was to let her decorate and extend the homestead. My sisters and I called it The Blob because it just kept getting bigger. Today the roof area is a quarter of an acre, which gives a good indication of how often Father was in deep shit. It was now looking more like a conventional home, with at least some walls. Staff quarters had been built near the abattoir so apart from guests and any overflow of staff we had the house to ourselves. Father employed Mad Max, the Yugoslavian stonemason, to work on the house every year. Because he was in particularly deep shit after the Simone and Julie incident he hired another Yugoslav, named Drako, to do the labouring work for Max so that Max could concentrate all his efforts on building stone walls. Drako certainly looked like he could work. He was not tall but solid as a brick, and had the appearance of someone who had been shovelling his whole life. Max and Drako unpacked to commence work as the stockcamp and I packed up to go out bush mustering, so our paths crossed only briefly.

I sent some of the men off in an old Toyota to drive to the Number Two bore, where we would be camping each night of the muster. I saddled one of my favourite horses, Mancho, a beautiful buckskin gelding I had brought over from Montejinni, a station owned by Father. I had ridden Mancho mustering on Montejinni and in my whole life I'm doubtful that I'll find a more surer-footed horse than he. He had not long arrived by truck from Montejinni and I was looking forward to mustering on him in the rough country. It was only a 20-minute ride to the Number Two bore and I expected to be there well before the Toyota.

When we came to the river the tide was still up; we would have a short swim across. Mancho was a little agitated by the sight of the river but I thought nothing of it and urged him on. When he saw the steep metre-high mud bank going down to the water he flatly refused to go any further. After trying patiently to coax him into the river I finally had to get a lot more forceful, whacking him with the reins. I was sure he'd be fine once I got him down the bank. He half slid down a couple of times but drew his front legs back like a cat. Then, at the very edge of the bank he took a deep breath and made the most spectacular leap I have ever witnessed. The daft horse was trying to jump the river. The girth strap snapped, the saddle came off and we all parted in mid-air. I ripped off my boots, which are impossible to swim in, and dived in after my saddle before it was lost forever in the murky brown water of the Bullo. I couldn't see anything, but feeling around the muddy bottom was lucky enough to bump into it before the current carried it too far away.

Dragging my wet, heavy saddle behind me I swam for the other side. I dragged myself out and looked around to see where Mancho was. 'Oh-oh,' I thought, 'this horse really can't swim.' He kept putting his head down in panic and coming up with a mouthful of water. I watched in horror as he went into shock, rolled onto his side and started floating down the river. In all my life I had never seen anything like it – I thought all horses could swim. I plunged back into the river and got hold of Mancho's reins, taking care not to get too close. Being in front of any horse in the water is extremely dangerous, let alone one that has completely lost the plot. I dragged him towards the shore. I spoke to him soothingly and as soon as he felt the bottom he sprang to life and took off for dry ground, dragging me along with him. I eventually pulled him up and settled him down, fixed my saddle, and in my sodden, mud-covered state rode on to the bore. The stockmen were waiting. They didn't ask what had happened but had big grins on their faces.

Over dinner I did fill them in on my river crossing, to their great enjoyment. They told me that desert horses, like desert Aborigines, are not the best swimmers. Mancho's home was right on the desert; he had probably never swum a stroke in his life. I would have felt terrible if he had drowned. I had him for many more years and he was the best horse to have in rough, hilly country, but I never did get him to cross the river again.

The next day the men and I worked on fence repairs, and in the afternoon I left and went back to the camp to start cooking dinner. It was a nice camping spot, well shaded by large, old bloodwood and box trees. I had the company of my faithful dog, Cozmo, a large and protective rottweiler who rarely left my side. I was peacefully pottering about the fire when Cozmo raised his head slowly. The hair on his back stood up and he let out a low, menacing growl. I looked up to see Drako the Yugoslav labourer walk into the camp. In all my life I had never had such a strong instinct that I was in grave danger. I heeded it and picked up my double-barrelled 20-gauge shotgun, checked that it was loaded, and cocked it. Cozmo kept himself between me and Drako, growling. Drako tried to appear casual, a rather difficult task in the presence of a big, unfriendly dog and a frightened woman with a loaded gun. I knew he had to have swum the river to have gotten here. He tried to make out that he had just been wandering by and had stopped for a chat.

'I just want to talk,' he said, trying to be engaging.

I looked him straight in the eye, and almost immediately wished that I hadn't, for I saw pure evil. I had looked into the eyes of a crocodile once and this man's eyes brought that memory back.

'I don't want to talk to you,' I said in a quiet, controlled voice. 'Sit down, don't move, don't talk, or I will shoot you.' I meant what I said and he knew it. 'Watch him, Coz,' I instructed my faithful dog.

Coz understood completely. He stood right in front of Drako with his eyes locked on him, the black hair on his back standing straight up like that of a razorback pig. Drako sat still, not uttering a word. I kept my loaded gun by my side and a very close eye on him at all times while I went about my work.

If he tried to move Coz would launch a full scale attack, giving me time enough to do whatever I had to do.

The men came back about a half an hour later – it had felt like an eternity. I wrote my mother a note of explanation that ended with 'Fire him or I'm leaving. There is something very wrong with this man' and sent a couple of the men back to the station with Drako and the note. She terminated his employment immediately. Later, I questioned my reaction. I had only seen Drako in passing the day before we had moved out to the camp and he hadn't done anything to indicate that he wanted to harm me, but my feeling was so strong I could not ignore it. I do believe that bush people, by necessity, take more note of these sometimes seemingly meaningless gut instincts. It was only after he had gone that we found out Drako had raped one of the Aboriginal girls working in the abattoir.

I returned to the homestead briefly to top up the stock camp's food stores. When the radiotelephone rang I answered it. It was Drako.

'I just want to talk to you.'

'Well I don't.'

I slammed down the phone confident that was the end of the matter, but he continued to ring for a year. In the end I was so freaked out I wouldn't answer the radiotelephone. The police were powerless to act because stalking laws had not yet come into being. Our unlikely saviours were the radiotelephone operators, who agreed to stop all Drako's calls. Each time he tried to book a call they said 'No, I'm sorry we can't get through.' I am extremely grateful to this day for their help. Once he couldn't ring any more I began to relax. 'That should be the last of the creep,' I thought.

———•••••———

Over the years our ugly old abattoir had not received much care. New, tougher rules on the standards of abattoirs were introduced, and we would have to spend very large sums of money on the facility if we were to comply with them and have our licence renewed. My father's health was continuing to deteriorate, and was not helped by the strain of running the abattoir. Cattle prices were again good which meant it was possible to survive solely as a cattle station, so my father decided to close the abattoir.

Nothing apart from a substantial lottery win could have pleased my mother more, but the day the old abattoir ground to a halt I had a strangely empty feeling I had not expected to feel. I wasn't particularly fond of the establishment, but like it or not, it had been a part of my life for a long time. The hollow feeling in my stomach came from the realisation that life had changed course irrevocably yet again. After the abattoir workers packed up and left the only people at Bullo were our family, a handyman, the stockmen and a cook on a seasonal basis. Suddenly it was a lot quieter at home.

The older I got the more difficult working with my father became. I had opinions and ideas that he didn't want to know about. If he was wrong about something, I told him, or if he asked something of me that I thought was unreasonable I dug my heels in. Since it was his nature to ask the unreasonable of everyone, not just me, I spent a lot of time in conflict with him. This was insubordination and no commander put up with that from his troops. However I was not one of his troops and so presented him with a unique problem. He knew what to do with troops, but what do you do with a daughter? As usual Father came up with his own special solution.

He called me into his office to tell me, in all seriousness, that he was going to arrange a marriage for me. He looked very pleased with himself, as if he had just given me some truly wonderful news that would delight me. Was he insane? The look on my face must have shown what I thought because he immediately started to justify his choice of husband. Intrigued, I listened. He had chosen an American, who was only 25 years older than me (I was 18), from an old, respected, moneyed family. Now the French lessons made some sense – they had been Father's attempt to refine me. I shook my head and laughed because it did strike me as being rather comical.

'I'll marry who I want when I want,' I said, walking out the door.

He bellowed after me, 'Murray Lee, I'm serious.'

He only used my real name when I was in trouble.

'So am I,' I yelled back at him.

My mother appeared from around the corner, wondering what all the shouting was about. She looked at me inquiringly.

'He wants to marry me off to someone 25 years older,' I said in disgust and kept walking.

'Oh Charles,' she said in an equally disgusted tone. I could hear them arguing as I left the homestead.

My father apparently saw a stubborn streak in me and had decided the best thing to do was to marry me off early before I became too much trouble. Why he even thought I would contemplate such an idea was beyond me. The term 'happily married' was a complete contradiction as far as I was concerned. The institution of matrimony seemed more synonymous with misery from my observations. I wanted to enjoy life at some point and I was certain marrying a complete stranger was not the way to do it.

I had had quite a few avid suitors in my young life. My father had a constant stream of people passing through the station on business, and his friends' sons who wanted to experience the outback lifestyle. My father also allowed the military to conduct training exercises on Bullo; having the station overrun with 300 or 400 men was a very interesting diversion for Bonnie and I now that we were older. I was not interested in getting serious with any of them. Like most people my age I was having fun finding out what I did and didn't like in the complicated world of relationships.

My mother and father had another major blow-up and Mother went to Sydney to take refuge with her sister Sue as usual. When she got to this point my father never tried to stop her; he knew it was easier to let her go and then bring her around later. My father, whose increasingly incapacitating illness, constant coughing and bad moods made him very unpleasant to be around, hired another woman he had met in Darwin, as a 'secretary' and moved her into the house. I was opposed to this and made my feelings clear to him in no uncertain terms. Not for the first time, we fought bitterly. Father, who didn't like to be told what to do at the best of times, but especially when he knew he was wrong, reacted by making my life hellish.

David had returned for another go at taking over the cattle empire so Father once again moved me aside, and assigned me an overwhelming load of menial jobs, the purpose of which seemed to be to keep me busy and out of the way. He had me trying to be a cross between a secretary, a housekeeper, cook and a stockperson. All these jobs conflicted and it was impossible to achieve everything demanded of me. I would get back late after a back-breaking day of stock work to be blasted for not serving his dinner on time. He did most things for a reason. Making life difficult for me would not only punish me but also make my mother feel guilty about leaving.

Apart from my problems with my father, Bonnie and David had formed a close-knit relationship from which they excluded me. Bonnie openly adored David and followed his lead, and I felt that she would be happy if I had nothing further to do with her. I was hurt. She had in effect abandoned the relationship we had as sisters. I had thought that we were close. We had been through a lot together and now it was as if as soon as she had found someone better she had discarded me.

I know David found it hard to catch up on a whole range of skills that Bonnie and I had grown up developing on Bullo, and to live up to Father's expectations. With the sort of pressures he was under perhaps he saw me as a threat. I was very direct with my opinions. If I thought something was wrong I said so, which could have seemed undermining in his eyes. I was interested in solving the problem, not how he felt, but I can see how he took it personally.

Despite my efforts, no matter what I did, my father never seemed to be pleased with me. I was good enough to do his bidding while David was away studying and when he had been on Kingston Rest but now that he had his son back again I wasn't needed any more. For the first time, I worried about my future. It was now clear to me that my father intended David to be his heir. In view of the bond between Bonnie and David, and the way they felt about me, my future at Bullo looked shaky. I couldn't think of another direction I would like to take with my life. I felt emotionally unstable, deeply depressed and alone. None of this was out of the blue, it had all been building for some time now and with Mother away for months trying to save her own sanity, it all came to a head. I believe now I was on the verge of breaking down.

It never rains but it pours. I missed my period. My fear that I was pregnant was confirmed by a doctor in Darwin. Never had I felt so alone. I didn't even consider talking to my father about it. My mother was still away and was absorbed by her own problems. I knew both of them would be scathing in their criticism and I didn't need that sort of judgement at this point. My sister, to whom I had once been so close, was distancing herself from me. I had absolutely no doubt that the father wouldn't want anything to do with the situation. He was a casual affair I had fallen into with all my wounded feelings, only to get into a bigger mess.

Emotionally I was a wreck and financially I had nothing. I had always worked at Bullo to keep our home together; I had never been paid wages. I was given a little bit of money for personal things when I asked, but asking was always uncomfortable. I was in no position to be a mother.

On the pretense of needing to see a doctor for a prescription I got my father to fly me in to Darwin again, this time to terminate my pregnancy. Emotionally I was very strung out; I was really just short of losing the plot. I went and saw my doctor, who later called my father to tell him that I needed to get away from the station for a while, and that perhaps he needed to lighten up on me in the future.

Early in the morning on my 19th birthday I went to the clinic. It was the only day that I could be fitted in on short notice. I had never felt so low and alone. My sadness about terminating my pregnancy was so great I didn't care about what I was doing. To the world I put on a brave face but privately I was consumed with emptiness.I retreated inside myself, and was to stay there a long time.

I could not face the dysfunctional chaos of our home. I had to leave Bullo, and quickly. I needed time to find myself again and make some sense of my life. While in Darwin I lined up a job in Victoria working on a mixed farm and pony stud. My father was not happy about me going away, mostly because it meant that someone else would have to do my work. By then I didn't care how inconvenient it was for him. I flew home and packed my things.

My mother was still away in Sydney so I spoke to her on the phone. It took no convincing her that father had driven me to the brink of a breakdown. She had frequently felt that way herself and understood completely. I never told her, or my father, my other reason for leaving.

I flew to Melbourne and was met at the airport by the

man who owned the farm, Alf Ferry. He drove me to his property about an hour outside of Ballarat, where I was to do general work and school the young ponies. I was the only person working there, which suited me. I didn't want any company; I needed time to myself. I needed to put the brakes on my life and sort through all my feelings – about leaving Bullo, and about my siblings, my parents, myself and my future. The decisions I needed to make seemed overwhelming; I decided that I would deal with each one separately in my own time.

Alf and his wife were good people and the quiet routine of the farm was welcome. Mrs Ferry was a wonderful country cook and very much the typical countrywoman herself. There was no beating around the bush for her. One day she said she had been watching me and thought that most of the time I seemed to be off in my own world. That was a fairly accurate observation. I am certain that she hoped I would open up and to tell her why, but I didn't explain. She did try again to find out why I was so sad and distant but in the end she gave up.

My mother eventually returned to Bullo after her rejuvenating break away from Father. I wondered why she returned this time because she never seemed to be happy with my father for any length of time. After a few months she and my father wrote to me and asked me to come back. My father promised not to be so hard on me and that he would organise for me to finish my flying training and get my pilot's licence. Bonnie and I had been doing a little bit of training each year with a qualified instructor but hadn't been able to afford to finish it. If I took him up on his offer at least I would have qualifications other than those of a stockperson. My mother promised to keep him to his word. They both said that they missed me, which I wanted to believe. I did miss the lifestyle of Bullo and thought passingly that it would be nice to see the sun again. The Ferrys had paid me a small wage, which I used to buy myself a ticket to Darwin, where my father picked me up.

I was a much more serious person when I returned. I was still sad deep inside but I was happy to be home and glad to thaw out in the warm northern climate. My mother and father seemed glad to have me back. Bonnie and David, however, didn't seem to be. Relations between us were still cold.

One of the first things my father asked me to do was to take the ten stockhorses out to Bull Creek, where David, Bonnie and the stockmen were camped. I headed off with the horses with my little sister, Danielle, helping me. It was good to be in the bush again. The horses gave us no trouble and we trotted into the Bull Creek campsite about three hours later. There was no camp. It seemed that Bonnie and David had camped somewhere else but hadn't mentioned it to me. What was it with those two? I couldn't traipse all over Bull Creek looking for them and Danielle, who was only 11, was tired by now.

We had ridden across tyre tracks heading towards the Victoria River, and I had heard that the portable yard for holding cattle was set up out on the salt flats. I decided to push the horses there; at least we could lock them in a pen until I sorted out where everyone was. It took another hour to get to the yards, which turned out to be dry. The horses were okay as they had had a drink at the last creek but Danielle and I were thirsty. I put the horses in a pen and settled down to wait while Danielle complained bitterly, as 11-year-olds will. Why didn't I know where the camp was? Why did we have to wait here? 'I'm thirsty.' 'I'm hungry.' It sure was going to be a long night if we had to stay here.

Just before dark David turned up in his Toyota. He had a smirk on his face. Danielle and I drove back to the camp with him, leaving the horses where they were as it was already dark. We would have to come back and get them in the morning. Back at the camp, which was a few kilometres from the old site, Bonnie was cold; she glanced at me and then turned her attention to Danielle. 'Well, things aren't off to a great start,' I thought. I went back home the next day and told my parents that I couldn't work with Bonnie and David. They clearly didn't want me in their camp, and in truth I didn't want to be there either. There was plenty of other work that needed to be done on the station that would allow me to stay out of their way. One thing I had come to realise while I was away was my distaste for conflict. I knew I couldn't avoid all conflict, but I made a conscious decision to do so where possible.

In contrast, David and my father were in constant and worsening conflict. They had another major row and David left, for good this time. I think they both felt that they had failed each other: David was not the son my father wanted, and our father was not the father David wanted. Bonnie was bereft at David's departure, and she became quite withdrawn. Our past relationship was never to be rekindled, though.

9

MY FATHER HAD BEEN IN PARTNERSHIP with his cousin Gus for more than 20 years, but during that time they had constantly argued, primarily over money. My father had always spent more than they had earned, and his wild ideas scared the hell out of Gus, who was deliberate, conservative and liked to save money. Finally, the friction became too great and they decided to part company. That was the end of Father's cattle empire dreams. He and Gus had bought numerous properties together and they would now have to be sold. Montejinni, one of the sweetest cattle blocks in the Top End, was the first to go.

The prospective buyers of Montejinni didn't want to pay the price set by Father and Gus because they didn't think there were as many cattle there as they had claimed. It was agreed that a bangtail muster, the only accurate way to count large numbers of cattle on a big property, would be carried out. Every animal that went through the yard would have the hair on its tail trimmed off, ensuring that no beast was counted twice.

Father employed a young Scotsman, Neil, to help with the muster, which would take a year. Neil, a 6'5" giant of a man, fell madly in love with Bonnie. He wanted to marry her and take her home to Scotland with him. Bonnie, who had always been a talented flier, had been doing aerobatic training and had set her sights on becoming a champion. She has always been single-minded about achieving her goals, and marrying Neil did not fit into her plans. Neil persisted, hoping she might change her mind, but it was not to be.

Every second day Father and I flew to Montejinni to check on the progress of the muster. Now that the abattoir had closed down Father had sold the old Beaver as it was too expensive to fly as a private aircraft, and he had purchased a Piper Super Cub, a fun two-seater. I flew while my father slept or read a book. He was now sick most of the time, coughing and wheezing despite being on all sorts of medication. He planned to settle all his business and then concentrate on regaining his health. I doubted that he would ever be well again but he expressed no such pessimism. He fully expected to regain all, if not more, of his former vitality once he could commit all his time and energy to his health.

The Montejinni bangtail muster ended in Father and Gus's favour; the count exceeded expectations and the sale went through. We settled back at Bullo to finish the cattle season and walk the last mob of cattle out to the highway. It was scorching hot and the cattle were very toey. For the first two days we battled to keep the cattle together. On the third day we had to walk them along a narrow stretch of road with a steep, rough sandstone hill on one side and the deep Rocky River on the other.

The steers were strung out for a kilometre and we were flat out keeping them together and away from the river. It is not a good policy to let cattle drink in the middle of the day because they bail up and won't walk well if they have too much.

Every now and then my father chose to assist with the cattle operations – much to my distress. He had never had much practical experience, so more often than not he was little help. He came flying around the corner in the Toyota.

His driver hesitated when he saw the cattle but Father motioned for him to drive right on through, honking the horn liberally as they went. The cattle went everywhere – up the hill into broken sandstone boulders, straight down the near-vertical bank into the river, up the road home, and out the road bush. The men instantly bolted off in all directions to get the fleeing cattle back under control. Seething, I pulled up my horse next to the Toyota and ripped shreds off my father. He went fire-engine red and bellowed 'You're fired!' to which I replied 'That's fine by me!' I looked him in the eyes, which he hated, and added in a very quiet voice, which he also hated, 'I will leave as soon as I have finished the job I started.'

'You'll leave when I tell you.'

'No, I'll leave when this job is finished and not before.' I swung my horse around and went down the river bank to help the men gather the cattle together. My father bellowed something after me. I couldn't hear what he said and didn't care. I did hear the Toyota roar off down the road home. It took over an hour to get all the cattle together and settled down enough to walk again; we had to push them hard to make up for the time we'd lost.

I didn't see Father again until the last day, when we were loading the cattle onto trucks at the highway. He had calmed down, and said that he didn't want me to go but that I should never speak to him like that again. I replied that as long as he didn't do anything that thoughtless again there would be no problem. He bristled. I stood my ground and stared right at him, and he backed down. It shocked me, quietly. He had never done this before. He looked tired, old and sick.

Bonnie was now devoting all her spare time to aerobatics. There was no doubt that she had a gift; she was a natural pilot. After she had completed her basic aerobatic training it was clear that she had a real chance of becoming a champion. What she needed now was an aerobatic plane to hone her skills in. Aerobatics was the sort of daredevil sport my father would have enjoyed doing himself, so he was very supportive. He sold the Super Cub and bought a Super Decathlon, a fully aerobatic two-seater. Bonnie was off and away chasing her dream. I definitely didn't share her passion for flying upside down and every other way for that matter. I did, however, completely admire her amazing ability. On a few occasions I went up with both Bonnie and an instructor and did some very mild manoeuvres, swiftly coming to the conclusion that I would need to take some shares in an airsickness bag company to make it worthwhile.

My mother pointed out that since my father was spending increasingly large amounts of time and money on Bonnie's aerobatic dream, to be fair, he should do something for me. I had a talent for art and had loved drawing and painting horses and other animals since childhood, so Father arranged for me to travel to Maryland and have private art lessons. He was actually killing two birds with one stone. My grandmother was having trouble finding someone suitable to live with and take care of her – I could live with her temporarily and take art lessons while I was there.

I arrived in Maryland in late 1982, at the age of 21. It hadn't changed; time certainly did move slowly in that place. Mister Marvel was still farming and still a bachelor.

I asked him one day, 'Have you ever wanted to travel and see the world?'

He replied, 'God put me here, this is where I'm meant to be and this is where I'm stayin'.'

He had not travelled more than 100 kilometres from his birthplace in his 60-odd years and that was only twice, to a nearby town called Salisbury, for medical reasons.

Despite being in her 90s, my grandmother was not at all frail. She had voluntarily given up driving so as not to be a danger to others so I immediately took a driving test and got my American licence. I helped her with household jobs, drove her to church, to the shops and to social engagements, and started the search for someone suitable to live with her when I left.

The following months passed peacefully, but compared to home the social life in Maryland was hectic. There was a never-ending string of parties, which in truth I found a little boring. I did start dating a fellow called Carol – apparently an okay Dutch name for blokes – Warfield. When I mentioned him to my grandmother she got very excited; she felt he would be the perfect match. He came from an old family, and on his mother's side was related to Dutch royalty and on his father's side to Wallis Warfield Simpson, who married Edward VIII.

My grandmother and my aunt contacted my parents and told them that there would be wedding bells any day now. My mother called me, wanting to know why I hadn't told them. I assured her there wasn't anything to tell. We were dating, that's all. Carol and his family thought that I would be a suitable addition to their family. Everyone wanted me to get married – except me. Apart from a long list of other reasons I had not to walk down the aisle, the Warfield family were strict Christian Scientists. I have never been a religious person and it was clear that anyone joining their family also joined their religion.

My art lessons had come to an end and I redoubled my efforts to find a suitable live-in for my grandmother. I had found several African–American women who would have been perfect, but my grandmother needed someone to sleep upstairs near her bedroom these days, and she was still stuck on the notion that coloured people had to sleep downstairs. I was very short with her but she refused to be swayed. Eventually, after conducting many, many inter-views, I found a suitable white person who she would allow to sleep upstairs.

I had stayed in touch with Neil, who had helped with the Montejinni muster, and he reminded me of his invitation to visit him and his family in Scotland. This seemed like an attractive idea as the pressure was getting too intense for me in Maryland. I booked my passage and a very forlorn Carol drove me to catch my plane.

I spent a month with Neil and his family, who made me feel very much at ease. Only a few days after I had arrived I got a letter from Carol. The next day I got another, and then the next day another. He was writing me a letter every day, all of them long. He asked me when I would return to the States and marry him. Neil teased me mercilessly about the letters, and I was a little embarrassed. I had never had anyone write to me regularly, let alone every day. I wrote back and told him that a letter a day was a bit excessive, but they kept coming, and Neil kept teasing me. I liked Carol very much, but I did not love him.

The Scottish countryside was glorious, steeped in history and tradition. I thoroughly enjoyed getting out and working on Neil's family's farm. It made me feel alive and I realised there with great clarity that I am happiest when out handling stock.

As the end of my visit drew near Neil took a few days off work to show me a little more of his beloved country. I was amazed at how small it was; we drove right around in a little more than two days. The north of Scotland was wild looking, dotted with deep, cold lochs, rough, windswept mountains and not a tree anywhere. Something about the wildness stirred me. I knew without a doubt that I could never live in a place like Maryland, beautiful as it is. I would slowly die inside if I had to stay there. I felt drawn back to the wildness and isolation of northern Australia. Sometimes you need to leave a place to fully appreciate it, and that's how it was for me. In Scotland I realised how much I loved Bullo.

I returned home, glad to be back in the bush and keen to get into the cattle work. I had been away for about six months in all and things had moved on in my absence. Bonnie had been put in charge of the stock camp. My father said that it was now her turn, which was fair enough. I'd had my go. Sadly, though, I didn't feel at all welcomed by Bonnie. In fact, I felt that she wanted me to stay out of her way. She had given my horse to one of the stockmen and taken my saddle; there were other horses and saddles, but she had wanted mine. I think she did it to drive a point home: she was in charge, and she liked it.

She had my father worked out. She would agree meekly to all he said and then would go ahead and do what she wanted anyway. I, on the other hand, would always argue a point if I didn't agree, so father thought I was trouble. I did not want to fight with Father or Bonnie, who seemed to be itching for it. I decided to find jobs that would be of help but allow me stay out of the way. I retrieved my horse and saddle and got on with my work.

Repairing old fences and building new ones were regular jobs for me, as was getting the killers. Getting a killer usually requires two people, but when I needed one of the men to help me they were now always too busy. I was not willing to beg, nor was I prepared to fight about it – so I worked out a way to do it myself. I would have to cut the bigger killers into eight pieces rather than quarters before I could lift them on the back of the ute by myself.

———

That cattle season we had started using a different company to supply helicopters and pilots for our mustering. When three helicopters landed one fine winter evening to take part the next day in a muster at Big Paddock, my father instructed me to go out and bring the pilots back to the homestead as he wanted to get their names and go over the muster plan with them. I walked across the lawn, looking over at the pilots with interest as they fuelled and serviced their choppers for the next day's work. I walked up to the first pilot and looked up – and up again. 'He's a big fellow,' I thought. Charlie Ahlers was 6'3" and well built. He looked down at me with his piercing green-gold eyes and listened to what I had to say in a businesslike manner, spoke to the other two pilots and then followed me into the homestead. His very presence made me blush in a self-conscious way; I wondered if he was single. Once we were inside and I could look at him again I decided there was no way he could be at a loose end. 'He's either married or has a girl in every port,' I thought. Helicopter pilots are notorious for having a girl at every cattle station they muster. It is easy to pick the ones that have a string of lovers. On show days, when all of the station people come together, they always make sure they're out of town.

Charlie returned for all the musters that season. In those days, the cattle were wild. Often when they bailed up in thick scrub or under trees the only way to get them moving was to fire bird shot near them from onboard the helicopter. The noise and the dust kicked up by the pellets usually did the trick. A good shooter was a real asset and translated directly into more cattle at the end of the day and therefore more profit for the station. The pilot decided who they would take up – if they deemed the shooter to be danger-ous or useless they wouldn't take them. Female shooters were not the norm, but I must have come up to scratch as Charlie was very agreeable to my flying with him and doing the shooting with his semi-automatic 12-gauge shotgun.

It takes a lot of practice to shoot well from a chopper because machine and beast are both moving. It's a chal-lenge just to hold the gun steady and, most importantly, you have to be constantly vigilant not to shoot the chopper itself. If you can anticipate the way the pilot flies then you are a much more effective shooter so it is necessary to build a rapport, something I was looking forward to doing with Charlie. It was not unusual for me to go through 400 rounds of ammo in half a day. Even with a rubber pad on the butt of the shotgun it kicked so hard my shoulder would be bruised black by the end of the day.

Although I certainly felt something between us when we worked together Charlie remained businesslike. I was beginning to think that perhaps he didn't have the same feelings for me that I had for him. Then, for about a month, during which we did several musters, he didn't come at all. I was disappointed each time the choppers landed and he didn't step out of one of them. I thought, sadly, that I must have been right; he wasn't interested in me after all.

A new pilot who hadn't been to Bullo before came in Charlie's place. Unlike Charlie, he wasn't on the quiet side at all. He started to pay a lot of attention to me and Charlie found out about it. Men *do* gossip, no matter what they all say. Unknown to me at the time, Charlie told his boss, Kerry, that he had to work at all the Bullo musters from then on, regardless of how far away he was. Some of the properties Charlie mustered regularly were many hours away and often it was not at all practical for him to fly to Bullo when there were other pilots closer. Charlie may have been quiet but he was determined, and to my delight he was at all the musters for the rest of the 1983 cattle season.

On his first night back at Bullo Charlie sat opposite me at the dinner table and played with my feet under the table. He had a twinkle in his eye and a smile on his face. That is how we finally connected and how I knew he returned my feelings. Not long afterwards, one evening when we were alone, he scooped me up in his arms and carried me very willingly off to his room. It was easy for me to fall in love with this gentle giant. He had all the qualities in a man that I admired. He filled the empty, sad parts of my life and made the future look bright again for me. Charlie was 32 years old, ten years my senior. The age gap seemed smaller, though, as in many ways I felt and acted much older than my years and Charlie was very young at heart.

I had written to Carol Warfield when I had returned from my travels and tried to explain why I so love the wilds of north Australia and why I could never live in America or marry him. I told him we were finished and if only he could see Bullo he would better understand. He apparently didn't understand and decided that he would have to see what I was talking about. He had been writing to me every week for some months and now he wrote to say that he was booked on a flight and was coming to Bullo.

I told Charlie the whole story and assured him there was nothing to worry about. Charlie didn't say much but he did get time off flying and moved out to Bullo for the duration of Carol's visit. He clearly didn't intend to take any chances. As he was a mechanic as well as a pilot he busied himself fixing things around the place. He never said a thing to Carol. He was just there. Carol did his best to change my mind but his efforts were in vain. He finally left. I still don't think he understood why I so loved this country, but he did understand that he didn't have a hope with Charlie in the picture. By now I certainly didn't have any doubts about how serious Charlie was, and it felt good.

One day I was busy doing my usual daily work when two policemen arrived at the homestead unannounced. I was stunned when they handed me a subpoena to appear in court in Darwin. I was completely at a loss about what it could be about until one of the policemen mentioned a name that sent a shiver through me. Drako the Yugoslav labourer who had so rattled me at the campsite at bore Number Two, had murdered a woman. She was a schoolteacher who had had a relationship with Drako and then broken up with him. He walked up to her at the Katherine Show and, in front of a crowd of people, drove a 40-centimetre knife into her throat, sliced down into her chest and rolled a cigarette while he watched her die. Apparently he was as calm as could be. In his statement to the police he said that Bonnie and I had taped the woman and her current lover making love and that each night we had played these recordings outside his door, and that was what drove him to kill her. I was flabbergasted.

Despite the fact that his statement was ridiculous I still felt tense about going to court. I was frightened. I had no wish to see that maniac again. Mercifully he pleaded guilty before I was called so I was spared confronting him in court. I was pleased he was now behind bars, where he belonged.

10

I HAD KNOWN CHARLIE FOR A YEAR and our relationship was blossoming. I was sure Charlie was the one for me, and I knew he was of the same mind when he invited me to go and visit his family property in north Queensland. He left just before Christmas, and I was to follow early in the New Year.

As my flight landed in Cairns I had mixed feelings. The thought of seeing Charlie again brought joy to my heart but the idea of meeting his parents made me a little nervous. Charlie met me at the airport and gave me a huge hug. We ran some errands around town and then drove up to the little town of Mareeba where Charlie's good friends, Sue and Noel, live. They were having a party that evening, which we joined. They were great people and I remember thinking that if all of Charlie's family and friends were like this I had nothing to worry about.

Late that evening we set off again as Charlie wanted to get home that night. He had had quite a bit to drink so I drove. The bitumen gave way to dirt and at 1.00 in the morning we came to the turn off for their station, Maitland Downs. I was pleased we were arriving so late as I'd have a chance to sleep before meeting Charlie's family in the morning. I drove up to the homestead and there stood

Charlie's mother, Joyce, in her nightgown, waiting for us, torch in hand. Alarm bells rang inside my head immediately. This didn't look like a welcoming committee. We got out and walked towards her.

Before I could say anything she shone the torch in my face, looked me up and down and turned her attention to Charlie: 'I've made up the guest room.'

'Marlee will be staying with me,' Charlie replied. He lived in a separate house on the property.

'She can't sleep with you; what will Granny think?' Joyce said.

'I don't give a stuff what Granny thinks!' Charlie was annoyed. Joyce pursed her lips, spun around and went back inside. 'Well, that went well,' I thought.

Still, I went to bed that first night feeling optimistic. I was sure that everything could be sorted out in the morning and we could get off to a fresh start.

The next day I met Charlie's father, George, a tough old bushman who had hunted crocodiles and worked cattle all his life. Though he didn't talk much I felt a bit more comfortable around him than I did around Joyce.

It turned out that my initial meeting with Joyce had set the tone for our relationship in the future. Charlie was the apple of Joyce's eye and I got the feeling I wasn't the type of woman she wanted to share him with. I tried very hard to change her opinion of me but all my efforts seemed to be in vain.

I don't recall any obvious warmth between Charlie's parents; George permanently slept out on the veranda. I did wonder whether they lived and worked together just to keep the property going. Charlie, being a man of few words, hadn't said anything about his parents. That's just the way they were; that was all there was to it.

Granny was fine. I got on extremely well with her. She had a ton of spunk and had no problem at all with Charlie and I sleeping in the same bed out of wedlock. Charlie's younger sister, Mary, and brothers, Steven and John, were

also great. Mary, who was a teacher and had her own property in Malanda in the Atherton Tablelands, and I found
something in common straight away – we both adored
Charlie. Steven was a mechanic and lived with his girlfriend
most of the time on Lakeland Downs, a large peanut farm
an hour's drive away. John, the youngest, was the only one
still at home working the cattle with George. I liked them
all and maintained high hopes that I could also melt Joyce
some day. In the meantime I was content to be with Charlie
and help around the place where I could. I stayed for a few
weeks and then headed home.

———————

Bonnie was still in charge of the stock camp, and I was
enjoying a more peaceful existence. I was very absorbed by
my relationship in any case. Father hadn't given any particular time frame for Bonnie to remain in charge, and nor
did I ever ask him about it. At this point in my life I really
was happy not to have the pressure and responsibility of
leading the stock camp weighing me down. It was both
liberating and a revelation for me.

My father liked Charlie. He was a real man's man.
However, I never envisaged Charlie living on the property
while my father was there. I knew without a doubt that
there was no way Charlie could work peacefully with my
father – he would never have put up with Father's unreasonable demands. To Bonnie, though, it may have seemed
that if Charlie and I married it could pose a problem for
her as the head of Bullo. She liked being number one and
intended to stay there.

While I was away in Queensland visiting Charlie's
family, Bonnie had done a saddle-making course at RM
Williams in Adelaide. There she met Peter Williams, one of
RM Williams's sons. They had a whirlwind romance and
Peter came up to Bullo to meet our parents and spend some
time with Bonnie. Peter was a tall, attractive young man.

The first thing that struck me was that he was far too gentle a soul. He was sensitive, considerate and so in love with my sister. Between my father and Bonnie bossing him about, and the fact that he put up with being bossed about, it was clear that things were doomed from the beginning. I felt sorry for Peter but it was not my place to say anything. He wouldn't have listened anyway; he adored the ground Bonnie walked on.

Around this time, the ABC were filming a documentary at Bullo. My parents organised a party to announce Bonnie and Peter's engagement. They were keen that Charlie and I make it a double engagement; I didn't even ask Charlie because I thought it was a horrible idea. While I was sure that Charlie was the one for me, I was not ready to get engaged yet – and when we did get engaged I certainly didn't want to do it on national television.

On the night of her engagement party, Bonnie seemed to have little time for Peter. I wondered whether she cared for him at all. They never did marry. Their relationship ended soon after and he left the property. That was the end of that.

At the end of 1984 Charlie and I decided to become engaged. It was more of a mutual decision than the traditional 'Will you marry me?'. My father and mother were happy for me. Bonnie was non-committal; she didn't make her feelings known either way.

My mother and I arranged an engagement party at a hotel in Katherine. All of Charlie's friends came but none of his family made the trip to attend. It didn't seem to worry Charlie but even though it was a long way to travel I did wonder why none of them had made the effort. It was a wonderful evening and everyone enjoyed themselves well into the next morning. I proudly wore the most beautiful engagement ring.

It was the last time my whole family was together. Father was there in body but not in spirit; he was not at all his normal feisty self. It was unsettling to see him like this.

The emphysema had a grip on him that I think he knew could not be shaken, even by someone with his pig-headed determination.

＊

Father had become very bitter with the world. He had always thought his destiny would be greater than it had turned out to be. Much greater, like that of a world leader. He realised that time was running out now and so he was spending large amounts of money from the sale of Montijinni, perhaps even more rashly than he would have before his illness.

There were some areas on the station that were so inaccessible we couldn't get the cattle out of them. Charlie convinced me that if we got a good-sized bulldozer we could make roads through the tricky terrain and get the cattle out. Since father was on a spending spree I approached him to buy an old Caterpillar D-8 bulldozer I knew was for sale in Darwin. To my surprise, Father agreed.

Charlie and I went and looked it over. Well, Charlie looked it over; I stood there, blown away by how big it was. She was a huge machine, weighing in at 38 tons. Charlie gave it the okay and I organised to have it delivered to our front gate on a low loader, a heavy-duty trailer made for carrying very heavy loads.

Our front gate is 76 kilometres from the homestead by dirt road. Charlie promised to drive the bulldozer in but when it was due to be delivered he was flat out flying elsewhere. He gave me all sorts of bulldozer-driving instructions over the phone, which I wrote down furiously so that I wouldn't forget anything. He finished by telling me that he was sure the low-loader driver would give me a run-down on the machine if I asked.

Having never driven anything bigger than a small tractor I drove out to the gate to take delivery of our bulldozer.

The low-loader driver was late coming, and rushing because he was also late for his next job. He unchained the dozer, started the engine and skilfully backed it off the float.

'There you go,' he said. 'Who's driving it?'

'I am,' I said, smiling broadly.

He raised his eyebrows.

'Would you be able to give me a quick lesson before you go?' I asked.

His eyebrows really went up this time.

'You haven't driven a dozer before?'

'No.' I shook my head. 'This is the first time and I really would appreciate it if you could take me through things once quickly.'

He rolled his eyes.

'I'm already late,' he said.

He really didn't want to give some girl a dozer-driving lesson in the middle of nowhere.

'Please,' I begged. 'Even ten minutes would help.'

'Okay,' he said, sighing heavily.

He must have decided that as he was late anyway he could spare a full half an hour to help me; I struggled to absorb the information he rapid-fired at me. When he left on his low-loader he was shaking his head, no doubt convinced that I was short a few kangaroos in the top paddock. I pulled out my notebook and furiously wrote down everything he had told me. All that day I crawled down the dirt road at a pitifully slow pace, terrified I might do something wrong and blow up the dozer. I was really struggling with the decelerator, which functions in the opposite way to an accelerator. If you put your foot down, the bulldozer goes slower. Take your foot off and it goes faster. I had made the mistake several times of taking my foot off when I wanted to slow down, only to find myself going even faster.

I planned to get as far down the road as possible by the end of the day and wait for Uncle Dick, whom I'd asked to come out and pick me up just before sundown. One thing

Charlie had been at pains to make clear to me was that at the end of each day I was to clear an area of grass with the blade and park the dozer on the cleared ground; this was to protect the machine in the case of an unexpected bushfire. When the end of the day came, exhausted from worry, I turned my attention to the blade controls, which I had been looking at all day but hadn't been game to touch. I identified the lever that controlled the dozer's big blade and moved it up and down tentatively. 'That's not too bad,' I thought.

I lowered the blade till it was just above the ground, feeling pleased with myself that I was getting the hang of things. I gently turned the dozer off the road, cutting across the metre-high pile of dirt, called a windrow, the grader had left in its wake when it was opening the road. The dozer's nose pointed sharply up as it climbed the mound of dirt, balanced for a moment at the top, then crashed heavily on the other side. The blade dug deep into the ground; I panicked and took my foot off the decelerator. All 300 horsepower went to work. Before I could gather myself and stop the runaway dozer, it had made an impressive hole. Charlie had said to make sure I got all the grass. I'd sure done that. There was definitely no grass left, not a blade – but I was sure he hadn't meant the dozer to be below ground level.

Now that my father's partnership with Gus had ended, Bullo was run as a proprietary limited company with my mother and father as its directors. The bills went unpaid while Father spent the remainder of the Montijinni money on unwise acquisitions. As Bonnie was now an exceptionally good aerobatic pilot, he bought a special aerobatic plane, in the company's name. This one-seater was purely for sport; it had no practical use. For himself he bought a yacht. He travelled especially to Sydney to buy it from Shirley Strachan, the former singer of The Skyhooks, who was to tragically die flying a helicopter some years later. Father hated rock and roll to the point that he probably wouldn't have bought the boat if he had any idea who The Skyhooks were. Shirl mustn't have mentioned that he had been a rock star; Father returned from Sydney and told us the owner was a carpenter who played in a band occasionally. A nice young man, my father said.

Sailing was my father's passion and he hadn't done much of it in a long time. He thought that a long rest and good sea air would help his lungs. Mother hated sailing with him and flatly refused to go. When he decided to hire an all-female crew she argued bitterly with him, but of course he got his way in the end.

Who was going to run the station, my mother asked in exasperation. My father still thought I was too difficult to deal with and favoured Bonnie over me to run Bullo. He planned to direct her from his ship somewhere at sea.

But Bonnie spent more and more time in Darwin flying and soon moved in with Arthur, a pilot and fellow aerobatic enthusiast who would later become her husband. She would come down to Bullo for each muster and leave as soon as it was completed. With Bonnie away most of the time, Father issuing directives from his yacht and both of them spending more money than the station could make, Mother was at the end of her tether. She could not deal with the everyday problems of running the station.

Father, who had been sailing along the Queensland and New South Wales coast for several months realised she was falling apart. He had docked in Sydney and had her join him there for a break. He called Bonnie and told her to get back to the station and stay there. Bonnie, having just won at the Australian aerobatic titles, refused. My father put the aerobatic plane on the market immediately and had a friend and owner of an aircraft company take the propellor off so Bonnie couldn't fly it. Bonnie demanded he reattach the propeller and when he refused she punched him, knocking him flat on his back.

Father sailed off to think about the situation and my mother came back to the station lost and depressed. There was no money in the bank. Between the running cost of Bonnie's plane and of Father's boat there was nothing left. The plane expenses came to an end when it was sold but Father was still spending constantly. Bonnie continued to refuse to come back to the station and made it clear she'd be staying with Arthur in Darwin, flying a borrowed aerobatic plane.

We still had one muster to go before the end of the cattle season.

'I can do it,' I told my mother.

She looked at me and I could see her thinking, 'What have I got to lose?'

There was an area known as Paperbark that we had never been able to erect a portable holding yard in because it was impassable for vehicles of any kind. With the dozer I was sure I could change that. I was becoming more confident on the huge machine and thought I could clear a road, build a portable yard, get a road train in and truck the cattle directly out. I spent a whole day on foot marking out a suitable route; I followed the red ant hills that indicated clay-based soil, a solid foundation for a road. It took me two weeks to construct it. As an afterthought I made a two-kilometre-long side cutting up on a steep sandstone hill that ran along the edge of the salt flats. The big end-of-year tides were due soon, which meant the salt flats might go under and we wouldn't be able to drive on them.

I consulted Charlie and his boss, Kerry, as to where we should put up the portable yard. In the past my father had usually ignored their advice, to his detriment. In all it took me about three weeks to get everything in place and bring in the choppers.

The muster was hard work. This area is full of permanent freshwater springs and thick, tall trees, and the cattle are experts at hiding. But they didn't expect the yard where it was; we got 400 cattle we had never even seen before. The men and I had them drafted in less than a day and

I had the road train standing by. The road crossed a few bad bull dust and sand stretches that there was no way around. I had Diesel Don use our little water trailer to wet down these sections for two days prior to trucking and I had the dozer parked by the one soft creek that worried me; if need be I could use the dozer to pull the road train through. I drove in front of the road train, indicating soft spots coming up with my hazard lights. The driver was excellent, took all my cues and gunned the truck through the trouble spots. We trucked 200 sale cattle out without getting bogged once. The tides did flood the salt flats but with the cutting I had put in we were not delayed.

This was a first for Bullo. My mother was over the moon. The muster had happened without any fuss or problems and, most importantly, she had money to get us over the wet season. She put it in a separate account so Father couldn't spend it. He called not long after we had finished the muster and packed up.

'Now,' he said to Mother, 'I will tell you what you need to organise for the Paperbark muster.'

My mother was not in a good mood.

'It's done,' she said and hung up.

He rang back, a little stunned, and said 'Who did it?'

My mother rubbed it right in, telling him how smoothly everything had gone and how many cattle we had got. She was still stinging over the all-girl crew my father had hired. He was silent for a moment and then told her to wire some money to his account. She told him there was no way he was getting his hands on any of it and hung up again.

My family was self-destructing around me. I was glad Danielle was away at school; she was aware that things were not good but at least she wasn't in the thick of it for now.

My father had planned to sail to America on his 44-foot yacht, *The Mary Blaire*, for Christmas so that he could visit his still strong and healthy mother, who was well into her 90s. But even he had to admit that he was far too sick to attempt such a trip. We convinced him to fly instead. He anchored the boat in Sydney and flew out. My parents' marriage had been on again off again my whole life but now it seemed that it was over forever.

With the last muster done the staff left and the station shut down for the year. Bonnie was still in Darwin and had made it clear she had no intention of returning, except under her terms. Charlie and I headed off to Queensland as we did each year to work on his family's property. My mother and Danielle, who was back from school for the holidays, had a quiet Christmas at home.

I had been planning to stay with Charlie until the start of the cattle season in March but a phone call from my mother changed that. Father had returned from America and was perilously ill; one of his lungs had collapsed. Mother asked me to come back and watch the station while she went to be with him in Sydney. I left immediately. It was still too wet to muster, but there was plenty to do. I cut and barked 200 fence posts so that I had a stockpile ready for the next season's fencing, and started repairing the flood-damaged fences.

My father was determined to have his health back and booked himself into the Royal Prince Alfred Hospital in Sydney for a risky lung operation in March 1986. Even the doctors were against it because of his weak condition, but Father insisted. He had not so long ago had two operations on his eyes to remove cataracts. The results had been spectacular and I think he expected the same of the lung operation. He so believed this that he started some very expensive improvements to his yacht.

'We don't have any money Charles, just wait,' pleaded my long-suffering mother.

Father fully expected to have his operation, get back on the boat and sail away; he wanted everything ready for immediate departure. He thought he'd sell the bulldozer and use that money. He contacted the dealer we had bought it from and told him to put it up for sale. I was mortified when my mother told me. The dozer made money, and she realised this too. I had three more areas I planned to push roads into, giving us access to thousands of cattle that we had never been able to get near up until then. I did a very bold thing. I called the dealer and told him to take it off the market. I said that Father had changed his mind. Father went into hospital for his operation thinking that the dozer was up for sale.

He only just came through the operation. My mother didn't once leave his side despite the fact that they fought like cats and dogs. After all the turmoil they'd been through they still had something binding them together. Father was permanently hooked to an oxygen bottle and was on painkillers and copious amounts of other drugs to fight infection. On my 26th birthday, my mother called me from his bedside to wish me happy birthday then put him on the phone. In a hoarse whisper that I could barely hear – his breathing was terribly laboured and it was clear that speaking was a great effort – he said, 'Happy Birthday Marlee, I love you.' My heart was in my throat and I burst into tears. That was all he was able to say and it was the last time I ever spoke to my father.

From April onwards his condition steadily worsened. One of his lungs collapsed. His body wouldn't respond to the antibiotics they gave him to control infection. His operation wounds would not heal properly. He was completely delirious because of all the drugs he was being given, including morphine. He called his family in America and told them the hospital was plotting to kill him and that a Chinese invasion of Australia was imminent.

In the midst of this my mother had a call to say that her mother had had a stroke. My Aunty Sue had moved up to Queensland and Nan had recently joined her there. In shock, my mother left my father's bedside and flew up there. Danielle, who still kept in contact with Bonnie, let her know about Nan's stroke. Bonnie and Arthur flew to Sydney straight away and paid a visit to my father in hospital. From his hospital bed Father made out a cheque for $50,000 to Bonnie. My mother only became aware of this when the bank contacted her to say that the cheque had been presented – and rejected because there were no funds to cover it. They warned her that Father would need to refrain from writing such cheques until there was enough money to cover them.

The incident did nothing to help the already strained relations in our family. Bonnie had not been to Bullo since late the previous year when she had come briefly to get some of her belongings.

At the start of the next mustering season Danielle was away at school, Mother had returned to my father's bedside and I was alone at Bullo but for a couple men I had employed. Time was running out so I asked mother what she wanted me to do about the first muster. She was understandably unsure about how to proceed but eventually told me to make a muster plan. She would show it to my father for approval and we would go from there.

In the previous years my father and Bonnie had moved the portable yards to 17 mustering locations on the property. Moving the yards is one of the worst jobs on earth in my opinion, and it cost a whole extra month in wages for the men moving them around. For all the effort the end result had not been very impressive. I sat down with Charlie and Kerry and picked just four yard sites for the year. When I presented my muster plan even my mother questioned the proposal, despite the fact that this wasn't usually her area. I was adamant that we could get the same, if not greater, numbers of cattle out of far fewer sites. She showed the plan to my father but he wasn't interested; he was off in another world. I am sure my mother had her doubts but she told me to go ahead. She emphasised how much we needed the money.

Because things were so desperate financially I asked my mother if I could purchase a short wheelbase Toyota that

I could turn into a bull catcher. Years before, my father had hired a contract bull catcher named Tommie to come out to Bullo, and I had learned the ropes from him. Bull catching is one big adrenaline rush. You hurtle through the bush at breakneck speed and once you have found a big scrub bull you knock him down and pin him to the ground with the vehicle. The strapper jumps out and ties the bull's front and hind legs together with thick leather straps so he can't get up. Then you cut the tips of his horns off and pull him up and load him into an old pick-up truck. You do this until you have a load of ten bulls. It is laborious, strenuous, hot and dangerous work but from the very beginning I loved it. In a little over a month, Tommie and I trucked out 400 big bulls, which meant a tidy profit.

I told my mother that I could make some serious money if she gave me the opportunity. I had been right about the dozer – it had made double the money it had cost by opening up the Paperbark area for mustering. My mother was at the stage where she would agree to anything that had the slightest chance of making money. Without consulting my father, she gave me the go ahead to purchase a second-hand vehicle for $3,000.

I found a suitable one advertised in Darwin and Charlie went up with me to check it over and then we drove it back to the station. Uncle Dick, one of the stockmen and I took the cab off, put roll bars all the way around, fitted belly plating to protect the sump and steering rod, and angled the bull bar to just the right position for pushing the bulls over. Finally we bolted two tyres to the bull bar to cushion the animals we pushed over. Bullo's first bull catcher was born.

My father was lapsing in and out of consciousness. In one of his more lucid moments he found out about our bull-catching venture. He was furious with my mother for not having consulted him and they had a vicious fight. He wanted to sell the bull catcher immediately and put the money into his boat. But in my first week of bull catching

I made $10,000 and I knew there was no way the catcher would be sold.

Father was so sick that he was hooked up to an oxygen bottle night and day. My mother and I spoke daily on the phone but he couldn't, and didn't want to, speak. Finally he arrived at the point where the doctors could do no more for him and arrangements had to be made to move him out of the hospital. My mother rented a house in Palm Beach that looked out over the water where Father's boat was moored; everyone hoped that the sight of the sea and his boat would encourage him to recover.

I hired some more stockmen so we could start the mustering at Nutwood Valley on the 14th of June, the same day my father was leaving hospital. The muster went really well. The yards were full to capacity, including large numbers of cleanskin cattle – unbranded cattle that have never been through the yards before. It's like finding money you didn't know you had. I called my mother that evening to tell her the good news, but she was distracted, and not at all happy about Father leaving hospital.

Aunty Sue's husband, Ralph, called the next morning to tell me that my father had passed away in the early hours. My mother was understandably a mess, so Uncle Ralph had offered to ring family and friends for her. Charlie wrapped his big arms around me and I cried quietly; he patted me gently without saying a word.

As much as I had fought with my father, he had many qualities that I loved and admired. He was my Father. I never expected him to die; he always battled on and came through in the end. It was only now that he was gone that I realised just how much I would miss him.

11

A GREAT FRIEND OF MY FATHER'S, General Ron Grey, arranged a military funeral in Sydney. The soul-wrenching bagpipe music made me feel even sadder. I was too shell-shocked to take in all the details but what I did notice was the great number and diversity of people who had come to mourn the passing of this exceptional man.

Bonnie had at first said she wasn't coming, which really upset my mother. She convinced her to come and paid for her airfare and clothing when she arrived. I had hoped that my father's death may have bridged the cavernous rift between my mother and Bonnie, and between Bonnie and me. It hadn't.

Bonnie had always sided with my father, who she saw as the strength of the Hendersons. Now that he was gone the politics in my complicated family had changed dramatically. In her obvious grief she kept to herself; I had the feeling that she was saying goodbye to the rest of her family along with my father. I felt hurt as she was still my sister. I know my mother was very hurt, something that has been well documented.

Bonnie left the funeral with an air of being the only one who had feelings for our father and the only one who had suffered a loss. Deep down she may not have felt that way, but that is how she came across to me. It upset me because we all felt my father's passing deeply.

I returned to the station after the funeral but my mother stayed to finalise things in Sydney. She thought it was right to take some of Father's ashes back to his home in America, and made the sad journey to Maryland alone. She also scattered some of his ashes at sea, and flew in a helicopter with Charlie to the mountains that run north of Bullo to bury the remainder of his ashes and mark the spot with a cross made by Uncle Dick.

Then my mother turned to the unpleasant task of sorting out the business. Knowing my father as she did she expected it to be a mess, but was not prepared for the magnitude of the problems we now faced.

She was still deeply grieving and reeling from the shock of discovering how bad our business problems were when Bonnie, within a month of my father's funeral, started legal proceedings to sue her for the $50,000 cheque my father had written in hospital.

My first task after my father's death was a muster at the Six Mile Yards. It went so well we ran out of yard space. We drafted nonstop like maniacs to try to clear the packed yards. Even after we had drafted 1,200 breeders into the holding paddock we still had 1,400 head of cattle for sale and branding in the yard.

As part of the business settlement that my father and Gus had agreed upon at the end of their partnership it had been agreed that we would deliver to him 400 head of breeder cows and a small number of bulls each year for four years. Gus owned a neighbouring property called Spirit Hill Station and the cattle were to help stock his property. Because our yards were bursting I had no place to draft and hold cows for Gus. I did, however, have a small pen for the bull quota. I called Gus and explained the situation.

He was very understanding and came over to inspect the bulls, which he liked and took delivery of. He assured me there was no hurry for the 400 cows, said how sorry he was about my father, and complimented me on what a good job I was doing. I gave him the approximate date of the next muster as the first week of July and he said it would be fine to deliver the cows then.

I had not seen the settlement contract nor was I privy to the terms; that was to be our undoing. It contained a clause stating that Gus, at his discretion, could refuse delivery of any cattle after the 30th of June. Shortly before the 30th I called Gus to reconfirm that the muster would be in the first week of July and that he would be over a few days after that, at his convenience, to inspect and draft his cows. He was again positive and supportive and said he looked forward to coming over. On the 30th of June he started legal proceedings for breach of contract. We were stunned; he was suing us for $500,000. My mother offered him more cattle, the value of the outstanding cattle in cash, interest in cash or calves – anything to settle reasonably – but he refused.

My mother was about as low as I'd seen her. She was ready to walk away from Bullo with nothing. And nothing is most certainly what it would have been – our debts equalled the value of the property. We had many long talks together and, despite everyone's advice to sell and walk away, we decided to give it a go. I managed to convince her that I could handle the outside work if she could do the office. After all, we really didn't have a thing to lose by trying and we might just pull it off. We would fight the legal cases against us and try to pull ourselves out of this unholy mess.

I felt deep pity for my mother. I wanted to support her, save Bullo from going under and prove all the doubters wrong.

Money – how to make more of it and how to save it – now occupied all my waking thoughts. One of the first things I did, on advice of Charlie and Uncle Dick, was replace the old abattoir generator that we had used to power the homestead with a smaller one. The old one was far too large for our needs these days and replacing it with a smaller one halved our fuel bill. We started turning the new generator off during the night, halving our fuel bill again. By doing our own bull catching, rather than relying on outside contractors, we gained 70 per cent on the sale of the bulls. The four yard sites we had chosen to muster that year turned off more cattle than the 17 yards the previous year. On the business side we were finding our feet slowly.

Charlie, who had been flying for many years now, was ready for a change and he agreed to come and manage the station. I was over the moon with his decision; I could think of nothing I wanted more than to work alongside of him. It made my mother very happy, too. She thought the world of Charlie, and having this exceptionally capable man on the station gave her a real sense of security, something she craved after such an erratic decade.

———

Charlie liked working on the land again, and he was still flying a little on the side for Kerry so he had the best of both worlds. While we had some daunting problems on the horizon, my mother had a great deal more confidence that, with Charlie and I working together and committing to a future on Bullo, we would all pull through.

Charlie and I had been engaged for nearly four years now; we always seemed to be too busy to get married. One day I approached the subject as subtly as only I can.

'Charlie, if you're going to marry me, you'd better do it soon before things get any busier.'

He smiled at me broadly. 'Yes, I guess I'll have to,' he said.

The only time we could possibly fit in getting married was over the wet. We sat down with Mother and settled on

January 1988. The next problem? Charlie's family all lived north of Cairns, my mother's family were in Bundaberg and Sydney, and most of Charlie's flying mates went to the Queensland coast over the wet. We decided to have the wedding in Brisbane as it was the most central place for everyone.

My mother made most of the arrangements by phone and we travelled down to Brisbane to sort out the final details two weeks before the wedding. I found an off-the-rack wedding dress that was perfect. My mother and I fell in love with one of Brisbane's first churches, a tiny wooden chapel with a welcoming atmosphere. We booked the minister, reception venue and photographer, and did all the last-minute coordinating, then collapsed briefly to catch our breath. Charlie arrived a week before the wedding, all the men went off for their suit fittings, and we took some dancing lessons so we didn't look completely hopeless doing the bridal waltz. The day before the wedding we discovered that the minister who was to perform the ceremony was ill with the flu but had arranged for another, Reverend Hall, to fill in.

Our wedding day unfolded wonderfully and smoothly. The church looked gorgeous, filled with sweet-smelling flowers. I walked out proudly as Charlie's wife.

I had been given away by the man who had given my mother away at her wedding many years before, Sir Jack Cater. After the ceremony Sir Jack and his wife, Lady Peggy, were chatting with the Reverend outside the church and mentioned that they had lived in Hong Kong most of their lives.

'My uncle was a bishop in the Far East,' said the Reverend.

'You wouldn't mean Bishop Hall?' asked Peg.

'Why, yes,' he replied. 'Do you know him?'

Peg and Jack were incredulous. Bishop Hall had been a personal friend of both my father and the Caters. He had also been my godfather, and had married my parents. Surely this coincidence was a sign that this was all meant to be.

It rained, only briefly, but enough to end any chance of the planned wedding photos in the park. Nothing bothered me though. I was too happy for anything to dent my euphoria.

We went to our wedding reception on a high and stayed until the early hours of the next morning. We were having far too much fun to leave. The next day we caught up on sleep and then headed up the coast in a leisurely manner towards Maitland Downs. We planned to take a honeymoon sometime in the future when we could fit it in. There was no hurry; we had the rest of our lives together.

Not much had changed on the home front at Maitland Downs, except that I had given up trying to win Joyce's approval. Until this point she may have lived in hope that Charlie and I would go our separate ways, but now we were married.

George had given Charlie a small block of land at one end of Maitland Downs that, when cleared, would be suitable for cropping peanuts. We planned to develop the block of land and then have a share farmer run it for us while we ran Bullo. We lived in a caravan on the block every wet season, returning to Bullo in February or early March, depending on the rains.

While we were away from Bullo our big grey stallion, Rastas, was bitten by a snake and died. Charlie and I set about finding another stallion to bring home. I listed my criteria: must be young, 16 hands high or over, not chestnut (I had come across a lot of bad-tempered chestnut horses in my life and decided that their colour had something to do with it) and as few white markings as possible. Horses with white feet often have soft hooves and feet problems; horses with big blazes and pink noses are prone to sunburn and skin cancer.

Charlie and I looked over a number of prospective sires, none of which caught my eye – until we saw Blazing Boots. The only thing on my wish list that Boots had was height – he was over 16 hands – but he had everything I'd said I didn't want. He was chestnut, had a full blaze, four white socks and was ten years old – but he had a beautiful nature and enough character for a whole stable full of horses. I instantly fell in love with him. Charlie laughed at me; all my resolve had crumbled with this one horse. I didn't have to convince Charlie, though, because he was quite taken with Boots as well. We had him delivered to Maitland Downs and bought an old horse float to tow behind the jeep back to Bullo.

Everything seemed to be going rather well, when the man we had bought Boots from called me and told me that he had forgotten to mention that Boots had had an accident in a horse float on the way to a race many years ago and that they had never been able to get him in a horse float since. He had been transported to Maitland Downs in a truck with a stock crate on the back, which is what is generally used to move cattle and sheep.

'It's been a long time,' I said hopefully to Charlie.

Charlie opened the float and I led Boots over. Without any fuss at all I walked him straight on. As Charlie clipped the chain in behind him we were both smiling.

'He has forgotten,' I said.

At that very moment he remembered. The normally mild-tempered stallion exploded. He squealed in hysterical panic and thrashed about madly. I had to dive out the front door of the float to avoid over half a ton of thrashing horse; the whole float was swaying dangerously. Boots lurched backwards against the chain with his full weight and ripped the bolts out of the float wall. He reversed at a gallop, stopping some yards away. Standing at his full height he let out several snorts of indignation. After that we couldn't get him near the horse float.

Now we had a big problem! I spent a lot of time thinking about it before I settled on a plan.

Boots loved food. Had he been a dog, he would have been a labrador or a beagle. I had Charlie park the horse float in an empty yard and set up two troughs in the float, one for water and the other for feed. I put Boots in his new

yard and left him to it. It didn't take him long to smell
the lucerne, molasses and oat mix in the trough. He was
all but drooling. Licking his chops and sniffing he took a
tentative step into the float and then backed off at the last
moment. He walked round and round the float but the only
way he could get that feed was if he went in. Once this had
sunk in he stood there looking forlorn for a time, getting
up his courage. Then he leapt forward into the float,
grabbed the biggest mouthful of feed he could and bolted
backwards, seemingly in one motion. He stood outside
munching on the feed. Each time he had to build up his
courage before he made his manic dash to gulp another
mouthful of feed. He did this for half a day; each time he
went in he was a bit slower coming out, until he didn't
come out at all. By the end of the week he was standing
in the float all day, munching away contentedly.

The time had come for another test run. I loaded Boots
into the horse float, clipped the chain in behind him and
went for a test drive, all the while expecting him to explode
in a spectacular fashion. He never did. Not once from that
day was he a problem. I left the feed bins in the float so
he could eat as we travelled home to Bullo.

I was so happy coming home that time with Charlie by my
side. I felt as though nothing could beat us. Despite all
the problems we had with the business, the future had never
looked brighter to me. After dropping off the horses and
resting a while we drove to Kununurra, where Charlie was
to help Kerry train new pilots. We spent a few days catching up with everyone, then Charlie flew off with Tony, a
young man who had been diligently working his way up to
being a chopper pilot. I watched as Charlie took him over
every nut and bolt on the chopper. Tony thought the world
of Charlie and I could see him enthusiastically absorbing
the vast amounts of information Charlie was firing at him.

They climbed into the chopper and disappeared in the direction of the training area.

I was reading a book when Pat, who worked in the office and was married to one of the other pilots, came to the door.

'Charlie and Tony have gone down,' she said.

She looked at me expectantly, waiting for a reaction. Fear gripped my heart, but panic solves nothing. I had learnt that a long time ago.

Breathing deeply to gather myself I asked, 'Are they all right?'

Pat shrugged. 'We don't have all the details yet, but we think they're all right.' I sighed with relief.

Charlie did not return until after dark. Both he and Tony had come through unscathed but the chopper was a write off. Not a good start to the season. Understandably, Kerry was not happy; I, on the other hand, was very happy to have my Charlie back in one piece. Yet again life had demonstrated to me the importance of making every day count.

———————

At the beginning of 1988 my mother was faced with the decision of whether to go to court and fight Bonnie's legal action in regard to the $50,000 or to simply settle. Bonnie claimed that Father had written the cheque to cover unpaid wages. My mother claimed that because over $100,000 worth of aeroplane running expenses had been outlaid in the last 18 months of Bonnie's training that she wasn't owed anything. In the end Mother's decision was a business one – it was cheaper to settle and so she did.

Bonnie clearly had no intention of returning to Bullo. The last time I had managed to speak to her was when she had come down to collect her belongings, after she had sued but before Mother had settled.

I had put it to Bonnie: 'This is your family. Don't do this. There must be another way.'

She turned and walked off without comment. I felt as if she didn't care if she ever set eyes on me again and that she had no interest in having any kind of relationship in the future.

Despite the fact that I disagreed with Bonnie's actions I didn't hate her. Bonnie was a complex person who reminded me of my father in a lot of ways. She could be exceptionally charming and great company, had several extraordinary talents, and was attractive to men in the way my father was attractive to women. Father had definitely favoured her; perhaps he too saw something of his own spirit in her. I think her contradictive nature, like my father's, meant she would find it hard to achieve balance in her life and relationships. In view of Bonnie's and my mother's attitudes, which appeared to be set in concrete, it seemed unlikely that Bonnie would be a part of our lives in the future. I felt a sense of loss. Despite our relationship problems Bonnie had many qualities that I liked and admired, and we were flesh and blood.

———————

Over the years, a number of Australian documentary makers had come to capture life on Bullo on film. Now, a German film-maker had expressed an interest in teaming up with a local film-maker to do a documentary on the station. Having to make the payment to Bonnie had stretched the bottom line considerably so my mother, for the first time, asked for money. After all, we really didn't need another documentary but we did need money. An amount was agreed upon; it wasn't a huge sum but it would help.

That year, our normally generous wets had not been forthcoming. It was now early August; no substantial rain could be expected for another four months. The situation became truly dire when a bushfire with a 40-kilometre front came over the northern range, threatening our best grazing country, where we kept most of our breeder cows. If we didn't stop the fire the cows would not survive – it would be at least four months before the rains came and the grass grew back, and we had nowhere else to put the cows. The stockmen, Charlie and I went to battle, grading firebreaks and backburning. The winds were often against us and the fire jumped our breaks many times. On about the third day, exhausted from lack of sleep and the monumental effort we'd made, we took stock. Most of the hill country had been lost but we had saved the river flats, where the best grazing grass was. There would be enough feed to see the cows through till the wet.

We had not even caught our breath when the film crew turned up. We had been in the middle of bull catching when the fires had forced us to drop everything and we still needed another 40 or so bulls to make a truckload, but it wasn't until the end of the first week of filming that Charlie and I found time get back to bull catching.

I left for Bull Creek in the dark driving the catcher, along with two stockmen who followed in the pick up-truck. Two hours later, just before daylight, the stockmen and I reached the agreed meeting place. I switched off the engine and caught a few minutes' sleep while we waited for Charlie. In the crisp morning I heard the familiar noise of the Bell helicopter's big rotors cutting through the air. I loved that sound. It usually meant that Charlie was coming, which always made me feel good.

Charlie flew over us and then peeled off up Packsaddle Valley to find a mob of bulls to push out onto the flat for me. He only went a few kilometres before he found a mob and disappeared below the trees to start them running. I turned the catcher on to warm her up, and checked that all the bull straps were ready. A tingle of anticipation coursed through me. I have often thought this must be the way a stalking predator feels before the kill. A mob of about 20 head came out of the thick scrub in single file at a fast trot. With my adrenaline at peak now I wheeled the catcher in alongside of the mob and isolated the boss bull. In just minutes we had him down and tied. Charlie kept them out on the salt flats while I peeled off cattle one by one until we had a full truckload.

It had been quite difficult in places; when the salt flats are wet with dew it's like driving on grease. The catcher was skidding all over the place and some of the country was too rough to drive over at all. Nonetheless we had got our load and the whole flat was covered with tied up and by now very aggravated cattle. Charlie didn't stay as he had things to do at the station. The men and I loaded the cattle and a few hours later started for home. On the way, four more bulls crossed my path. I caught them and tied each of them to their own tree; we would return later with an empty truck and pick them up.

Bull catching is mentally and physically demanding, and after the days we went without sleep while we were fighting fires I was exhausted. It was mid-afternoon by the time I had finished unloading the truck. The men went for a break and I escaped the film crew by going to our bedroom for some much-needed peace. They wanted to shoot the classic 'wild horses galloping' scene with my sister Danielle riding behind them on a motorbike. They were in Bullrush Paddock trying to make this happen but Danielle was struggling to push the horses to where the crew needed them to be. She came back to the homestead upset, hoping that Charlie could come and help her. Charlie smiled. He liked Danielle, and he liked helping people generally.

I watched from the bedroom window as he went out the back gate and got on his motorbike. He had been a bike enthusiast all his life and was highly skilled. I, on the other hand, was completely hopeless. Charlie had patiently given me lessons on a very mild-powered bike but even that gave me trouble. He looked so good on a bike. 'Well,' I thought, as I watched him roar off, 'if I keep at it I'll get better.' But I knew I could never hope to be as good as Charlie.

I lay down on our bed and closed my eyes to rest my weary body; my mind was still going over the next few days' work when Danielle knocked at the door about an hour later. She and the film crew had been waiting for Charlie to bring the horses but he hadn't turned up. Danielle had looked everywhere but couldn't find him. 'Oh God,' I thought, 'what if he's had an accident and is lying somewhere and needs help?' I drove out to Bullrush. I looked everywhere without success. I was really feeling panic rise inside me now. The quickest way to find him would be to look with the chopper because the grass was so long it would have been possible to drive within a metre of someone and not see them on the ground. Tony, the pilot Charlie had helped train, was at the homestead with a chopper.

My mother saw the look on my face. 'What's the matter?' she asked.

'I don't know yet,' I replied, not stopping. 'I'll tell you as soon as I do.'

I went out to Tony and asked him to take me up straight away. We started at the far end of the paddock, flying in a systematic pattern.

'There he is.' Tony said.

My heart leapt. We'd found him. Everything would be all right now. I could see that the motorbike had skidded quite a way on its side and Charlie was lying motionless in the long, golden grass. I had my seat belt unbuckled and was halfway out of the chopper before Tony was anywhere near the ground. He tried to get me to wait. He seemed reluctant even to land. I tore my eyes from Charlie for a moment, glared at Tony and shouted, 'Land!' He did, and I was out and running before the skids had found the ground. Panic engulfed my whole soul and being. I called to Charlie as I ran through the grass. 'I'm here, Charlie, it's okay, I'm here.'

I fell to the ground beside him and rolled him over so that I could see his face. My heart felt it would burst when I saw him. His skin was blue, and his beautiful green-gold eyes were lifeless. All I could think of was that he needed oxygen. I had to save him. I immediately started CPR. His mouth was full of vomit. I didn't care. I wiped it out and kept going. If I kept going until we got him to a doctor he'd be fine, I said over and over to myself. Tony came to us quietly, knelt down and took Charlie's big arm to feel for a pulse.

'Marlee,' he said gently. I didn't hear him. I was doing CPR obsessively. 'Marlee.' Tony took me by the shoulder gently. 'He's dead, Marlee.' I paused and saw Tony for the first time.

He had tears streaming down his face. 'We have to get a doctor! Go now, get help quickly!' I said.

'Please come with me. I don't want to leave you out here alone,' he pleaded.

'I can't leave Charlie. I have to keep going. You go get help. We need to get a doctor. Go!'

Tony backed away. He didn't know what to do. But he did know there was no way I was going to leave Charlie. I just kept doing CPR. I didn't hear Tony take off in the chopper. I couldn't feel anything. Time stood still. If I kept going he'd be all right, I thought again and again. I was alone with Charlie in the long, golden grass for over an hour.

Tony never came back; he was a wreck by the time he got back to the homestead. Danielle and her boyfriend David were driving around looking for Charlie and finally came upon us. Danielle dissolved, her beautiful eyes filled with tears.

'Oh Marlee,' she said and came to me.

'We need to get a doctor. We have to get help,' I said to her.

David felt for a pulse and shook his head at Danielle. Danielle knew I was in my own world of denial. She led me along with such kindness.

'We should get Charlie home, Marlee,' she said gently.

'Yes, yes, and hopefully they'll have the doctor there by then, I sent Tony to get help,' I raved on.

It took all three of us to lift Charlie's 240 pounds into

the Toyota. I refused to have him lying on the hard steel
tray on the back but sat him up on the front seat and held
him in my arms to steady him. He wasn't blue any more
– that had to be good. It was going to be all right, I kept
telling myself. Back at the homestead we lay Charlie on our
bed and I lay next to him.

'Will the doctor be here soon?' I asked.

No one answered. They didn't know what to say. My
mother came to the door and collapsed with a wail.

'Marlee, oh Marlee, no.'

My poor sister Danielle picked her up and led her off.
From there on everything is a blur. Everyone tried to get me
away from Charlie but I furiously resisted. I was waiting
for the doctor and I was not leaving Charlie. He needed me.

Finally, Kerry came. Charlie and I both thought the
world of this man. I looked into his eyes and saw tears well
out of terrible sorrow and pain.

'Why do all my friends die?' he asked and put his arms
around me firmly.

'Marlee, you have to leave him now,' he said, and led
me away.

I didn't get far before I swung around and went back.
I had to stay with him; he couldn't be alone. Kerry caught
up with me at the door as I saw the police zipping up the
black body bag and reality intruded swiftly and brutally.
There and then I wanted to die; I wanted to go with him.
The nurse from Timber Creek had come out with the
police. He gave me something that took all my feeling away.
I knew nothing and felt nothing. I drifted off into a grey,
timeless void.

———

I drifted for days. The pain and depth of my despair when
I did come back were unbearable; and I couldn't escape
from them anywhere. The thought of death was irresistible
to me. I would do anything to escape the relentless agony

and be with Charlie again. When I could think those were my only thoughts. Were it not for the drugs I was religiously fed I would have committed suicide in those first days after I lost Charlie.

In the blur of the half world I was living in I remember my Uncle Ralph coming and Charlie's father and brothers coming. I wanted to bury Charlie on Bullo but his father wanted him buried in Queensland. I wavered in and out of reality, and in the end I gave in. We flew to Cairns and drove up to the little town of Mareeba where the funeral was to be held. I don't remember much. There were a lot of people there but I saw them only as ghostly shapes. I couldn't see through my veil of tears. I couldn't hear through my pain. My memories are hazy. I cried and cried. I didn't care about anything any more.

After the funeral my mother took me down the coast to my aunt and uncle's home in Bundaberg and we stayed for a while. I took the tablets every day willingly; I waited to slip into the blissful fog where the pain could not reach me. Each day I felt like I was sinking lower and lower. My mother was very worried; she didn't know what to do with me.

Finally we went home. Kerry was on my flight and endured my raving at him. He made me promise to pack all of Charlie's possessions up and put them away until a time when I was strong enough to deal with my emotions.

I did do what Kerry asked but I sobbed convulsively for days afterwards. Being home didn't help me feel any better but it did bring me back fully into my emotions from the half world of the previous weeks. Everywhere I looked there were things that brought gut-wrenching memories flooding into my mind. I blocked them out as much as I could. I would deal with them in small doses when I could face them. The cattle season was not yet over. I threw the pills away and put my head down and started working. Each day I went till I could do no more. In the end work was my salvation.

I had set up the portable yard at Twenty-two Mile when

two policemen from Timber Creek came out to take a statement from me. I was sobbing so much I couldn't talk. They
were kind and apologetic and offered to come back another
time.

'No,' I said, 'I'll finish now.'

In truth, the pain it brought back to me was unbearable
and I didn't want to feel it again soon. I wanted to forget
everything for now. When they left I lay down in my swag,
drank enough alcohol to dull my mind, and sobbed myself
to sleep.

The coroner's report said that Charlie's death was accidental; he had broken his neck when his bike hit an ant hill
at high speed and had died instantly. The fact that he had
not suffered was important to me and the only small
comfort I had.

Before Charlie's death we had secured a bank loan to buy
a thousand Brahman heifers from Queensland to boost our
herd. When the last muster was finished my mother
reminded me of the loan sitting in the bank. We contacted
the cattle agent and I caught a flight to inspect the first
lot of 300-odd cows. The heifers suited our purpose and
so the wheels were set in motion to transport them to Bullo.

Charlie and I had bought a bulldozer to use on Maitland Downs. I got a phone call from the people who had
sold it to us – they were interested in buying it back. I had
no use for it now and agreed to sell it. I used the money
to purchase 80 head of high-quality stud cows, which I
could use to breed bulls for the Bullo commercial herd. The
cattle agents found an excellent line of young cows in calf,
with calves at foot, and three good-quality bulls. I followed
the cattle truck home and everything was going smoothly
until heavy rains hit. The manager of a nearby station let
me put the cows in their yards while we waited to see if the
rains would ease long enough for the road to dry out. They

didn't. It poured for over a week; our road would not be open to trucks until the next year.

I had Danielle get together some horses to meet me and the cows at the front gate. Danielle, Rex, an excellent half-Aboriginal stockman who had worked for us some years before, and I settled the cows down for the 76-kilometre walk home. It was awfully slow going the first day. The cows had a lot of very young calves at foot. Most of the cattle had been living with an extended drought and had never seen a flowing creek. Even the rain unsettled them, because this was the very first time they had experienced it.

The first creek we came to was running fast and deep. The cows all stuck their tails straight up in the air and sniffed nervously at the swirling flood waters. We had to push them hard with stock whips to get them across. The cows came out the other side sopping wet, shaking their heads. Twenty creek crossings later they were more blasé about the whole water thing.

By about halfway through the first day I realised that the smallest calves were slowing up the mob so much that we wouldn't make it to our night yard at this pace. The station handyman, Stumpy, was following along in my jeep with feed for the horses, swags and food for us. We pulled up the cows, caught all the straggler calves and put them on the back of the jeep. The cows were understandably upset but once they realised that their babies were in fact right there they settled down and we made up for lost time. It was a drizzly, miserable night but by some miracle Rex managed to get the sodden wood to burn, which helped to keep some of the billion or so mozzies at bay.

Overnight one of the cows had a calf. It looked strong and was drinking well. After a scant breakfast we caught the new calf and all the stragglers from the first day and started off again. There were at least four more that looked like they were going to have their calves any minute, which turned out to be the case. By lunch a heifer had gone down calving and we had to pull the mob up and wait for her. An hour later I was looking at my watch wondering what to do. If she didn't have it soon we wouldn't make the next yard. Not ten minutes later the most gorgeous little Brahman calf was born. I gave the cow time to lick the calf all over and then crept up on all fours to help the calf find his feet. I steered him towards the heifer's swollen udder and he sucked like a pro the first time. The cow wasn't sure what to make of me, but must have decided I wasn't a threat because she begrudgingly put up with my presence. As soon as the calf had his fill I trussed the little fellow up and put him in the back of the jeep with the other calves.

We got to our second camp on dark. Pushing cows all day is hard work, especially cows with calves. They don't like to walk, and certainly not fast – they prefer to stand under trees or eat.

When we reached the upper Bullo River crossing it was in flood. I had anticipated this so on the trip out I had Stumpy leave a Toyota and a small tin boat on the other side of the river. I parked the jeep up high out of the flood's reach and left it to bring home later if the flood waters dropped. We swam the cows across and then got everything else across in our little tinny, including the calves, and loaded them into the other vehicle. That night another two calves were born, and on the last day of our journey another. The cows were so used to the calves being in the vehicle that they were no longer distressed. At the end of each day they would line up next to it and wait for Stumpy to let their babies go.

We were damp and tired by the time we had reached Bullo, put the cows in the home paddock and let our horses go. I was glad we had got the cows and calves home, and glad to be home myself. I still wore a heavy cloak of sadness that I felt would be with me forever.

It had been five months since Charlie's death. Everyone kept gently reminding me there were things I had to sort out. Charlie and I had had a house on Maitland Downs in which we had kept a lot of our personal belongings, and on top of that something had to be done with the land that Charlie's father had given him. Every fibre in me didn't want to face going through and packing up our life and dreams just yet, but I thought it would be better to get it over and done with. I left for Queensland, my mother coming with me for company and support. The closer I got the worse I felt. By the time we got to Cairns I was a wreck. All the memories I had tried to keep deep within me until I could face them had come flooding back; I was a blubbering mess. The thought of packing up our personal belongings was torturous. I realised I couldn't face it yet. Everyone has a different opinion on how soon after the death of a loved one you should pack up their things. For me it was still too early. My mother didn't push me; she understood.

I called George and told him I couldn't face packing up our things but would return at the end of the coming cattle season and he seemed fine with that. The land that Charlie and I had cleared and started to develop for growing peanuts on I gave to Charlie's sister, Mary. I thought Charlie would have liked me to do that and I felt that the land should stay in his family. I knew how hard they had worked to get and keep their property.

My mother and I had discussed many ways to make extra money on the station. The most obvious one, and the one with the most potential, was tourism. Our part of the territory is scenic and diverse, and our large, rambling homestead perfect for entertaining. We had started constructing three double guest rooms with en suites in the homestead. I didn't want the whole trip to Cairns to be a complete waste of time and money so in place of Charlie's and my belongings we filled the truck with mattresses, and slate and tiles to finish off our new guest accommodation.

It was a relief to leave Queensland and the painful memories it brought back. On the first day of our trip back to Bullo I drove for 22 hours straight. The further away we got the better I felt.

On one of my trips to Queensland to buy cattle Danielle had come with me, and had met a young man named Martin Jennings. They had clicked instantly, and had kept in contact since then. Love was definitely blooming for them. Martin packed up and moved to Bullo to spend some time with Danielle and break a few horses over the wet. Having Martin around really brought some joy into Danielle's life and I was glad for her. She had been such a pillar of support in all the tragedy of recent times; she was deserving of her piece of happiness.

By the end of the wet season Danielle had decided that Martin was the one for her and she had made plans to live in Queensland with him in the New Year. My mother feigned delight when Danielle told her the news – she was in fact very upset, I guess because she was losing her baby and had decided that she didn't like Martin. Danielle's departure with Martin was awkward and uncomfortable. She left with the air of a guilty person when she had nothing to feel guilty about.

With Danielle gone my mother and I settled into another cattle season. I was still a sad soul deep down but found some solace in my work. My mother didn't say much about losing Charlie, but she was there and supportive, which is all you can be in such situations. Business-wise we were slowly pulling ahead, which was both a credit and a comfort to my mother and me.

But as the cattle season came to a close I felt panic engulfing me. I didn't want the wet to come and the cattle season to finish because I would have to face going back to Queensland to pack up our house and belongings. My mother and Jim, the man from whom we had bought our bulldozer, had become good friends. Jim offered to come to Queensland with his truck to bring back the caravan Charlie and I had lived in on the land George had given Charlie to develop for peanut farming. Danielle also offered to come over and help me pack up. I gratefully accepted all the support that was offered. I drove our seven-ton truck and picked Danielle up on the way. My mother and Jim travelled together in Jim's truck. When we reached Cairns my mother and Jim stopped for a few days' break while Danielle and I went up to Maitland Downs to start packing the truck.

I had called Joyce to tell her of my plans and this made me even more nervous than I had already been about the ordeal ahead. I stopped in Mareeba on the way to Maitland Downs to buy all the family Christmas gifts. When Danielle and I arrived, I hugged George, Joyce and John and gave them their presents. John was genuinely welcoming but George and Joyce seemed ill at ease and I got the distinct feeling they didn't want to accept my gifts. They took them awkwardly, their only comment being 'You didn't need to.' I replied that I bought them because I wanted to, not because I needed to. They made no further comment and disappeared hurriedly.

I steeled myself and went into Charlie's and my old house to start packing. I walked from room to room, tears welling in my eyes as memories flooded back. As I settled down and started to look more closely I felt that something wasn't quite right. It only took me a moment to put my finger on it: everything had been moved.

I couldn't see a number of very personal things, such as cards and letters we had written to each other and keepsakes of Charlie's. I confronted Joyce and she responded by becoming wildly angry.

George said that it was my fault that Charlie's and my possessions had been moved because I had left it so long to come back. He also told me he thought it was disgusting that I had been 'Going all over Queensland spending money like a drunken sailor.'

I was incredulous.

'What are you talking about?' I asked.

He mentioned my purchase of breeder cows for Bullo. I shook with anger.

'For God's sake,' I said in as measured a manner as I could muster, 'I bought breeder cattle, not Ferraris. We have a cattle station; cattle are our business.'

He stared at me, blinking occasionally, then changed the subject: 'You'll be leaving all Charlie's belongings.'

'No George,' I said, 'that will not be the case. I'll decide what I leave, if anything, and who gets what.' I think George was unused to a woman speaking to him in that way.

He responded: 'I'll be calling the police in that case.'

I told him that he could go right ahead because as far as the law was concerned he was the one who was out of line. He made no response and just sat there staring blankly.

It was clear that civil communication was not possible. I got up and left with tears streaming down my face and ran back to our old house. Once in the door I sobbed inconsolably. I understood the pain they were suffering – they had lost a son – but their hostility was hard for me to come to terms with as I was lost in my own grief. Danielle didn't know what to do but she was there for me.

I never spoke to George or Joyce again. John helped us pack up and load the truck. I gave him all the parts and engines that Charlie had collected over the years. He had sheds full of them. There were some of Charlie's personal things that John wanted so I gave him those too. I gave Steven one of Charlie's two lathes and one of Charlie's guns that he particularly wanted.

I didn't eat anything for the three days I was there as I wanted nothing further to do with George and Joyce. I cried most of the day and night. My mother and Jim turned up to load the other lathe and the caravan; she was horrified by the way Charlie's parents had behaved. As we drove away poor Danielle sighed in relief and commented that it had to be one of the most unpleasant weeks she had had in a long time. I completely agreed with her.

12

THE JOURNEY TO QUEENSLAND had left me feeling violated and drained, and I sunk into a depressed state. The bad thing about the wet season was that I had time to think for days on end when up till now I'd kept myself pretty well permanently busy since Charlie's death.

Mother asked me if I wouldn't prefer that she sell the property so we could move somewhere more comfortable. Who could blame her after all the years of struggle? I was adamant that I didn't want to live or work anywhere else if I had the choice. Things were going well enough business-wise, so we agreed that as long as I was happy to do the manual work we would continue on in our so far successful business partnership as co-directors. I had been a director of the company since my father's death, but my mother always handled all the accounts and money.

I decided to throw myself into work even though it was still the wet season. I was lucky enough to get a contract bulldozing job on Spring Creek Station just across the border in Western Australia. I would mostly be clearing fence lines. I hired a truck and low loader to float the bulldozer to the station, unloaded it and introduced myself to the manager, Barry. He looked curiously at me on the big old dozer, as everyone always does. I could see him thinking, 'She doesn't look like a bulldozer driver.' I am sure people who employ me sight unseen as a bulldozer driver expect me to be rough, tough, and an extreme feminist. I'm not rough, although after ten hours on the dozer I must admit I look a bit that way. I am tough – one has to be a little resilient to drive a bulldozer for weeks at a time in the bush. As for being a feminist, I believe in equal rights but I know, having worked in many predominantly male jobs, that women are not generally physically equal to men. However, even when I have come up against a job where my lack of physical strength was a problem in most cases I've found another way to get the job done.

My reasonably feminine appearance combined with my strength and my knowledge of traditionally male jobs often leaves men, in particular, a little confused. To the credit of most men, once they realise that I'm not on some mission on behalf of women, but rather are there to do a job well, they treat me as an equal. At least in the bush I haven't come across any glass ceilings I couldn't circumvent.

Barry had hired a helicopter to do an aerial survey of the fence lines. It landed, Barry got in and he and the pilot disappeared over the hills. I waited on the side of the dusty road by the dozer, trying to be positive about the job ahead. I had two months of dozer work in unfamiliar country ahead of me. And I really needed to get it right. Just getting work as a female driver is quite a task; I knew everyone was watching and that my chance at future work depended on how well I could pull this job off.

The helicopter returned after 40 minutes or so and Barry told me that the pilot would take me up and show me where to put the fence lines. In a little under 30 minutes the pilot showed me the next two months of work from the air. My brain was in overdrive trying to take in all the information. The chopper dropped me off next to the dozer and left me in a cloud of red dust. I went straight to pastoral maps I had brought with me and started drawing lines furiously in all directions, with footnotes about where I had seen suitable drinking water. When I had finished I studied the map with a sigh. Now all I had to do was make those lines on the map into fence lines on the ground. One of the problems with an aerial survey is that a route that looks excellent from the air can be a different story on the ground.

I had hired an English backpacker, Dave, to help me out. It was his job to pack up the camp in the morning, cook dinner and follow the dozer in the Toyota until I stopped and we set camp again for the night. I taught him how to make bread and cook it in the ground, a skill he was so proud of he nearly burst with pride the first day he dusted off a beautiful golden loaf. I had to take a picture that I am sure his grandchildren will look at in wonder some day – Grandpa Dave in the middle of the Australian outback with his first loaf of camp-oven bread.

I started work as soon as I could see and finished only when I couldn't. The days were long and back-breaking. I didn't stop except for a short lunch break. When I could get ten hours of dozing in I was making $1,500 dollars a day, which was awesome money at that time. Barry came out every week to check on my progress. Occasionally he would turn up at morning or afternoon tea time and on those odd occasions I did take the luxury of a break. Barry would bring out biscuits or cake and pour me a cuppa from his thermos. We would sit and chat about all sorts of things, the low rumble of the dozer the only sound in the otherwise silent bush. I was still a bit of a mystery to Barry.

One day over a cup of tea he asked, 'Why do you do it? Is it a power thing?' I smiled good humouredly, which put him at ease.

'No Barry, nothing so deep. I do it for the money and no other reason. I have to tell you that I don't feel the least bit powerful driving a dozer. It's loud, hot, dusty, rough work. At the end of a day I've been shaken up so much I feel like I've been in a tumble dryer for ten hours. But right now we really need the extra money.'

Every two or three weeks I would take a day off and

drive the 250-kilometre trip home to check on things and stock up on food supplies. Mother was genuinely delighted by the cheques that I brought home.

After I had finished the dozer work on Spring Creek Dave and I packed up and went to say goodbye to Barry. He never really commented on my work, but he did tell me that he would like me to come back next year to do another couple of months work, which was enough praise for me. Outwardly I accepted the work in a grateful but businesslike manner; inwardly my heart was bursting with pride. I had done it. I went home like the returning conqueror. I hung up my dozer driver's hat and put on my Akubra to start mustering the cattle for the season.

Having finished our three guest rooms we were now accepting paying visitors, who brought in welcome extra money. One particularly memorable group arrived in their own Citation jet. The group was made up of men in high-stress jobs, among them a surgeon and a stockbroker. I took them up the Bullo Gorge for swimming, fishing and bull catching, and showed them around the property. A few days later they were different men. The stockbroker came to me on the eve of their departure and said, 'I'm sunburnt and every bone in my body aches but I can't remember feeling this great in a long time. I actually slept two full nights in a row.' I remember thinking that tourism, if you got it right, could be a great business. You got paid to do a job that made people happy, and they thanked you for doing it as well.

The court case with Gus had come and gone, and we had left the triumphant winners. My mother and I were just beginning to feel like we were getting on top of things when Gus appealed the decision. My mother was certain there was no way he could win an appeal, but such is the law that one judge can make a decision and another can completely over-turn it. This aspect of the law I have never been able to grasp.

He won the appeal. My mother was in a state of shock for some time. We did not have the resources to fight the appeal, so despite the fact that we had delivered all but 400 cows we had to pay Gus. My mother made up a payment schedule that we hoped Gus would accept and to our surprise he did. I think the only reason he cooperated was because it was better to get the money in instalments than to go to court again.

My mother called on everyone who might be able to help us. One of our most unlikely knights in shining armour was Ernesto, my father's Filipino boat boy, who had gone on to become a wealthy shipping businessman. My father had taken Ernesto under his wing, employing him first as a boat boy on his yacht and later in his shipping business. Ernesto had adored my father because he had given him the opportunity to make something of his life. He had always called my mother 'Mummy' even though he was quite a bit older than her. Mother hadn't spoken to Ernesto in 25 years but she called him and explained the situation.

'Yes, I understand, Mummy. How much do you need?' he said without hesitation.

He wired money straight into our account and told my mother to pay him back when she could. The money Ernesto lent us gave us the time to get the rest of the money together for Gus. Things looked a little bleak but it did appear that we would be able to scrape through with the cattle sales and my bulldozing work.

With that situation under control I set out with about eight men to build a lane way – a narrow, fenced corridor used to contain and direct cattle – across the Bullo River from an area of the station that had always been a problem to muster. The river was so densely timbered there that every time we tried to bring cattle across we lost most of them. I recall once having 800 head go into the river and only 400 come out. The pilot lowered the chopper down over the water between the dense river foliage and there, swimming in tight circles under Pandanus palms, were some of the missing cattle, up to their necks in water. Bush cows are not dumb.

Work on the lane way progressed well. I left the men to put the posts in and went to the homestead to order parts for my chainsaw. While I was waiting for a phone call from a supplier I flipped through the *Bulletin* magazine. The *Bulletin*/Qantas Businesswoman of the Year Awards caught my eye. The year before they had required a written nomination, including a list of the reasons why your nominee should win. I had started but after ten pages had given up – I thought I'd just about have to write a book. This year, however, you could fax a nomination with less supporting material. That was more my style. I filled in the form while I was waiting by the phone, and faxed it off there and then.

My mother came by not long after. I told her what I had done and that I had no doubt she would win. I had the strongest gut feeling about it. She laughed.

'Marlee,' she said in a 'let me tell you how life really is' tone, 'these awards are all bought and paid for. There is no way I can win.' I listened with a 'not another lecture' look on my face and told her that in my opinion not all awards were rigged and that she had more than a good chance of winning. We left it at that, both agreeing to disagree.

A few weeks after I had faxed through the nomination my mother received a call from the *Bulletin*. They were doing profile stories on some of the nominees and wanted to do one on my mother. It didn't come as a surprise to me.

'You are going to win. Mark my words,' I said, nodding sagely.

My mother responded with 'Oh Marlee' and a shake of her head. But there was just a glint of excitement in her eye.

The judging panel contacted her for permission to check the company's financial position, which she gave them. Despite the company carrying large debts it was heading in the right direction and the future looked promising –

both to us on the land and to the judges on paper. Next came the news that Mother was one of the finalists.

'I told you,' I said.

'No Marlee, they just put people like me in to make it look fair.' I gave her the look that daughters give their mothers. Outwardly she scoffed at having any real chance. I could see that inwardly she was hoping I was right.

I was out working at the Twenty-two Mile camp when my mother received the news that she had won the award. She was in a state of jubilant shock when I came in that evening. She hadn't won anything since her early tennis career, certainly nothing as prestigious as this award. Floating on cloud nine, she looked happier and more animated than I could ever remember. Even if the award came to no more than an enjoyable evening at the awards ceremony in Sydney, it was absolutely enough for me to see my mother's spirits so lifted. She had been through more than enough over the years and I had long felt she'd been handed a raw deal by my father.

My spirits were very much lifted too. But what I didn't know then was that my mother's winning of the Businesswoman of the Year Award would change our lives forever, subtly at first and then with more drastic consequences.

In the weeks leading up to the awards ceremony we weren't allowed to tell anyone Mother had won. This was not difficult for me as I was out in the bush most days, but Mother, who spoke to friends and family on a daily basis, found it hard not to let her news slip. My Aunty Sue would ask if anything new had happened and it was difficult for Mother not to blurt it out.

'No, nothing much,' she would say.

'Any news about the award?'

'No news yet.'

When the time finally came to fly down to Sydney for the

awards presentation Mother was beside herself with excitement. I accompanied her, and Danielle flew down from Cloncurry. I had just finished mustering – it was quite a leap to go from my swag to the Regent Hotel. It all felt a little surreal for me, as if I was hovering off to one side taking in the spectacle. I marvelled at the huge difference between my workday life and the scene at the awards. I might well have been on a different planet the gap was so big.

The award organisers screened a film clip they had made at Bullo. The stunning landscape of our station sprang to life on a screen that nearly took up one whole wall. It took everyone's breath away; there was a collective gasp from the guests. My mother was announced the winner by Hazel Hawke and a deafening applause filled the ballroom. The beautiful award was presented by Mrs Hawke, who dropped it on the stage. My mother scooped it up and made light of the incident. Everyone chuckled politely and I think this helped a little to calm my now very nervous Mother. Mrs Hawke departed and left my mother to bravely deliver her first public speech, which she did with great style. I was proud of her.

After the formalities were over everyone relaxed. It was a great evening that went on into the early hours of the next morning. We retired to the bar, where we had the biggest bowl of Beluga caviar I had ever seen. Everyone was on a high and it felt like it would last forever, but eventually the reality of the next day had to be faced and one by one we all trailed off to bed. At home we would have started work already.

I caught a little sleep before we had to be ready for the interviews that had been lined up for my mother that day. I was to take part in some of them, and to keep her company for the others. I opened my hotel room door to get the morning newspaper – and found my mother smiling at me from the front of the *Sydney Morning Herald*. All the way down the hall I could see the smiling face of my mother. I took the paper in and plonked it down in front of Mother.

'You are wall to wall,' I said, but she was already glued to the article in complete fascination and awe.

No one had quite expected the media response that followed my mother's award. Something about our story and lifestyle had really struck a chord. From then on things happened very quickly that day. The one interview that was to have a lasting impact on our lives was on morning radio in Sydney with Andrew Olle, who sadly died some years later.

Andrew had been at the awards presentation and had immediately booked Mother for an interview. Driving to work that morning and listening to Andrew Olle's programme was James Fraser, a publishing executive. As soon as he got to the office he put the wheels in motion.

'Find out where that woman is staying in Sydney. I want her to write a book!'

He made an appointment to meet us the following day, Saturday, at our hotel. I guess my mother was so excited by the amazing turn her life had taken that she wasn't in a state to absorb any of the finer details. She assumed that we were to meet at the publisher's offices. My mother and I turned up at the appointed time to find the building shut. The cleaner very kindly let us in and we waited and waited before concluding that there had been some sort of a mix up. I found James's phone directory in his office and called his home, where his wife kindly sorted out the misunderstanding. Meanwhile, James had been waiting patiently at our hotel. Finally we did meet, and laughed heartily at our mistake. Mother and I instantly liked James. We discussed the book he was now proposing, and when we came to the bit about how much of an advance she would be paid Mother had to excuse herself for a trip to the ladies room. This was something she always did when she was nervous. While my mother was taking refuge in the toilet I negotiated James's original offer of $5,000 up to $20,000. My mother returned and was beaming when I told her. James bid us good day and said he would get the contract drawn up as soon as possible. We spent the rest of the day shopping and catching our breath. My mother was in a well-deserved happy daze.

I was glad to be home and back to work after our trip to Sydney. I find the city overwhelming with all its people and cars. The awful-smelling air gives me a constant headache and everyone seems to be going a hundred miles an hour night and day. After being in the city a while I crave the solitude of the bush; I feel very much at home there.

My mother was lost in her new dream world for a time; she was flooded with phone calls and letters of congratulation from people she did and didn't know.

'I suppose I'll have to write that book now,' she said tentatively. She dug out her old manuscript, *Through the Saltbush Backwards*, dusted it off and started working. For several months, whenever I came back in from bull catching, I would find her sitting at her desk writing longhand of her turbulent life. Sara Henderson the author was about to be born. She settled easily into the new role. All her life she had done things because she felt obligated to, and now she had found something that she really enjoyed doing. It seemed to liberate her instantly. I think she found the whole process cathartic.

I wanted to get up into the Mickey Creek fault valley where there was a large number of bulls that choppers had never been able to move. I set off on the dozer and made a road and a dozen creek crossings for 40 kilometres. Then I used a grader to smooth out the road.

I set off with five men in the bull catcher and two trucks at 4.00 one morning in order to arrive at the fault valley by dawn. The weather was oppressively hot and humid, but we hadn't had a drop of rain yet. It looked like it was going to be a late wet. We had only driven a kilometre into the valley when we ran into a mob of ten bulls, bullocks and dry cows – all exactly what I wanted. I roared off after the leader and in an hour had all ten tied up. We had a full load and it was only a little after 8.00 am. I was in high spirits; it was going to be a good day.

We were loading the cattle onto the pick-up truck when I felt a change in the atmosphere; sharp blasts of chilled air sliced through the thick humidity as a north breeze began to pick up. In the distance I saw the blackest, lowest front of cloud I have ever seen in my life. It was approaching at an alarming speed. The clouds were skidding along the tops of the sandstone valley, their blackness contrasting startlingly with the red stone. The men and I dashed about to load the last of the cattle, by which time the clouds were overhead. I had one of the men start up the bull catcher while I started up the grader. I didn't want to have it stuck in Mickey Creek all wet season, and I reasoned that I would be able to get the dozer out in far worse conditions than those in which I'd be able to move the grader.

The rain came down in a wall of water. The first creek we came to was rising so fast that in another ten minutes we wouldn't have been able to cross. The next creek had burst it banks and the crossing I had made with the dozer was ten feet under water. It had gone from bone dry to ten feet deep in 30 minutes. Our only option was to follow the creek up towards its source until we could find a shallow enough crossing. I led the way through the torrential rain, making a track for the others to follow as I went. It wasn't until we had gone a few kilometres that I found a suitable crossing. With every creek we came to it was the same story. They had all burst their banks.

By midday the ground had soaked up enough water to get boggy and the vehicles started to go down, particularly the heavily loaded truck and the 16-ton grader. We struggled on in the relentless rain, stopping to pull each other out as we went. Finally it became impossible to go on with the grader. I parked it up on a hill where it would be safe from floods and we went on with the bull catcher and the pick-up truck loaded with bulls. At the second-last creek before the Bullo River I could find no place to safely get the truck over and it was now too boggy to go up higher to the creek source to find a shallower crossing. I made the decision to leave the truck and the bulls. The creeks came up and went down quickly in this area and once the water was down we would be able to get the truck across. I slacked off the bulls' head ropes so they were a bit more comfortable.

We all piled onto the catcher and after two more bogs made it to the Bullo River, which was about 20 feet higher than in the morning. We looked solemnly at the gushing, foam-topped flood waters. Swimming across was completely out of the question; I doubted that we would make it a metre into the river before we were swept away.

It was nearly dark now and we would need to do something quickly or spend a long, wet night by the river with the mozzies. I had a lot of ropes in the back of the catcher that I used for dragging reluctant bulls out of creek beds. I thought that if I tied them together there would be over 100 feet of rope available, enough to get us over the flood waters. David, voted the most agile in our group, shinnied up one of the huge trees at the river's edge. He had the long rope tied around his middle so that if he slipped and fell into the river we could haul him back to the shore. We watched in the fast-failing light as he crept along the branch that reached furthest across the river. The branch bowed dangerously. He made an enormous leap and grabbed a branch of a tree on the other side. It was a spectacular effort; he had the hugest grin on his face as he struggled to hold on to the wildly swaying tree branch. We all whooped and cheered him on. I couldn't help thinking that the day so far had been like an Indiana-Jones-style obstacle course – and it was not over yet.

David made it down the tree and secured the rope to it. One by one we dragged ourselves across. The current was strong and it was hard work. It took a few minutes for each of us to cross, although it felt a lot longer.

Once safely on the other side we had one more flooded channel to cross. It was deep but not flowing anywhere as fast as the main river. We joined hands and tentatively waded in. The night was pitch black, without starlight to help us make our way. The rain was still coming down steadily. The water came up to my neck and for a stretch the men, who were all a lot taller than my 5'2", had to hold me up so I didn't get washed away. Our hearts were pumping flat out as we were all expecting a crocodile to appear at any moment. Fortunately we were spared that additional trial.

My sodden bull-catching crew eventually squelched their way up out of the riverbed. Our skin was wrinkled like prunes as we had by then been wet for 12 hours. We were freezing and hungry as we set off on the three-kilometre walk to the road where we had the second truck parked. On the way we had to wade through half a kilometre of swamp that was up to our waists. It was hard to fathom that all this had been bone dry just hours earlier.

For some reason getting to the truck made us feel like everything would be fine now. We climbed in and started down the road home. The first creek we came to was too deep to cross. The rain had stopped so we decided to try to get a little sleep. Between the mozzies and being teeth-chattering cold none of us actually slept; we sat up and talked instead. Five hours later, at 2.00 am, I waded across the creek to check the depth and found the flood waters had fallen enough for us to cross.

We crossed it, and another two creeks, then we were stopped yet again. We waited two hours for that creek to drop enough to get across. By 6.30 am we came to Dingo Creek, the last creek we had to cross, just five kilometres from the homestead. It was over three metres deep and didn't look like it was going down in a hurry. What the hell, we had another swim. We had a kilometre to go when the first rays of the sun warmed our wet, cold, tired bodies.

My mother was tremendously relieved to see us. She had

been in a state all night worrying. We changed into fresh clothes; it was unexpectedly luxurious to be dry again. We had a big breakfast and the guys were all about to collapse when I asked for a volunteer. They looked at me in horror, as if I was a madwoman. I needed someone to go back with me to either get the pick-up truck home or let the bulls go. A big, good-natured chap who never complained said 'I'll go' and the rest of the men sighed in relief.

I packed up a four-wheel drive bike and off we went again. Most of the creeks were still up but with the two of us we were able to float the bike across. It took us until late morning to get back to the truck. By now I knew there wasn't a hope of getting it back for days. The bulls were fine. We pulled their head ropes off and dropped the gate. The bulls were out of the truck and off into the scrub in a moment; what they thought of the whole experience I can only guess. Dog tired by now we forded the river and creeks and were home again by mid-afternoon. I went straight to bed; I don't even remember my head touching the pillow.

<hr />

I started the 1991 cattle season with more contract bull-dozer work, and went on to get a respectable number of cattle from our mustering. Meanwhile, my mother spent the year finishing her book, which was looking very promising, and discovered a flair for motivational speaking.

Towards the end of the cattle season most of the men I had working for me had to leave because they had other commitments. I still wanted to muster the cattle at Paper-bark and do some bull catching so I advertised for two tall, fit men. It does sound bad, doesn't it? However, there are practical reasons for imposing such criteria. The nature of our work is very physical and fitness is important, especially in the intense heat leading up to the wet season. And

I needed the men to be tall so they could lift the steel panels that make up our portable yards and stack them 30-high on the back of a truck – for anyone under about 5'11", it is an impossible task. I had ended up with a few guys who were not only shorter than me but had trouble lifting a knife and fork let alone steel panels. Having been caught out a few times I now made my requirements clear.

Several people applied. I was out at Paperbark doing the muster when my mother called me there on the radio with the details. Two Dutch fellows and two Austrians had applied. I told her to give the go ahead to the two Austrians because they had their own transport and sounded the most organised. They agreed to come the next day as with only two guys I was struggling to process the cattle. I left instructions with one of the girls at the house, Katie, to drive the Austrians out to the camp when they arrived as they would never find the way out themselves.

I went to the yard the next morning with the two men I already had working with me to start branding, dehorning and castrating the cleanskin mickies – wild young bulls that have never been mustered before. It was oppressively humid and hot; there wasn't a breath of wind. By the time we had been working for an hour the sweat had soaked our shirts and was dripping steadily onto the deep, fine yard dust. The dust stuck to the sweat on my body. I had blood from the dehorned mickies all over me. And my hands were covered in blood from castrating. We looked like we'd stepped off a bloody battleground. I glanced up and saw the Toyota approaching, Katie battling to control the old vehicle in the bull dust. 'Good,' I thought. 'We could use some help.'

I shall always remember the first time I saw Franz. He was tall, extremely fit, with long, rusty-red hair and an earring in one ear. He was wearing an impossibly white t-shirt that read 'Save the turtles'. He walked up to me and did not even hesitate to take my bloody, dirt-covered hand. He looked at me with the cheekiest twinkle in his eye and the most amazing smile I had ever seen. In that instant he filled my world with light. It was like I had waited my whole life for that moment.

I was wholly confused by my unexpected feelings. I was the one in charge. I was a level-headed, mature woman of 30. There wasn't anything fuzzy or romantic about me these days and yet I suddenly felt like a befuddled schoolgirl. How could a complete stranger walk up, shake hands and turn me into a disoriented mess? I got hold of myself quickly. In a businesslike manner I shook hands with Roland, who had no such effect on me, and got on with the work. Neither of them spoke much English but enough to get by.

Franz was quick. I would show him something and he would get it straight away. I watched him when I was sure he wasn't looking. What was it about him? I was instantly, madly in love with a complete stranger. I had heard of love at first sight and, frankly, had thought it was complete crap.

In the five years since I had lost Charlie I had resigned myself to a single life; having affairs with men who passed through my life to keep myself from complete loneliness. I could have married again – I'd had opportunities – but I'd made my mind up that it had to be the real thing or nothing. I was not going to marry just for the sake of having someone. But I didn't believe I could ever find true love twice. It was hard enough finding it once.

Every time Franz was anywhere near me I felt electricity between us. I tried to talk myself out of it: this is ridiculous; he's not going to stay out here; don't even think about getting involved if you like him even half as much as you think you do; when he leaves, which he will, you will die. That's what one half of me argued very convincingly. The other half said: opportunities for love come by rarely in life; take the opportunity with both hands; it is truly better to have loved, if only for a brief moment, than not at all; if you can accept the worst-case scenario then be brave, enjoy your time, however long or short it is, and be grateful. My thoughts raged back and forth for weeks.

Each night I lost myself in the infinite pleasure of contemplation of what might be between us.

———

We had finished at the Paperbark area and were rebuilding the portable yards back home. I had just finished using the backhoe to move the calf crush; I stopped the backhoe, jumped to the ground and turned over on my ankle, twisting it badly. The pain took my breath away and I couldn't put any weight at all on my foot. It was nearly morning tea time anyway so I told the guys we'd stop for a cup of tea while I tried to strap my ankle. We all drove to the homestead, which was only ten minutes away, and from the back gate I was hopping on one foot, tears streaming down my face because every time I hopped it jarred my ankle. Franz came and scooped me up in his arms. I blushed beetroot red and made some feeble comment about being too heavy, which he ignored, and he carried me into the homestead. I remember thinking that it was worth the pain to be in Franz's arms; it felt like heaven. I completely forgot my ankle for a moment and wished that he would carry me around all day. He gently put me down on a couch. 'Marlee, you are in deep, deep trouble,' I thought. And I wasn't referring to my ankle.

My ankle was going to be a problem for some time. Even tightly strapped it was excruciatingly painful. I pulled out a set of steel crutches that Uncle Dick had welded up for Diesel Don many years ago. The crutches were a torture all on their own; they were gruesomely heavy. I discovered that they had all sorts of other uses – you could use them like a crow bar, and they were strong enough to lay across a couple of stumps and use as a seat. Swinging the crutches I was certain I'd have bulging biceps by the time my ankle had repaired itself. But there was no use complaining as they were the only ones we had and they were definitely better than nothing.

Both Franz and Roland were cheeky fellows. Roland fancied himself as a ladies' man and one evening after a few beers offered me an Austrian back rub. Apparently they are the best. Franz gave me a cheeky look and also offered to rub my back but told me I'd have to pay him. I laughed at both of them and declined. The truth was I seriously doubted that I could control myself if Franz started rubbing my back.

Franz's English improved rapidly in the first couple of months and we began to speak more. He was 22 years old, came from a farm in southern Austria, near the Italian border, was the third of four children, and had trained as a cabinet-maker. It was not his ambition; he was yet to discover what that would be. He was passionate about travel and had done so at every opportunity. This was his second trip to Australia; there was something about the vast wildness and free spirit of the country that captured him. He had already decided that he would most like to live in some isolated place. 'God, I wish this was the place,' I was thinking.

In the short time that we had been working together our feelings had become mutual. While we had not spoken at all of these feelings, the attraction between us was undeniable. Still, I hesitated to get involved, afraid of being hurt when Franz left.

The year came to an end; Roland wanted to move on, which meant that Franz would go as well. My heart plunged into despair. I was in a quandary as to whether I should tell Franz how I felt and beg him to stay – when he came and told me that even though Roland was going he would like to stay a while. My heart soared, and did multiple somersaults and other acrobatics of happiness. My mother and I were going up to Darwin and he asked if he could come along to sell his motorbike and extend his visa. 'Yes,' I said, smiling so broadly I thought my face would split.

In Darwin Franz attended to his business and was ready to go back to Bullo to plant hay. My mother and I had to stay on for a week longer to do a few bits and pieces, including the Christmas shopping, so Franz decided to catch a bus back to Bullo. I drove him to the bus station. We were early and stopped at a cafe, both ordering iced coffee. I expected to get a tall glass with some embellishments, but instead a short-tempered waitress plonked down two cartons of Paul's Iced Coffee. Not even that fazed me. The feelings between us were so strong now, we might have been in the most romantic cafe in Paris. I saw Franz off and floated around Darwin.

A week later I drove the 850 kilometres home, thinking mostly of Franz. My mind was made up. I would take the plunge and start a relationship. I would enjoy every moment of happiness it gave me, day by day, for however long it lasted. When we pulled up to the homestead Franz was there waiting with his cheeky smile. 'I'll take you up on that back rub now,' I said. His smile enveloped me in warmth. I knew that I had found my soul mate. I had loved Charlie deeply and had never expected to love or be loved in quite the same way again. The feelings I had for Franz were different, but then so was I. The past years had changed me; I was a different person in many ways.

Christmas passed in a blur of happiness. I had never felt in such harmony with any man before. I was so high that I was afraid to look down. Every time thoughts crept in like 'What will I do if he leaves?' I pulled myself up: 'Stop, Marlee. Just enjoy the time you have; don't spoil it. Go higher; don't look down. Soar, fly, be happy. Don't doubt and don't look down.'

13

I LISTENED TO THE POSITIVE ME and enjoyed every moment I was with Franz, until February 1992 when, by necessity, reality had to be faced. The time on Franz's visa was running out and we would have to do something soon if we were to stay together.

I was living in Australia on an American passport with a permanent residency visa but had long ago decided that I wanted to become an Australian citizen. I loved Australia and it was where I wanted to make my home. Franz and I went up to Darwin – me to attend my citizenship ceremony and Franz to try and extend his visa again.

The Immigration Department made it clear that Franz was to leave the country as soon as his visa expired, in about three months. He could apply to return, but they could deny his application without any explanation. Under no circumstances were we to consider marrying. Franz and I had not talked of marriage anyway. We had only known each other for four months; at this point all we wanted to do was spend more time together. I dissolved into a blubbering mess. All I could think of was that I couldn't bear to lose Franz as I was so, so in love with him.

I attended my citizenship ceremony. The woman who swore me in was particularly nice and for some reason I felt that she may be able to give me some advice. I blurted out my dilemma.

'Marlee I'm not allowed to give you advice,' she said, and my heart sunk. Then she went on, 'Do you know, however, that the registry office is two blocks along on this street?'

I knew immediately that marriage was the only way I could stay with Franz. I didn't feel helpless any more; I knew there was a solution. We discussed it and agreed that marriage was essentially a social and religious custom, and a legal piece of paper. It was not what made a happy relationship between two people. That being our mutual view we decided to marry now. If it worked – great. If it didn't, we would go our separate ways.

Next we found that in order to marry, Franz needed to have at least 90 days left on his visa. He checked his passport – he had 91 days. That put me into a panic. My God, we would have to get married the next day. We went to the registry office, where the celebrant reminded us that you normally have to give one month's notice of intended marriage, though she could, at her discretion, marry people with less notice. I burst into tears and begged her to marry us the next day. Bless her soul, she agreed.

I was feeling a little exhausted by my roller coaster emotions. Franz and I met my mother for lunch at our favourite restaurant; she had also come to Darwin as she was due to fly to Sydney in a couple of days. I had a look on my face that made her take notice.

'Franz and I have decided to marry,' I told her.

She was a little shaken but responded with, 'Oh that's nice. Have you set a date?'

'Yes, tomorrow,' I said with a smile. That did shock her.

'Tomorrow . . . Oh Marlee, you're a tease,' she said, her alarm subsiding as she assumed I was saying it in jest.

'No, I'm not joking; we really are getting married tomorrow.'

Mother went pale and asked in a weak voice if there was

any reason we needed to do it so urgently. I explained the situation. I could see on her face that she wasn't at all sure about what I was doing, but she knew me well enough to know that she wouldn't be changing my mind. She gave me her support.

I think a lot of people thought that Franz and I were crazy for getting married after only knowing each other for four months. In my opinion, living and working under difficult conditions strips the varnish from people very quickly. You see what the real person is made of and then some; it's like seeing them through a powerful magnifying glass. Franz and I are both definite people – we both knew what we wanted and liked in a partner – so marrying after only four months together wasn't quite as frivolous as it at first sounds. However, the future is never certain, so Franz didn't call his parents when we decided to get married. He waited to see how things went before breaking the news to them.

Mother swung into action, arranging everything she could in one afternoon to make our day special. Franz and I went out and bought some clothes to wear to our wedding – we kept them pretty simple – and wedding rings. Then we met my mother back at the apartment we were renting. It was late afternoon. I needed another witness for the ceremony and as Danielle was planning to come up to Darwin anyway I thought it would be nice for her to be there. I called her up and asked if she could get on the early bus to get to Darwin by the morning.

'Yes, but why?' she responded.

'Well,' I said happily, 'I'm getting married tomorrow and I want you to be here.'

There was silence on the other end of the phone and then she said 'Bullshit!' Danielle has never been one to mince words.

'I really am Danielle. I'm not joking.'

'Bullshit! Why didn't anyone tell me?' She was very, very put out. I told her that we'd only decided a few hours earlier.

'Bullshit!' she said again. I wanted to hear 'How fantastic' or 'I'm so happy for you'.

I handed the phone to Mother and said, 'She's your daughter, you talk to her!'

My mother got much the same and had to hold the phone away from her ear. In the end Danielle finally believed my mother that it was not a practical joke we had dreamed up. And then I doubt anything would have stopped her getting to Darwin. She had to see the penniless backpacker – Franz was not penniless, but that was the image she had in her head – her irresponsible sister was going to marry.

When she arrived the next day she was none too friendly. She looked Franz up and down without comment and looked at me as if I had lost my mind.

I was way too happy to be bothered by what Danielle thought. For a hastily organised ceremony in a registry office, it was unexpectedly moving. It was held in an attractive wood-panelled, private room and my mother had brought along a cassette player and some suitable music. She even managed to hire a photographer. Franz, who is normally reserved about expressing his emotions, had the biggest grin on his face, only matched by my own. To the credit of the good old grapevine, an acquaintance, Lynette Ainsworth, had turned up. As we walked outside as Mr and Mrs Ranacher she showered us with frangipani petals. I hadn't felt such happiness and contentment in a long, long time.

As our wedding gift, my mother and Danielle had booked Franz and I a suite in the Beaufort Hotel, the best in Darwin. We lost ourselves in the joy of each other's company for the afternoon and then wafted down to a restaurant for a beautiful dinner with my mother and Danielle, who was starting to thaw a little.

My second wedding was a perfect, no-stress, no-fuss, feel-good day. I was full of positive emotions and surrounded by people I loved. Not for one moment did I have any reservations about marrying Franz. When I woke beside him the next morning I felt how right it was; every hour that passed only made the feeling stronger.

Franz and I drove home to Bullo with a load of supplies in the seven-ton truck. We didn't have time for a honeymoon but I really didn't care. I was wallowing in happiness and planned to do so for as long as possible. My mother flew off to Sydney for a meeting with her publishers. She had finished writing her book at Christmas and it was due to be published in time for Mother's Day. Danielle went to visit Bonnie, whom she still kept in close contact with. Bonnie had made no effort to make any contact with me or my mother in the many years since she had left – nor had I, for that matter, made contact with her.

The Immigration Department were not at all pleased that Franz and I had married. They told us that his permanent residency would not be approved for two years, during which time they could kick him out without explanation and deny him re-entry forever. These words over the crackling radiotelephone struck fear into my heart, as well as instant rage and determination that I would never allow the Immigration Department to destroy our life together. They were never to carry out their threats but we were to have an axe hanging over our happiness for two years, until Franz's permanent residency was approved.

———

While I had been in Darwin becoming an Australian citizen, loading the truck and getting married I had also squeezed in an appointment with my gynaecologist to have pap smear. One day I returned from work to find a message from him that I needed to come back urgently. My heart skipped a beat. I phoned him straight away. He told me that my pap smear had found cells in my cervix that were only one stage away from cancer. I would have to have an operation to remove the pre-cancerous tissue, and to make sure that there were no cancerous cells there. I hung up the phone, numb. Why was life so hard? Why did it give so generously with one hand and take so brutally with the other? I had only been married for six weeks, was madly in love with my husband, and had gone so far as to think of having children down the track. The future, which had looked so bright, suddenly became dark and unclear. What if I wouldn't be able to have children? And what if they couldn't stop the cells developing into cancer?

I dissolved into a pathetic heap of tears and that was how Franz found me. I sobbed my way through an explanation, terrified of how he might react. Franz listened quietly and patiently and then put his arms around me. I felt stability and strength in his embrace; all my fears vanished.

'I'm here with you,' he said, and he meant it. Every day I had passed with this remarkable man I had found more qualities I loved him for. Today, even in the misery of that moment, my heart caught as I realised that in times of trouble he really would be my rock. I would always be able to count on him – not everyone can say that about their partner. With Franz's quiet support I pulled myself together. 'One step at a time, Marlee,' I told myself.

My mother didn't know what to say. She had never been good with medical problems of any kind. I told her not to worry. She was attending a conference in Darwin at the same time I was going into hospital for my operation, so we went to Darwin together. Franz was to come up in the truck later. Mother offered to miss a day of her conference to be with me when I went in for surgery but I declined. I knew she would just get upset sitting waiting in the hospital and I couldn't see the use of that.

However, when they wheeled me into the operating theatre I felt lonely and wished I'd accepted. Not for long, though, as I drifted off into the oblivion of the anaesthetic. My mother was there when I came out; she was upset because the operation had taken twice as long as expected.

After the doctor had finished removing the suspect tissue, the medical instrument that was holding me apart collapsed and two sides of the wall of my vagina were cut, from the cervix all the way out. They had to stitch me up, which took quite some time. I was in astonishing pain. Literally every movement hurt. Just sitting upright was unbearable; sneezing was excruciating. My anticipated few days in hospital stretched into ten. My birthday came and went.

60 Minutes was due to come to Bullo to record a segment about my mother and her soon-to-be-published book. The publisher had told her the book world was abuzz over it, and that a favourable *60 Minutes* segment would help to make it a bestseller. My mother returned to the station while I was in hospital. I called and begged her to put the filming off; I knew they wanted high action, which I would not be able to provide in my current state. My mother said she had tried to put the filming off but just couldn't.

Franz came to Darwin in the truck to pick me up. It was a long and difficult trip home. I lay down on the truck's uncomfortable bench seat with my head on Franz's lap all the way because sitting up was too painful. We arrived home to find that mother had arranged to have Danielle travel from Queensland to help with the action scenes for *60 Minutes*.

The house was a mess. We had one young woman working for us at the time and I helped her put things back in order before the film crew arrived, although I wasn't supposed to be working at all. The work I normally flew through was slow and difficult. I felt weak, as if I was about to faint at any moment. We didn't have a cook at the time, which meant I also had to cook for everyone.

All I felt like doing was lying down in a dark place until the pain went away. I couldn't keep the thought from my mind that I may never be able to have children. To fall pregnant while there was the possibility of cancer posed many complications, and if I did develop cancer, who knows, maybe my whole uterus would need to be removed to save my life. I was very tearful. Through all of this Franz was there for me. At night he just held me and settled me down. During the day he went about the business of keeping things going on the station.

The *60 Minutes* crew arrived. Like most film crews they had four days in which to complete a week's worth of work; they were all on hyper drive. I soon doubted whether they knew how incapacitated I was. They wanted me to ride horses, leap about in the yard and so on. At that point even going to the toilet left me in tears and I was still bleeding heavily. I was beyond frustration.

The producer was the only one who asked how I felt. I snapped back at her: 'How do you think I feel? I've just had an operation and everyone expects me to perform on command.' I regretted my outburst; it wasn't her fault. I was so overwrought it didn't take much to set me off.

My mother came to me the day after my outburst.

'Darling, could you please just milk the cow for them, and they also want you to drive the grader.'

I milked the cow with some of the tourist guests we had staying at the time and pretended that there was nothing I'd rather be doing. Franz had to lift me into the grader; there was no way I could climb into the cab myself. I did the grader scene and Franz lifted me back out afterwards. I went back to the kitchen and continued my pathetic hobbling about.

Once the film crew had left I retreated into our bedroom, where I rested and recovered. It was the first time I learned how debilitating pain can be. As soon as it subsided my outlook on life became much brighter.

Despite the tension of their few days' filming, the crew from *60 Minutes* put together an excellent snapshot of life on Bullo that catapulted my mother's book sales into orbit. The publishers were elated. Mother was flooded with congratulations and thanks from friends, family and a great many complete strangers who had read and loved the book. She was proud of her achievement, had a new-found confidence in her abilities, and was happier than she had ever been.

It was the beginning of a new life for her, full of opportunities she had never dreamed of. Mother had become a great motivational speaker since becoming Australian Businesswoman of the Year; she could move any audience. Her sudden fame as an author put her in even greater demand on the speaking circuit. The money she was offered took her breath away. Initially she was paid $3,000 plus expenses per speech. Soon she was earning $10,000 plus expenses per speech. Never had she imagined she could earn such money just by speaking to people.

The extra money my mother was bringing in was an unexpected and welcome bonus, but the consequence of her new profile was that she was away more and more frequently for longer and longer periods. Book promotion and speaking engagements became the predominant part of her life. We encouraged her wholeheartedly, because not only was she very good at it, she genuinely seemed to be enjoying it.

Back at Bullo daily life was running smoothly. Mother had never been involved with any of the outside work so her absence didn't have too much impact on the day-to-day running of the station. I was fully mobile again and glad to be out working. The tourism side of our business was slow, but it was profitable when we did have guests. What we needed to get things moving was more exposure.

The *Holiday Show* contacted us to do an episode on Bullo – thanks largely to Mother's high profile, I'm sure. After speaking to them on the phone to get details of who was coming and what they wanted to film I hung up in amusement. The interviewer's name was Sarah Henderson. On the trip out to Bullo she encountered a few problems. When she was checking out of the Kununurra hotel she said she was Sarah Henderson, to which the manager responded, 'No you're not. I know Sara Henderson.' The misunderstanding was cleared up and the manager now knows there are at least two in Australia.

The film crew were good to work with and we packed as much into the segment as we could. It went to air soon after and we all thought it was excellent – so, apparently, did the viewers as we had many bookings as a result.

Our guests came from all walks of life. From the extremely well-heeled arriving in their private jets, to retired farmers driving up our dusty road. What they all had in common was a wish to see more of the real Australia. My mother entertained them with endless stories of life in the outback and I took them bull catching, fishing and sightseeing. They loved the spectacular country, and the fact that there weren't a million other tourists around. In most cases it was just them, and that made them feel special. It was sort of like they had a national park all to themselves.

By October we had finished the mustering and it was time to start our yearly bull catching. It was also time for me to have another pap smear to see if my operation had been successful. I was dreading what the answer might be. My doctor was as calm as ever.

'In most cases the results are good, and we did get it early,' he said with a smile.

It felt like an eternity to get the results back but when I did it was an enormous relief – they were all clear. This was by no means the end, however. I would have to have checks every six months for the next five years. I felt that day in the doctor's office that I was off to a flying start, though, and my spirits lifted immediately.

October was also time for the Businesswoman of the Year Awards. My mother and I were invited to attend, and gratefully accepted. It was really nice that we could do something like this together. More and more these days our lives seemed to be going in opposite directions. We had been through so much together in getting Bullo back on its feet and I missed our closeness.

The awards were my first social engagement for the year and probably my mother's hundredth public appearance. She was so busy during our stay in Sydney that there wasn't much time to talk. When we did have a moment we marvelled at how one event – such as my mother's winning of the award the year before – could so change the direction of your life. We also talked about our plans for developing Bullo – the possibilities were tantalising.

———————

Franz and I had decided that it was time for me to meet my in-laws. I hadn't even spoken to them on the phone because they didn't speak English and I didn't speak German. We would fly to Austria in the New Year, so I bought some German books and studied as much as I could so that I wouldn't be a complete mute when we got there. I was excited, yet terrified of meeting my in-laws, as my in-law experiences hadn't been great. I explained my feelings to Franz, who just laughed in a good-hearted manner.

'You will like my mother and she will like you,' he said with total confidence.

'How do you know that?' I said.

'I know what they like and they will like you. If you're not comfortable we can stay in a hotel,' he added to put me at ease. This did put my mind at rest and I stopped worrying so much.

My mother, while she didn't openly say a lot, made it clear she didn't want me to go. When I ran through our travel details with her she pursed her lips and gave me a look that made me feel like I was irresponsible for going. She made a point of telling me how long it had been since her last real holiday. Why couldn't she be happy for me taking my first holiday in more than ten years? She had a full-time housekeeper and a mechanic, and Danielle was coming over from Queensland to keep her company. The station was shut down for the wet season so apart from the chores of everyday living there was nothing for her to do but write her second book.

In February, in the midst of Bullo's wet season, we flew into Frankfurt in Germany. It was amazing to go from Bullo, with a wet-season population of four people and 10,000 cows, and 40-plus-degree temperatures, to Frankfurt with its population of over half a million people (I have no idea how many cows), and temperatures that hover around zero. One of Franz's best friends, Gephardt, picked us up and we set off on an 800-kilometre drive through Germany to southern Austria and the little village of Ober Millstatte, where Franz and Gephardt had grown up.

Ober Millstatte is built 900 metres up a mountain that overlooks a picture-postcard lake. I was in awe of the beautiful old architecture there. Many of the homes, including Franz's family home I was later to discover, were 400 years old – twice as old as white Australia. The little village church, which was still used daily, was 900 years old. Mountains towered above the village.

As we neared Franz's home I started to get the jitters about meeting his family. Franz, who has always been able to read me well, drove right past his house and took me to a nearby pub for a few beers to loosen me up. Finally the time came and we drove up to the house. Outside was a huge sign that read 'Willkommen Daheim' (Welcome Home). The warm, smiling faces of Franz's parents, sister, niece and nephew melted all my fears on the spot. The rest of his family came later. I liked them all instantly and I felt that they liked me in return. It was as if I was coming home rather than meeting them for the first time. It warmed my heart to see Franz with his family; they were such open, genuine people.

It was obvious that Franz loved his family and his country. Later, when I knew enough German to hold a broken conversation with his mother, she told me that she always knew Franz would live somewhere else, and that although he loved his home there weren't enough challenges to hold him here. His friends and family weren't surprised that he had chosen to settle in Australia. However, they were surprised that he had married – he had had a wild past and they were keen to see what kind of girl had got him to the altar in four months!

Our five weeks in Austria was the best holiday of my whole life. I was more relaxed and had more fun than I had ever had. Franz bought me skis and gave me my first skiing lessons. I loved it from the first moment, even if I didn't actually spend much time upright.

He also took me to my first sauna. Before we went he told me that in Austria no one wears anything in the sauna; it is mixed sex and everyone is naked. I thought he was pulling my leg, but sure enough, when we got there, it was full of completely naked men and women wandering around as calmly as if they were in a supermarket.

I was too much of a prude to go in without a towel wrapped around me, and as a result everyone stared at me, wondering what I had to hide.

I had just come out of the sauna when Franz said, 'Now we go outside and jump in the spring pool.'

'We do what?' I asked in horror.

Sure enough a group of naked men walked outside in the –15 degree weather and jumped into a small, spring-fed plunge pool. They came out, steam billowing from their bright pink skin, resembling just-cooked lobsters. I was certain that Franz would contract pneumonia and foretold his grim fate. Franz continued to go from the sauna to the plunge pool our entire holiday and didn't get so much as a sniffle. I rugged up and refused to do anything so foolhardy, and caught a cold that had me in bed for over a week.

I called my mother every week to check on things at the station. I came to dread these calls. She complained about everything, made mountains out of molehills, and usually ended up with '. . . And *when* will you be back?'

The more I got to know Franz's family the more I liked them; despite the fact that I didn't speak their language I felt completely at home with them. Our time in Austria passed all too quickly. We had quite an emotional farewell. Franz and the other men did not break down and cry but the rest of us did. We boarded the jet in –10 degree weather for the long flight home.

As we disembarked in Darwin the 38-degree heat and 90 per cent humidity made it feel like we were walking into an oven. We chartered a light aircraft to Bullo. From the air we could see that it had been a good wet – all the wetlands were full and the creeks were still high. My mother was very glad to have us home; there wasn't a trace of her former cold disapproval. There was no doubt that she had hated us being away. I was happy to see her, while deep down I was still resentful about her attitude before we left and her tone on the phone.

———

Franz had been considering getting his pilots licence for some time now so I called Ron, the instructor with whom I had completed my own pilots licence many years ago and booked Franz in for lessons. I ordered the books he needed to study for the exams and left him to it. Franz is a most determined person. He ploughed through the gruesome amount of information he needed to learn, with his German dictionary by his side. I explained the technical terms that weren't in the dictionary. It didn't faze him in the least and he passed all his exams first time. With the theory out of the way he started his flying lessons. There was no doubt he was a natural and he gained his restricted licence in the minimum number of flying hours. Over the next couple of months he continued his flight training between musters and other work.

My mother's books were truly going from strength to strength. She was being swept along in a heady rise to

celebrity status at an alarming pace. She was already booked
out for the whole year with book tours and speeches. No
longer the long-suffering wife of the notorious Charlie
Henderson, as he was locally known, she was Sara Henderson, bestselling author, and famous in her own right. But
she was still my mother. She still had her feet on the ground,
was still humble and appreciative of her good fortune. I was
terribly proud of her.

My admiration was more from a distance these days,
though, as she was away most of the time. Such was her
profile that she had been invited to drive in a celebrity race
at the Grand Prix in Adelaide. She was slightly torn by the
invitation. She really wanted to do it but the fact was she
hadn't driven in the last 20 years that I knew of – and even
before that she had never been a confident driver. As young
children if Bonnie and I so much as moved when she was
driving us somewhere she freaked out. We were definitely
not allowed to talk to her when she was at the wheel.

In America, which was the last place she had driven, she
had only driven an automatic, and had next to no experience driving with gears. My mother and I talked about it
and decided that she ought to give the Grand Prix race a
go. She asked me to go out with her and take her through
a refresher course. We headed down our 76-kilometre road
to practise – at least traffic wouldn't be a problem. My
mother was extremely nervous. She tortured the poor four-
wheel drive's gearbox for 40 kilometres along the road. I
kept her on the flat; I didn't think she was up to hills at
that point. On the drive home she actually started to get
it together and finally began to relax. As we approached
a gate I cued her to slowly gear down, and with great confidence she whacked the four-wheel drive straight into first
from top gear. The gearbox screamed in agony and my
mother completely panicked; all the confidence she had
painstakingly built up disappeared in an instant. I was
wondering if the celebrity race was such a good idea. If she
was this nervous now how would she be with 20 other fast

cars and a few hundred thousand people watching?

Shortly after this she was off to Sydney again on business and, with a couple of days spare, she booked into a race-driving school. She said she had a great time but driving the real racing car was even more difficult than our old four-wheel drive. She hadn't backed out of the celebrity race yet but by the time she graduated from the racing car driving school she was looking for a good excuse. She knew she was going to look bad out on the field, and how she looked to others had always been very important to her.

The four-wheel drive had to go to town to get a new gearbox fitted, and as it turned out fate provided the excuse for my mother to pull out of the celebrity race . . .

Franz, Gordon, a kiwi chap who was working for us at the time, and I were mustering Bullrush Paddock for the last steer sale of the year. We had left the muster until late in the afternoon because the weather was so hot. We were damp with sweat before we had even started work. A short burst of rain from one lonely cloud drenched us – now we were hot and wet. We started to push the reluctant steers from the cover of the scrub out onto the open river flats. Franz and Gordon were pushing a large mob of cattle about a kilometre from me and I was battling to wheel around a small mob that were trying to break and go back into the scrub. I was riding Napoleon, a big, grey thoroughbred gelding – not the smartest horse but he had a comfortable gait and was fast enough to keep up with the Brahman cattle. Napoleon was at a gallop, when he hit a wet saltpan. His feet went from under him and he crashed down hard, rolling right over the top of me.

From a distance, Franz and Gordon saw Napoleon go down – and struggle to his feet, riderless. I was breathing but unconscious when they got to me. Franz sent Gordon home to bring a vehicle out while he unsaddled his and my horses and let them go. It would be dark soon and there would be no way of bringing them back – they would have to find their own way home. Gordon and Franz picked me up as carefully

as they could and put me in the Toyota. When they got me
back to the homestead it was 5.00 pm; there was still time
for the air evacuation plane to pick me up if they came
straight away. Franz called the hospital, who said they would
get back to him, but by the time they did it was too late for
the plane to come out. In desperation he called Ron, his flight
instructor, and asked him to come in from Darwin to fly
me out, but he had had a few drinks and couldn't fly.
However, he did call a friend at the air evacuation service
and made sure that they would be at Bullo at first light. Franz
tried to contact my mother in Sydney with no success.

I drifted in and out of reality all night. I was speaking
but most of it didn't make sense. Apparently, I asked the
same question – 'What happened?' – a thousand times.
Franz would give me an explanation. I would listen quietly
and then immediately ask the same question again. If he
didn't answer I got quite agitated. After Franz had reached
his limit Gordon very generously sat with me, answering
the same question again and again. I don't remember any
of this.

The next morning the evacuation crew came, carefully
put me on a stretcher and asked me who I was. By this time
I did know who I was, which was good. I wished Franz
could come with me on the plane to Katherine but they
wouldn't allow it. At the hospital they x-rayed everything.
I had severe concussion, my shoulder had been dislocated,
I had heavy internal bleeding around my shoulder, and a
damaged elbow. (Even after months and months of physio
my shoulder and elbow were never the same again and they
still trouble me today.)

Franz managed to contact my mother that morning and
she cancelled all her engagements and flew straight to
Darwin. From there Ron flew her to Katherine in his tiny
two-seater trainer aircraft. Having her there pleased me; I
didn't feel so lonely.

A week later, when I was well enough to leave hospital, Franz and Ron hired a Cessna and flew down to

Katherine. The plan was to pick my mother and I up and take us home, and the flight could double as Franz's graduating flight. I had missed Franz terribly and was very pleased to be going home. Franz took the little plane up high where it was smooth and cool and I slept most of the way. I still felt weak and disoriented. At least the accident had happened at the end of the year; I could afford to take time to rest until I was more myself.

On our landing at Bullo Franz became a fully licensed pilot. I was a little hazy in the head but congratulated him. I felt so proud of him as I drifted off to sleep in our bed. My mother had never liked flying – largely because father was always crashing, I suspect – but was reminded by my accident of how useful having an aircraft on the property could be. Franz could have flown me out that night if we had had our own plane. The delay turned out not to be a problem, but if my injuries had been more serious it could have been a much different story. We decided to keep the Cessna on hire for now and look into purchasing our own aircraft.

My mother's fame had brought all sorts of people into our lives, and one of them was Jim Hazelton, of Hazelton Airlines. Jim offered to help us find a suitable plane, and with his assistance we looked all over Australia and New Zealand. After two months of searching we hadn't found a plane of the right type in good condition at a reasonable price.

Jim looked further afield and located two that sounded perfect in the USA. I booked Franz and Jim tickets and off they went, hopefully to buy a plane and fly it back. They did the necessary test flights and checks on the first plane and everything looked good. We were only a hair's breadth away from transferring the money when Franz, as a final precaution, took out the oil filter and cut it open to inspect for any metal fragments. This gives some warning of internal problems with the engine. He found large pieces of metal. It is normal to find fine pieces of metal from engine wear but large bits mean trouble. They opened up the engine and found that the crankshaft was well on the way out. The plane may have flown another 10 or 15 hours and the engine would have self-destructed – Jim and Franz would have been somewhere over the ocean between the mainland of the USA and Hawaii. Franz's thoroughness had in all probability saved their lives.

The second plane checked out okay so they bought it, fitted extra-large fuel tanks and set off for Australia. Their six-day journey took them to Hawaii, Christmas Island, Samoa, Pago Pago, Norfolk and Lord Howe Islands, the Australian mainland and finally Bullo. I had worried about them all the way; apart from the fact that I missed Franz's company dreadfully the thought of them going down somewhere over all that water plagued me. It was a relief to have them home.

We had to register the plane in Australia, and we could choose our own call sign so long as it hadn't already been taken. As a surprise Franz and I nominated SBH, my mother's initials, and to our delight it was free.

14

BY 1994 FRANZ HAD SETTLED INTO LIFE in the north as if
it had always been his destiny. I was still madly in love with
him; each day was better than the last, and I found more
and more attributes to love about him. When my regular
pap smear came back clear again, for the first time we
talked seriously about having children. I was 34. My
biological clock was ticking away and we would have to
decide one way or another soon. I had decided that I
wouldn't have children unless Franz was 100 per cent with
me on the idea, and to my delight he was. We agreed that
it was time to start trying to raise a family.

We also planned to visit Austria again in the New Year;
we wanted to visit every second year or so to keep up with
friends and family. My mother was writing her third book
by now, and her first two were still selling strongly. Her
first book was due to be released in England and South
Africa. She had a three-week break between her book tours
of the two countries so it would fit right in for her to stop
over in Austria for a break. We put this plan to her and she
was delighted.

Austria was every bit as wonderful for me the second
time. We spent the first week catching up with friends and
family, and then I eagerly headed for the slopes. At the

conclusion of her English book tour, my mother flew from London to Munich, in Germany. Franz and I picked her up at the airport for the three-hour drive to Ober Millstatte. She was on quite a high, having just been launched as an international author. On the way to Ober Millstatte she commented that Ausgang must be a huge city as we had been passing highway exit signs for it for an hour. Franz and I burst into laughter. 'Ausgang' is German for 'exit'. My mother laughed along as well. It was the beginning of a lovely holiday for her. She had a pleasant routine, spending the mornings writing and the afternoons with us playing indoor tennis, sightseeing, or going to the sauna for a massage.

Franz's mum spoilt my mother; she brought her tea and cake while she was writing, did her washing and basically took care of everything. I couldn't help but notice the difference between them. Franz's mother and father were hands-on working people as opposed to my mother, who was more the lady of the house. Franz's whole family went out of their way to see that Mother was happy. I remember thinking that increasingly these days that was the way she liked things.

All too quickly she had to leave to do her South African book tour. 'That's just the way it is when you're a famous author,' I teased her.

———•—•—•———

Earlier in the year the owner of a Brahman stud in Rockhampton, Queensland, had contacted my mother. He was selling his stud due to health problems, and was determined that we should buy the last of his bulls. My mother told him she would love to buy his bulls but we were not in a position to spend that sort of money. He was persistent, and put a deal to us that we couldn't refuse.

Franz and I set out to Rockhampton to inspect the bulls. We stopped to top up our tanks with extra fuel in Cloncurry, where Danielle lived. She came out to meet us, and brought along her first child, Natalie, who was eight months old and whom I had only seen in photos. Danielle was full of pride. Motherhood seemed so natural for her and I wondered if I would be like her when I had children – Danielle had always been far more maternal than I.

At Cloncurry we discovered there was a problem with the propeller on our plane; we had to hire another one to make the journey to Rockhampton while ours was being repaired. It was like going from a Rolls Royce to a Mini Moke. It was slow, and the artificial horizon didn't work, which meant that we would have to be careful not to get caught in any bad weather. The window seals were gone, so it was freezing. I immediately came down with the worst cold I'd had in a long time. Apart from my cold symptoms I was also feeling nauseated as well. I suspected that I might be pregnant but it was a little early to tell yet so I hadn't said anything to anyone except Franz. I would reserve my excitement until it was confirmed.

We inspected the cattle; the beautiful, well-natured Brahmans would have improved any herd to which they were introduced so we went ahead with the purchase. Then we flew to visit my Aunty Sue and Uncle Ralph for a couple of days in Caloundra, where they had moved to from Bundaberg. By the time we returned to Cloncurry our plane had a new propeller, and I was feeling sick in the stomach every day.

When we returned to Bullo I took a home pregnancy test, which revealed that we were indeed going to be parents. Franz and I kept it to ourselves for the moment because we knew that the first three months can be dicey. Nevertheless, both of us had a glow of deep pleasure. I went and saw my doctor, who gave me a general briefing on what to expect. He told me there were some things I had to abstain from doing for now. Riding was not a good idea, lifting the portable yard panels or anything else heavy was not recommended, and he really didn't like the idea of me bull catching. The poor doctor rolled his eyes as I reeled off the list of things I normally did, shaking his head and saying over and over, 'No, Marlee, that's not a good idea.' Franz and I had recently been talking about getting our helicopter licences.

'Do you think I could do my chopper licence while I'm pregnant?' I asked hopefully.

'Marlee,' he said with a look that answered my question, 'I don't think it's a good idea.'

'Yes, I suppose you're right,' I said, sighing in resignation. 'I'll just have to slow down for the moment.'

Apart from my occasional bouts of nausea and my work limitations, pregnancy didn't affect my life greatly in the early months. I still worked in the yards; I was just more careful and took no chances with the welfare of our little one, now my responsibility.

Meanwhile, Mother had returned from one of her engagements on the speakers' circuit and told me that a man had all but got down on his knees begging her to take his 15-year-old daughter into her care. Alesha was disappearing, sometimes for days, and her parents had no idea where she was or who she was with. The man said that she was out of control and he and his wife had grave fears for her future. My mother told him that he would need to speak to me, as I was the one at home all the time and the bulk of the responsibility would fall to me.

Despite our heavy workload it was hard for me to sleep at night thinking that if I had made the extra effort I may have helped someone take a better direction in life. In short, I found it difficult to say no. I rang and spoke to Alesha, and her father and mother. I could hear real desperation in the parents' voices, and real sadness in Alesha's. I made it clear to Alesha's parents that she could only come and stay with us if she agreed to it – we weren't in the business of holding rebellious 15-year-olds hostage until their hormones levelled out.

She did agree to come, because she loved the country

and loved animals, and would be working with me outside with the cattle and horses. Alesha's family had lived in the country in her younger years but her father had sold up and moved to the city due to work commitments, and that was when all the trouble had started.

Alesha looked a good deal older than her 15 years. She was taller than I by a good couple of inches and had a strong, well-developed build. She had dark, almost black, hair and a stubborn-looking jaw line, but it was her eyes that I remember most – they were so sad and betrayed her many problems. Her manner was defensive and reserved.

I gave her hand a firm shake and reiterated what I had already gone over on the phone with her: 'No smoking. No drinking. No fraternising with the men. I expect you to do as I ask. I won't ask anything that is unreasonable. If you think something is unreasonable speak up. No backchat. Questions, however, are fine. I expect you to do each and every job to the very best of your ability. If you're going to bother doing something, bother to do it well. We work and live together closely here so it is important that everyone is considerate of each other. No matter how grumpy or tired you feel I expect you to be cheerful, or at the very least, to be good at pretending. Other than the smoking, drinking and men restrictions I will treat you as an adult and be completely straight with you in all regards. If at any point it all becomes too much and you aren't happy you are free to go. I don't want anyone working here unhappily'.

Alesha stood silently, taking in all I said, and nodded at the end that she understood and accepted. From that point Alesha was to have her ups and downs, as we all do, but it was the beginning of a remarkable metamorphosis.

Over the next few months she battled with herself and the tasks I set her. I think it may have helped her that life was so vastly different out here compared to the city that she didn't have set responses to draw on from the past. In addition she was surrounded by good people who set good examples. By the time she found her feet osmosis had done its job and she had started to change. It was a bit like putting the wild cattle in with the coachers – eventually they settle down and start to behave like the others.

I knew that Alesha was truly changing one day when I had her and another young woman, Sally, out cleaning the cattle's water and molasses troughs. When they came back from their day's work Alesha had a rather twisted look on her face.

'Man, that was the grossest thing I've ever had to do,' she said with total conviction.

They had found a dead steer in the molasses trough at Nutwood Paddock. In the tropical conditions at Bullo it takes only a few days for a carcass to rot – and I mean really rot. Sally and Alesha had tried to tow the carcass out of the trough but had only managed to get a part of a leg – the animal was too rotten to pull out in one piece. They then faced the horrendous task of getting the animal out one bit at a time and cleaning out the trough.

Outwardly I congratulated them both for getting this extremely unpleasant job done. Inwardly I smiled. A few months ago Alesha would have probably let out a string of unmentionable words and refused to go within a mile of the carcass. Now she had her mind on the job; she cared about the work she did.

'Marlee, I think we should do the trough checks more often so that if we have to get rid of any more dead animals they aren't as rotten,' she said.

When she had first arrived my advice to her was that a job is a job; no matter how hard or disgusting it is someone will have to do it, and if it ends up being you, it's best to get it over and done with quickly to the best of your ability without complaining. Who knows if pulling dead animals out of molasses troughs will hold her in good stead in the years to come? I do know that after working on Bullo for a year not much will stop her.

It was a hot October day when we started muster preparations at Bull Creek. I was five months' pregnant now but not showing at all; most people had no idea I was expecting. I had told my mother by now, and her reaction had been rather reserved. This didn't surprise me, as she never had a positive view of child-bearing. In any case, she had feigned pleasure at my announcement.

These days I was feeling very tired. I had an over-whelming desire to curl up and go to sleep most of the time. It was a real effort on long days to keep going. This year at Bull Creek we were building a new holding paddock. I had already cleared the fence line and graded it and was now working with two of our stockmen to cut, bark and put in the fence posts. Neither of the men were experienced with a chainsaw, so I took the job of cutting trees into lengths that the men would then remove the bark from to make fence posts. Pre-pregnancy I could cut 70 to 100 posts a day but it was a very different story now. I only had 20 posts to cut and was finding it hard going. I had to sit down and have a rest between every tree, sharpening and adjusting my chainsaw as an excuse to stop. The heat was affecting me badly and I was having bouts of dizziness. Luckily the guys barking the posts weren't that quick – using the back of an axe to remove bark from a tree is really hard, physical work – so I was still able to keep just ahead of them. Within a few days the fence was up and Franz, Alesha and two other stockmen had put up the portable yard.

The muster went well enough and as usual for Bull Creek, we got a lot of scrub bulls and mickies. Having so many dangerous cattle always makes the drafting a slow process. Most of the time we had to work perched on the top rail of the yard panel for safety. Once the cattle were sorted we started loading the sale cattle onto trucks. We were all spread out around the back of the mickey pen, trying to push them through a gate into another pen used for loading; all but two deadly-eyed mickies went through. In such cases we stand where we don't want the aggravated beasts to be, and yell and shout at them every time they go the wrong way. When they go the right way, towards the open gate, everyone backs off and are quiet. In the end the animals realise the only way they will get peace is to go through the gate, and in most cases that's what they do.

These mickies were out for blood today – our blood. Alesha was in one corner of the pen, on top of a big, round hay bale. Each time the furiously mad bulls came to her corner she enthusiastically swung a long piece of polythene pipe at them to drive them from her corner. A young bull was standing right below her, hooking furiously at the hay bale with his horns, trying to get at Alesha, who was safely out of reach. She took one almighty swing at the bull with her pipe, her feet went from under her, she slipped on the hay and landed right on top of the bull's head. She let out a scream that made us all jump several feet into the air and that will remain indelibly printed on my memory for as long as I live. The second mickey's ears flapped in acute distress and he bolted through the gate; he had no intention of facing a creature that could make a sound like that.

Alesha was still sitting on the first bull's head. Fortunately she was a healthy-sized girl and the mickey was small, which meant that so far all he was able to do was lift her up and down. I was running towards her, trying to make myself heard above her Olympian and unrelenting screams. Alesha was right up against one of the yard panels; she only needed to grab hold and step off. This she finally did, by which time all of us had arrived at the scene to draw the bull away from her. I went to her and held her in my arms. She was shaking and crying in fear. I checked her all over and found her to be in one piece. Her tears had made mud tracks through the dust that was caked on her face. I washed her face, gave her another hug and then teased her a little to lighten things up.

'In future all we need to do is get Alesha screaming and all the difficult cattle will run in terror.'

Alesha couldn't help herself but burst into laughter at the thought. After her initial fear had subsided she almost had a bit of a swagger in her walk. She was a seasoned stockwoman, having come off on the better end of her first run-in with a bull.

The following week, an old mare, Mark of Gold, which I had bought with Charlie just after we were married, had her last foal. I brought her in from the paddock as she was weak and needed some tender loving care. The foal seemed healthy and quite strong. Having settled them down in the yard nearest the homestead, I went off with Alesha, Sally and the men to finish off some drafting work.

When we returned at lunch I went to check the foal and was shocked to find the little filly gravely ill. She was lying in the sun and had obviously not had a first drink from Gold – she was severely dehydrated. I made up some electrolyte replacement fluid from my vet supplies and started what looked like a mission that was doomed to failure; I really thought she was too far gone to save. I managed to get some fluid down the little foal's throat, and every few minutes for the next six hours. The baby foal was so close to death that she was having convulsions. Alesha, who loved animals, was by my side the whole time helping me. The old mare seemed happy with us being so close to her foal; she knew we were trying to help.

As dark fell I thought that if the little foal could make it through the night she would be all right. Alesha offered to sleep outside next to the foal and keep up her fluids during the night. I went to bed with a smile on my face. The picture of Alesha lying next to the foal, the old mare on the other side nuzzling both of them occasionally, was in my mind. I had told Alesha to wake me at any time if she was worried or needed my help. In the very early hours of the morning she called that I had to come urgently. I woke with a fright and dashed out expecting the worst.

My heart warmed – the foal was trying to find her feet. Alesha and I rubbed her legs to get the circulation going and helped hold her up until she found her balance. Next we steered her into place so that she could have her first drink of milk from the mare. Alesha had tears of joy streaming down her face. That was when she decided she wanted to go back to school and go on to do veterinary science.

We kept a close eye on the little foal over the next week. Once she was up and drinking there was no stopping her. Now that we were confident that she was going to live we gave her a name. After much thought we settled on Monsoon because her arrival had coincided with the first rains of the wet season.

With the road closed and the cattle season over for the year it was time for Alesha, and most of the staff, to leave. Alesha had soggy eyes as she went home to her family. She had learnt so much in her time here and we would miss her. I was proud of the person Alesha had become and even felt maternal towards her. I was pleased we'd been able to show her another way of looking at life and I hoped with all my heart she would have the strength to stay on track.

My mother had paid Alesha a small wage for her work. A few weeks after she had left Bullo she called me for a chat.

'I spent $200 in town yesterday,' she said and paused.

The little monster knew exactly what I'd say.

'Alesha! You promised me you'd put some of your money aside and start saving.' On and on I lectured her about squandering her money.

'I bought a suit and shoes for my job interview next week. I'm working until school starts in February. Is that all right?' she asked innocently.

'You, you, you . . . Okay you got me! You know damn well that's okay. In fact, that's very good.'

Alesha was cackling away on the other end of the phone.

My mother, Franz and I had a quiet Christmas. I was seven months' pregnant but still not showing much at all; I could still fit into my normal clothes. My doctor had been worried that my little one was not growing properly but after an ultrasound, during which he measured the baby every which way, he was quite satisfied that all was as it should be. I was just one of the lucky ones who was not going to get big in pregnancy. He told me that sportswomen who remain active throughout pregnancy often don't get particularly large, and he suspected that because my work was very physical I fell into a similar category.

However, I was very tired and the wet season heat was affecting me badly. I had been given stern lectures by my doctor about the dangers of getting overheated in pregnancy so I tried to take it easy. Our little baby was making its feelings known by now too. I was still regularly mowing the five acres of lawns and whippersnipping around the house and the baby didn't like me to do more than two hours at a time. After that it started kicking up a fuss. That suited me because by then I was tired anyway.

In mid-January Franz flew me into Darwin for a check-up and my doctor told us that we were having a boy. Franz grinned broadly and seemed immensely pleased with the news – I think most men, deep down, want a son. But like me – and most first-time parents – his greatest wish had been to have a healthy child, regardless of gender. We went and had a celebration lunch at our favourite cafe, Franz chatted away about all sort of things, but I was only half listening because I was so overwhelmed by feelings of happiness. Franz was a wonderful, supportive husband, and we had grown even closer with our impending parenthood. I knew instinctively that he would be a wonderful father.

Back at home I busied myself around the house, painting and generally succumbing to an obsessive nesting urge.

In the first week of March my mother and Franz flew out together to catch flights south. My mother was going to a speaking engagement and Franz was starting his helicopter training in Maroochydore, Queensland. It was the only time that Franz could get away, as the mustering would start in the next month or so. Franz' excitement about getting his helicopter licence was infectious leading up to his departure. Once he had gone, though, I felt flat and lonely. As the plane lifted off from the Bullo airstrip I missed his company already. We spoke daily; he gave me detailed accounts of his progress while I listened wistfully on the other end of the phone. I wished I was getting my helicopter licence too.

While Mother and Franz were away I had a call from Jane, my mother's publicist in Sydney. The popular TV programme *This is Your Life* wanted to do a show on my mother. As anyone who has seen it knows, surprising the subject is the key element of the show. There was to be no consulting Mother. The programme's makers had lots of questions about Mother's life. I answered as many as I could, but I would need to ask her for some of the information. How to do this without arousing her suspicion consumed my thoughts for some time – until I came upon a perfect solution.

When my mother returned from her speaking engagement I told her I was sorting through a heap of old photos that were unceremoniously stored in a box and was putting them into albums. This gave me the perfect excuse to ask questions about all the people and events in my mother's life. I gave the *This is Your Life* production people all the information they needed, and plenty of photos, and they started to put the show together.

The excitement of organising *This is Your Life* for Mother took my mind off missing Franz a little. He was progressing, but not as quickly as he had hoped because bad weather frequently made conditions unsuitable for flying. By the end of March I felt like my time was close. Franz had been away for about three weeks and if the weather continued he would need at least another month to complete his licence. I was desperate for him to come home, so he decided to finish off his licence at the end of the year and came home, to my delight.

At the beginning of April I had another check-up and my

doctor told me that I would have our baby within the next two weeks. Franz and my mother lived in fear that I would go into labour on the station in the middle of the night in bad weather and they wouldn't be able to get me to hospital, so we decided that I would move up to Darwin for the last two weeks. I flew home and packed my bags. I planned to spend the last days of my pregnancy shopping at a leisurely pace for all my baby requirements. At this point I had one packet of cloth nappies my mother had brought back from one of her trips and a red plastic baby spoon someone had given me some months before. That was it.

Franz flew my mother and I up to Darwin on the 7th of April and we rented an apartment for the wait. Franz stayed with me for my birthday the next day. We ran some errands in the morning and went for a quiet walk along the waterfront at sunset. I would have normally enjoyed it but I started to feel dizzy, faint and sick in the stomach, and had Franz take me back to the apartment. I definitely didn't want to go out anywhere for dinner, so we stayed in for the night. Franz flew back to the station the next day to keep everything running. I had planned to start shopping then, but felt so bad I put it off and called my doctor, who told me to come in the next day for a check-up.

When the doctor checked me over he found my blood pressure to be alarmingly high and rising, which explained why I had felt so ill. He said he wanted to induce the birth the next morning. I had so hoped to have a natural birth but he explained that if my blood pressure continued to rise my baby and I could die. It certainly wasn't worth the risk and I agreed to have my labour induced. He sent me straight to hospital, where I could be monitored.

I called Franz and he flew back to Darwin to be with me. First thing in the morning my doctor came to see me and said that I should have my baby by lunch time, all going well. It didn't go well. For some reason I didn't respond to the various methods of inducement they used until late that afternoon.

My mother, who had to fly out of Darwin that night to Perth for a speaking engagement the next day, said to Franz, 'Typical! The one engagement I have for April and Marlee has her baby. I knew this would happen.'

Mother had never had a very encouraging attitude to childbirth and had, over the years, told me many times about how bad it was and how much she had suffered. Her attitude was, 'You'll see how bad it is, just wait.' When my labour started and my contractions came closer together she got up to leave saying she had to catch her flight.

My labour dragged on. I had dreadful lower-back pain and Franz rubbed there diligently. Little did he know how long he would have to do it. At dinner time there was no way I could eat the meal the hospital provided but Franz was starving and very happy to eat it in my stead. Every time he stopped rubbing my lower back I begged him to keep rubbing. There he was eating with one hand and rubbing with the other. He went on rubbing into the night, complaining that his hand was about to drop off. His words fell on deaf ears. I was merciless. 'Keep rubbing!' I commanded.

Finally, at 11.30 pm, my doctor put a suction cup on our little baby's head to pull him out – I couldn't push him any further myself. The first attempt was a failure. The suction cup came off and our baby slipped back again. His head was so big there was no room to use forceps. My doctor told me he would try once more with the suction cup, and if that didn't work he would have to do an emergency Caesarean section. I had been in second stage labour so long now that the baby was becoming distressed.

At that moment a man supporting a pregnant, very upset woman struggled past my door into the other delivery suite. One of the two female midwives who had been attending to me asked if I would mind if a male midwife came in to help the doctor in their place, as they had to rush off to attend to the unexpected arrival. Anyone who's had a long labour will understand why the gender of the attending nurse was definitely not on my list of concerns right at that point.

Moments after they had left one of the female midwives returned to tell the doctor that the woman in the other suite was hemorrhaging and needed an immediate Caesarean section. He told the nurse to get the paediatric specialist on call up there straight away, and to prepare the other woman for immediate surgery, then turned his attention back to me and again put the suction cup on our little baby's head. Franz and the male midwife supported my back and lifted me upright slightly.

'Now Marlee, on the next contraction, push as hard as you can.'

I pushed with every fibre in my body. There was a loud cracking noise as I felt my tailbone break, and our little boy was born at quarter to midnight.

The doctor put him on my chest and I looked into the sage eyes of our son. I can't adequately describe how I felt in words because there is nothing in the world like holding your own child for the first time. It is more than spiritual, more than awesome. An undiscovered part of me opened and released emotions I had never felt.

Franz looked in wonder at our son. Through all the drama Franz had never wavered. He had remained calm, helping both me and the doctor where he could; as usual, he had not been the least bit fazed. It was so typical of his quiet strength, which I so admired. His being there had given me so much comfort.

I sighed heavily. At least my part was over. My doctor's work was not yet done. He barked instructions to the nurses to give me an injection to help slow down my heavy bleeding. He cut the cord and checked our baby quickly before handing him to the paediatrician and dashing into the other birthing suite. It was only a few minutes later that I was pleased to hear a baby crying next door. My doctor returned not long after from the other birthing suite, wearily mopped up the blood on the floor of my birthing suite and stitched me up. I felt ghostly and weak from my long effort and blood loss.

My mother was on the phone as soon as she had landed in Perth. Franz gave her the news that her first grandson had been born but spared her all the gory details. Franz told me that she seemed very pleased. I didn't have the energy to talk to her. I was so cold and tired; one of the nurses came in and put a heated blanket over me that felt like heaven. Franz and I had chosen a few boys names and finally we agreed on Ben. Then Franz called all his family in Austria, who were delighted with Ben's arrival.

After resting a while I managed to walk back to my room without the wheelchair I was offered. It had been a difficult birth but I had so prepared myself for the worst that it hadn't been as bad as I was expecting. In fact my broken tailbone was proving to be much more painful than the birth. Little Ben was placed in the nursery. He was healthy but because he was two weeks' premature they were checking him over carefully. I sank into a blissful state of sleep and Franz went back to the apartment to have a shower and catch his breath. He hadn't left my side. The way he had picked up and held Ben with such ease and confidence touched my heart. I could see he was a natural.

The next day I felt like a whole convoy of trucks had run over me. I was told that the main difficulty had been Ben's big head. He had a Ranacher head at 36 centimetres. Because I had been in the second stage of labour for so long my bladder had literally gone on strike. The nurses put a catheter in, which was more painful than childbirth and my broken tailbone combined. I was sobbing by the time they had finished. By now my milk had come in as well; enough for the entire nursery. To add to my woes I had painfully engorged breasts. The staff asked me to partici-pate in a study on how effective cabbage-based products were at reducing the discomfort. I was quite a sight with cabbage leaves sticking out of my bra, and various drips and bags hanging off me. My blood pressure was still up which made me feel terrible as well.

My mother returned from Perth in high spirits. It was good to see her; I had forgotten all about being annoyed with her the day before. She was attentive and sympathetic, and brought me beautiful gifts and edible goodies. I was glad to have her company and she seemed pleased to have her first grandson. My room resembled a florist shop by now. I was deeply touched by all the flowers, notes, and teddy bears that everyone sent.

Ben was with me in my room and feeding well. He was a model baby from the start. I kept him next to me in bed except while I slept and I could tell this comforted him. The nurses were impressed with his placid nature. They were surprised that he was my first baby because normally first mothers are uptight, and their babies pick up on those vibes and cry a lot. They thought I was remarkably calm. I told them I had raised a lot of calves and maybe that had helped. One very serious Dutch nurse was alarmed by this comment.

'It's all right. I know that babies are a little different to calves. I promise I won't pull his tongue out and pour the milk down if he doesn't drink,' I said cheerfully to put her at ease.

She only looked more concerned.

Just over a week after Ben was born I was given the all clear to leave hospital. Franz drove me straight to the Baby Barn, Darwin's number one baby shop. I walked in and put sleeping Ben in the cot we intended to buy and then strolled around picking out other things we needed. The shop assistant appeared by my side and asked if she could help. I pulled out my long list and started reading it out. I was halfway through when she asked how I knew I'd need things for a boy and commented on how organised I was to get all these things so well in advance. I laughed.

'Not exactly, I had my baby a week ago. He's right over there.' Little Ben was fast asleep in the cot.

Somehow we managed to stuff all our luggage and the amazing amount of baby requirements into our little plane and flew home to our new life. I was reminded of my first trip to Bullo with my mother all those years ago. At least we'd be taking our son to a slightly more established life than the one that had greeted us. Ben never made a peep, sleeping all the way. I was very, very glad to be home. Franz assembled the cot while I fed Ben and then I put him to sleep for his first night at home. Apart from being extremely tired I was happy and relieved to find that motherhood felt so natural.

15

I SPENT THE NEXT COUPLE OF WEEKS resting and finding a routine that suited Ben and me. He was an amazing baby. He just ate, slept and grew daily. He almost never cried. I thought he looked just like Franz, with his red fuzz that would eventually be hair, but my mother said she could see me in him as well. He was a long baby but being two weeks early had weighed a tad under seven pounds at birth. He was making up for lost time. With his several chins he was definitely chubby now.

About three weeks after Ben was born, Franz fitted the baby car seat in our grader for me and then together Ben and I started grading our 76 km road to repair the damage from the wet season rains, as I did at the beginning of each year. He gave me the strangest look when I put moulded ear plugs in his ears, like 'What are you doing?', but he loved bumping along in the grader. On our first day I discovered that the manufacturers had not taken nappy changing into their design considerations. There was nowhere to change Ben. I parked the grader in the work-shop and asked my ingenious husband to find a solution, with complete confidence that he would. Franz made a hinged, drop-down change table that rested on the back of my seat and could be clipped up out of the way when it wasn't in use. It worked perfectly. I am sure I had the only baby-friendly grader in the north.

I was happy enough to have Ben with me while I was working on the first 40 kilometres of our road as it was a flat gravel surface. Once I hit the hill country, however, it got very rough in the grader – way too rough for Ben. Mother, Franz and I decided that we would get a nanny so that I could continue doing most of my work. I advertised and couldn't find anyone suitable who wanted permanent work, but Judith, a young woman from Israel, agreed to take the job for six weeks, enough time to finish grading the road and find a permanent nanny. We set off each day in the car loaded with nappy buckets and other baby essentials. Once we got out to where the grader was parked I would get in and start grading, with Judith and Ben following behind me in the car. Every two hours when Ben woke up hungry she would flash the headlights and I would stop grading to feed him. Judith did an excellent job, and commented that it was probably the most unusual one she was ever likely to have.

While Judith, Ben and I were on the road, Franz harvested the hay and started building new permanent yards at the homestead. I must say all was going smoothly on the home front. My mother was busy with her books and speaking engagements, Franz and I were busy with our son and work, and everything was bubbling along quite well.

In early June, I was 65 kilometres out on the road and only had one more day of grading to do when burn-off fires purposefully lit on the adjoining Auvergne Station as a bushfire precaution came over the mountain range, the flames fanned by a 30-knot wind. In less than 12 hours the fire was burning into the holding paddocks right at the back of the house. Auvergne's manager came with his station's grader to help us fight back at least some of the 100-kilometre fire front and save some of our grass. I brought our own grader back 65 kilometres to help too. Over the next four days we fought the fire with both graders and our bulldozer by making fire breaks and back burning. I only paused to express milk, which I sent home in an esky for Ben, who must have wondered what had become of his mother.

We only managed to save two paddocks, as the wind was so fierce it drove the fire over our breaks again and again. We had lost 250,000 acres of cattle feed to the fire – half of Bullo's area. This was very serious indeed. We could not realistically expect rain until November or December – five to six months away – and then it would be another month after that before there would be enough grass to be useful.

It was to be the beginning of a long, hard year. We had to jam as many cattle as possible onto the northern side of the property, which wasn't burnt, and sell as many as possible, as quickly as possible. We couldn't afford to hold cattle for a better price; everyone knew this and capitalised on it. The effects were to be far-reaching. The shortage of feed resulted not only in us losing stock in the short term but also affected the number of calves born the following season. The cows were in such poor condition from the shortage of feed that they didn't have normal reproductive cycles and therefore didn't get in calf.

It was time for Ben and I to fly down to Sydney for the *This is Your Life* sting on my mother. She had already flown down a week earlier, thinking that she was to attend a meeting with her publishers. Ben and I met up with Danielle and Natalie at the hotel. Danielle and I both needed things for the big night so we set off to David Jones. We were walking along chatting when who should we run into but Mother. The *This is Your Life* producers were paranoid about secrecy. I did some fast thinking as my mother, who had a very puzzled expression on her face, walked over to us.

'Marlee? Danielle? What are you doing here?' she said.

I had one of those epiphanies that seem to regularly save me from strife. My mother's 60th birthday was coming up.

'We, the whole family,' I blurted out, 'were planning a surprise party for your birthday. I'm not saying any more and you'd better look surprised for them or they will all be so disappointed. I'll see you later. Go!' I commanded her.

She seemed happy with this explanation and did go immediately, with a pleased look on her face. The *This is Your Life* office found out about our accidental bumping into each other in DJs – to this day I don't know how – and were in some state. They were going to cancel the show. I told them that was entirely their decision but added that the excuse I had made was a good one, and that I didn't think their cover had been blown. It's not as if people go around expecting to be on *This is Your Life* is it? They settled down and decided to go ahead as planned.

I wasn't there for the sting, of course, but those who were said my mother was blown away, as I imagine most people are. The show went very well and everyone seemed happy with the outcome. I felt immensely proud of my mother and all her achievements, and I thought she shone on the night.

There was a party afterwards but little Ben was so tired that I took him back to the hotel so he could sleep in peace. By then we both needed it. The next day I flew home and Mother left for the world's biggest book fair, in Frankfurt, Germany, still on a high after her *This is Your Life* experience.

Not long after that my mother became busy writing a cookbook, the latest suggestion from her publishers, as an addition to the series of books she had written for them. I thought this one was a bit ironic since Mother hated cooking. I gathered up all my recipes for her, as did Aunty Sue and Aunty Frances – the wife of Mother's brother Todd, and an exceptionally good cook – to help her put together what turned out to be an excellent country cookbook.

It was about this time that Mother found out Bonnie was writing her own account of life in the outback. That news really upset her. She stewed over it for days although there was, of course, nothing she could do. My mother had not spoken to Bonnie in nearly ten years, since after the court case, when she said she had 'lost a daughter'. About the only time she had spoken of her was after Bonnie had published an article in one of the women's magazines. Her bitterness towards Bonnie was still very evident. Finally my mother picked herself up and continued with her own book but I could see it was in the back of her mind all the time.

———

Every year we were determined to stay up and see the New Year in but every year by ten o'clock we were sound asleep. For a change, Franz and I did manage to stay up to see in 1998 and opened a bottle of champagne to toast the future. In hindsight, we should have gone to bed; it was to be a terrible year.

The first disaster was the horrific floods the town of Katherine suffered. We all watched in horror as the town disappeared beneath flood waters and the traffic on the main street became boats not cars. However, the people of the north are tough. Everyone rallied, cleaned up the shocking mess and got on with life. We had excellent rain on the station but were spared being flooded out. This meant that the cattle would have an abundance of feed. I remember thinking despondently that it didn't make much difference, though, because the Indonesian economy had collapsed and we had lost an excellent market for our cattle virtually overnight. We had almost no buyers, and no one saw any hope of the situation changing that year.

In mid-February Franz was paving and putting up a fence around our swimming pool because Ben was up and toddling about now and I lived in terror that he would fall in. Franz had a backhoe parked next to the pool with the bucket out over the water. It was the end of the day and the sun had already sunk below the horizon, yet it was still very hot. Franz climbed up and dived off the bucket into the pool. When he came up his face was covered in blood. He had hit his head on the bottom; it was a miracle he hadn't broken his neck. My heart caught when he walked in the door. Head wounds always look bad because they bleed so much. This one looked particularly gruesome; he had blood streaming down his face, neck and chest.

I got the first-aid kit out and cleaned him up so that I could see where all the blood was coming from. He had split his head open just along the hairline. It looked like it needed about four stitches but it was too dark to fly into hospital now, plus there was bad weather everywhere. Luckily I had all the stitching equipment and local anaesthetic on hand for such occasions. I called Wal, our family doctor, at home in Darwin and consulted with him before going to work on Franz's head. Franz complained bitterly (he says now he didn't) about the anaesthetic needle but I continued on. It would hurt a lot more if I tried to stitch without it, I assured him. My ungrateful patient wiggled and complained (he says now he didn't) all the way through my stitching job; I was very glad to finish.

It was our wedding anniversary and Franz had promised to cook dinner for me as a treat.

'I don't know, the lengths men go to to get out of cooking. I suppose I better go make something for dinner,' I said.

Franz's neck was stiff and sore, and at my insistence we flew to Darwin the next day to have Wal check his spine. To my relief, Franz was given the all clear.

On the positive side, my mother's career was still going strong. She had just been asked to be an ambassador for the Sydney 2000 Olympics, which pleased her enormously, and her year ahead was fully booked with social and business engagements. She had even been approached to make a miniseries based on her books and had signed an option with a production company.

The other really good news was that she had been chosen to appear in advertisements for Biozet soap. She had a three-year contract and would be comfortably remunerated in the six-figure bracket. Mother was rightly very chuffed to be pulling in such money.

The Biozet commercial people descended upon us in early May in three planes. There were 16 people and 43 pieces of luggage. They had wardrobe, make-up, lighting and props men – the works. My mind boggled that they needed all this for a 30-second commercial. What must they need for a whole movie? Franz, Daryl and Wayne, two of our stockmen, appeared in the ad wearing the most impossibly white moleskins on earth; they were so bright you could hardly look at them. We all thought it was highly amusing. None of us would ever wear white jeans. They'd only be that way for an instant – and then never again. In reality, no soap could ever make white jeans white after a serious day in the cattle yards.

While the cattle markets were abysmal our social calendar was full for a change. My father's sister, Aunty Margaret, and her delightful friend, Chrissy, spent a few days with us. Next came Hugh, my half-brother, with his son Teddy. Their visit coincided with the arrival of John, Bullo's former manager, whom I had not seen since I was a child. Still a man of few words, he said to me in a quiet moment 'You have done well.' These few words meant more to me than I could have ever imagined they would. I felt a deep flush of pride.

Next, Franz's parents came to visit for six weeks. They fitted right in. Franz's dad helped in the workshop and his mother in the house and garden. Neither Mama or Papa Ranacher spoke much English and although they had both taken an English course were still a long way from conversational, so they didn't get to talk much with my mother. When they did persevere, Mother would nod and acknowledge everything they said and then ask me what the conversation had actually been about. I enjoyed having the Ranachers there, and Ben warmed to them straight away, often following Mama Ranacher around the garden.

Franz and I were determined to take his parents somewhere during their visit, and thought that a day-long Argyle Diamond tour out of Kununurra was a good idea. We asked Mother if she wanted to join us, but she wasn't interested. We went ahead and made a booking and told Mother that we were going to take a day off to go on the tour. She was clearly unimpressed with this plan and became distant towards me. I recall being confused, but also annoyed. I was beginning to get the impression that she didn't like us doing anything that was remotely recreational. Apart from our trips every second year to see Franz's family we hardly ever went anywhere socially. Most years I could count the outings I took on half of one hand.

I ignored her this time and went on the trip, which we enjoyed greatly. My mother didn't say much on our return. She was still distant towards me, and didn't seem interested in hearing about what we had seen. I had the distinct feeling that she expected some sort of apology – for what was a mystery to me.

After Franz saw his parents off from Darwin airport we went back to the depressing job of trying to find someone to buy our cattle. A new market into Egypt had just opened up as a result of the mad cow disease outbreak in Britain. Egypt had sourced their steers out of Ireland but now had to look elsewhere. The problem was that they wanted the same standard of cattle they had gotten from Ireland. We have completely different breeds in the Northern Territory, and to get the weight for age they required was close to impossible. They refused to take any cattle with four teeth, an indication of age. I had 400 steers all in good condition and of the required weight, but when the buyer inspected their teeth only 90 were acceptable. I was devastated. The buyer called me the next day because he knew how upset I'd been.

'Don't be too hard on yourself, Marlee. I just went through 2,000 steers and not one came up to specs.'

Things were desperate. We couldn't sell cattle anywhere. No one could. The cattle market showed no signs of rallying and we speculated that it may take years to recover. We would need to do something, and quickly. The obvious solution was to expand our small tourist enterprise to make up for the shortfall. In the long term it would also stabilise the business. With the correct marketing there was no doubt there was good money to be made.

Franz, my mother and I agreed to build 12 double bedrooms with ensuites just away from the homestead. Franz and I drew up plans and wasted no time in getting the Bessa blocks, cement and other materials on site. Franz and a bricklayer undertook the huge task of laying the foundations, and began construction.

Franz had finished his helicopter licence a year after he had started and was now fully commercial, which meant he could legally fly passengers and charge money. Now I was finally following through on my dream to get my helicopter licence. I studied and passed my exams, then Franz flew me and my helicopter instructor, Graeme, to Victoria River Downs Station to pick up a training helicopter, a dual-control Bell 47, just like the helicopters in the program *M*A*S*H*. I was apprehensive – and wildly excited. Graeme and I got into the helicopter, and he took off, then handed control over to me, asking me to fly straight and level on the flight home, not an easy task for me at this point. My pilots licence was of little value to me in this new endeavour – flying a helicopter is completely different from flying a fixed-wing aircraft. I wobbled all the way back to Bullo and Graeme was ever so patient. Just when I thought I was the most hopeless trainee pilot in the universe it all came together. At first it was only for a fleeting, glorious moment, but once I had found this harmony between myself and the machine everything looked brighter and my progress became more rapid.

We flew every morning and afternoon until, after 20 hours' flying time next to Graeme, he told me to do 50 minutes on my own. I took off on my first solo flight, all of Graeme's training comfortingly echoing in my subconscious. When I landed safely, Franz had the biggest grin on his face. He congratulated me and complimented me on how steady I had looked. I smiled and thought how very unsteady I had actually felt.

My mother returned from one of her trips to Sydney and I proudly told her about having soloed in the helicopter. Mother, who normally would have been quite enthusiastic about this achievement, didn't seem interested. I asked her what the matter was, to which she replied 'Nothing'. I was sure this was not true but she was not in a conversational mood. I said nothing more but was hurt and quite confused by her strange demeanour. She seemed distant, and as though she didn't care about anything.

The third book in Mother's series about life on the station, *The Strength of Our Dreams*, had a photo on the cover of my mother and I, which had been taken by Franz. The publishers thought it would be good if I was with my mother for at least some of her publicity tour when the book was released. My mother had written a great deal about me over the years and the general public were apparently interested to see this Marlee whom my mother spoke of so often. I also think it provided them with the point of difference they needed at that stage because Mother had been pretty well exposed over the years. While I was curious about this side of my mother's life, I hated the thought of being away from Franz and Ben for so long. I was torn between my feelings.

Mother started her tour in Perth and went on to Adelaide and Melbourne, where I flew to meet her in mid-October. Over the years my mother had described the amazing suites she had stayed in while on tour. For the first time I saw what she meant. The suite in Melbourne had a private sauna, spa, kitchen, grand piano, two bathrooms and a living room; it was bigger than a lot of houses. There was a control panel by the master bed that looked like it belonged in a jet. Press one button and you could open or close all the curtains in the suite. Press another and a TV screen the size of a small cinema appeared. Another button adjusted the bed – and on it went. It was utterly luxurious and I was impressed and excited to be staying there.

Our days were packed with back-to-back book signings, lunches and dinners, at which she and I both spoke. My Mother was totally amazing. She powered on at an extraordinary level, and even seemed to thrive on the fast pace. It all felt surreal for me. I was observing an aspect of my mother's life for the first time. It gave me a new insight into my mother that was both positive and worrying.

On the positive side I could see she was a fantastic public speaker who inspired many people; the adoration of her fans was tangible. But for the first time I saw things about her that I didn't particularly like. We flew into Canberra one evening for a dinner speech and book signing; we would be out the next morning at 6.00. My mother had been telling me that her Canberra suite was even more luxurious than the Melbourne suite we had just vacated. How that could be so, I couldn't imagine but I took her word for it. When we arrived at the hotel though, they had made a mistake and put us in a much less impressive room. It was still very nice and more than adequate for our needs, but it wasn't the much-anticipated suite Mother had told me about. Her publicist, Jane, sensed that she may be put out and said she'd go and sort it out. My mother was very gracious to her. 'No, no. It's only for the night,' she said, smiling. Jane looked relieved. Book tours are hard work for everyone and we were all tired. I think Jane just felt like having a shower.

Jane left us to get ready for the evening. The door had

just closed behind her when my mother made it clear to me that she was not happy at all. I said that it really didn't matter – we were only here overnight and all we needed was a bed and a shower. 'Heavens,' I thought, 'we've been in much worse over the years.' The mother I remembered and thought I knew would never have been upset by such a thing. I realised that she had changed and I hadn't noticed it happening.

We spoke to at least two or three hundred people that night. We had developed a rather good system of both being up at the microphone at the same time, throwing stories back and forth for up to an hour. It worked well and the audiences seemed to enjoy it. Afterwards we had question time, which was also popular. My mother was a polished speaker and was quick to come up with witty answers to questions. I was really in awe of the skills she'd developed.

As it was my first time a great many questions were directed at me. One that I particularly remember was from a young woman who said that she had a child and couldn't find time to do anything but care for her baby, and asked how I managed motherhood and all the work I was doing. I was just about to answer that I wasn't Superwoman, and that I had a nanny, without whom I would be in exactly her position, when my mother cut in over me and said with apparent sincerity, 'She has her mum.' The crowd murmured approvingly. I was silent – I couldn't say anything without making her look bad in front of her adoring public. I kept my mouth shut but was disturbed by this, and other such statements, my mother made while I was with her on the tour.

Sydney was the next stop, where Mother's publishers had arranged a swish cocktail party to celebrate her astounding achievement of one million book sales in Australia. This really is rare and remarkable in our country. Family, and friends from the past and present, came to celebrate with her – except for Bonnie, and Danielle and

Martin, who weren't able to come because of business commitments. My mother glided around the plush room, which overlooked the Opera House and harbour. She socialised with and charmed everyone, from her nieces and nephews to executives, with equal ease; she literally shone. I marvelled at how easy she made it all look. We stayed in Sydney for a few days attending book signings and then flew on to the Gold Coast, where I left the tour.

Upon leaving Mother I felt strangely confused and empty. I had hoped that going with her on tour would bring us together more as I had felt we were drifting apart of late. I went home feeling a little sad that in fact we seemed more distant than before. And I felt an odd mix of admiration and disappointment in her.

I was so glad to see Franz and Ben at the airport. Warmth flooded back into my heart seeing my gorgeous two-and-a-half-year-old son. Ben had a bunch of roses for me and the biggest smile on his little face. I melted on the spot. I had missed them so much.

When I got home Franz had a surprise for me – he had finished our bedroom. My whole life on Bullo it had had a concrete floor and no ceiling. In the wet season the wind used to howl through the space between the wall and the roof, and we were joined by millions of bugs if we turned a light on. Now I would be able to read at night, which was an incredible luxury. For the first time in my life I had a real floor and ceiling, and an air conditioner in my room.

My mother returned to Bullo a week after I did and looked at our room with a critical gaze that made me feel most uncomfortable. She was clearly not pleased that Franz had taken the time to fix our room. She didn't say anything, just looked displeased. Years ago as a surprise for her, I had finished off her room when she was away. Her room had a ceiling, it just needed some finishing touches. I had a tradesman put a slate floor down over the old cement in her room, and had personally painted the walls for her in one of her favourite colours, salmon.

In mid-November I finished my training and got my private helicopter licence. Everyone except my mother congratulated me. Instead, she called me into her office to tell me that she couldn't afford to have me on the insurance policy for the station's helicopter. Because I didn't have a commercial licence, I couldn't legally fly guests, so I couldn't make any money from my flying. I was by no means planning to fly hundreds of hours, costing the station money; all I wanted to do was fly enough to retain my skills until I could afford to upgrade to a commercial licence. It would cost about $40,000 to get a commercial licence, plus extra costs such as airfares south, food and accommodation.

Mother made it clear she wouldn't compromise about including me on the insurance policy and I had a feeling she wanted to provoke an argument – something I did not want. I turned and left her office feeling her glare on my back. I didn't fly the helicopter again.

When I finally managed to have a proper talk with Mother a little while later she said she felt that I didn't care about her any more and never spent time with her like I used to. I sighed and told her that of course I cared for her but I had less time to spend with her now. I didn't have much time any more because I had a child. There was also the usual cattle work and the new tourism business to deal with. Most days I had to leave the homestead before my mother was up and I rarely came back until dark. If I had any time I spent it with Ben, as I should. My mother was never a children person, nor was she a warm, fuzzy grandmother, so for her it wasn't really an option to spend time with me and Ben together. I say this without malice – I knew what she was like and accepted her that way. In addition, there were Mother's many trips away from Bullo. As often as I could I sat down and chatted with her but these days it was getting harder and harder to find the time.

I knew Mother was lonely and I could understand that the changes in my life impacted on her, but what could I do but my best? Did she really want me to spend less time with Ben and Franz? I was not willing to do that. This was my chance at family life and motherhood. I was already feeling guilty that I didn't spend enough time with them because of all the work that needed to be done on the property. Franz and I generally worked on different jobs these days as we got more done by splitting up and supervising two sets of workers. I saw Ben briefly at lunch time if possible and caught him quickly again at night.

Danielle and Martin were coming for Christmas with Natalie, who was now three-and-a-half years old, and the latest addition to their family, their son John. Franz and I thought it would be great for Ben to see his cousins over Christmas because seeing other kids was a rare event for him. I also thought Danielle would be good company for Mother. She feigned happiness to Danielle on the phone about their visit, but in fact was not at all happy. She said that 'having three screaming kids at Christmas' was not her idea of enjoyment.

I ordered the festive food, after going over what my mother wanted for Christmas dinner with her, and began to prepare. The Jennings clan arrived just as Ben was coming down with the flu. On Christmas afternoon, while I was cooking dinner, he was in our room being looked after by Franz. I was worried because he had a high fever and we were having trouble controlling it. Ben had always been quite sooky when he was sick and wanted me to be with him. Franz finally came out to the kitchen with a look of defeat on his face.

'I can't stop him from screaming, he wants you.'

'Everything is ready here,' I told Franz. 'All you need to do is make the gravy, serve it and eat. Could you bring me in my dinner a little later?'

Franz nodded and started to make the gravy. Franz is an excellent cook and I had no qualms about handing over the Christmas dinner to him. Poor little Ben had a raging fever of nearly 40 degrees and was sobbing when I came into the room. I gave him Panadol, calmed him down and swabbed him to cool his hot little body. I was sitting beside him thinking that I would take him into town the next day if the fever didn't break, when I heard pots and pans being crashed about in a very purposeful way in the kitchen.

Next Franz appeared at the bedroom door.

'What's going on?' I asked.

'Your mother,' he answered, and gave me an ominous look.

I left Franz to watch Ben and went out to the kitchen. It was evident that Mother was not happy at having to help.

'What is the matter?' I said. She wouldn't look at me, turned her back and marched off. I pressed on: 'What is the matter?'

She spun around and told me she didn't like having all the cooking dumped on her without notice.

'What are you talking about? I've cooked everything. All you have to do is serve it onto plates and eat it for God's sake. Franz was doing it,' I said.

I was sick of Mother's behaviour at this point, but I was also worried by it. This was supposed to be Christmas where everyone pitches in and helps. Danielle braved the kitchen to help serve and I went back to looking after Ben. My mother refused to speak to Franz or me for the rest of Christmas.

16

FRANZ AND I WERE TRULY HOPING that 1999 would be a happier year at Bullo. Martin called to ask if we could come to a surprise party he was arranging for Danielle on her birthday, early in the New Year, in Darwin. Family meant a great deal to Danielle, and Martin wanted to get everyone together. I wasn't sure that was wise considering the yawning abyss that seemed to divide my family, but his effort was noble and, most importantly, he was doing it to make Danielle happy.

I was getting the distinct impression that Mother felt I had failed her in some way. I think she wanted me to apologise to her and make a bit of a fuss of her but I acted as if everything was fine and normal, because I honestly felt that I had nothing to apologise for. My thoughts were consumed by the question of why I had fallen out of my mother's favour and why this gulf had opened up between us. In hindsight, perhaps she felt displaced from my changing life and perhaps she had difficulty switching from the total adoration of her fans to the very normal way I treated her as my mother. Whatever the reason, I felt like I was losing her and it filled me with anguish.

I told her what Martin was planning for Danielle's birthday but she didn't want to go, particularly when she found out Bonnie was going to be there. I finally convinced her to attend, with truths such as 'You know how important family is to Danielle'. I gave many such arguments, and the fact that they were all true made it hard for her to say no.

Danielle had a lovely time and seemed genuinely happy to be surrounded by all her family, and Martin was pleased with himself for having pulled it off. Bonnie for the most part ignored me, although not too obviously, and lavished her attention on Danielle. 'Well, it's her party,' I thought bleakly.

On our return to Bullo my mother was distant and cold. Franz, Ben and I were going to Austria again to see the Ranachers and my mother was going down to stay with Aunty Sue and Uncle Ralph in Caloundra while we were away. I hoped that a good break was what my mother needed.

As usual we had a great time in Austria. Ben was old enough to have fun in the snow now. I will always remember the delight of watching him run about catching snowflakes in his mouth; it was the first time he had seen falling snow. I called my mother a few times but she was rather distant and I hung up from our conversations feeling uncomfortable. When I did ask her what the matter was she was short: 'Nothing.' We both knew that was complete bullshit. I left the subject for later, hoping that she would eventually reveal all and that we would have it out and continue our lives peacefully on Bullo.

When we returned to Bullo, we started the musters and attended to the many guests who were now coming for overnight stays and day trips. We had tour buses coming in once or twice a month with up to 60 people for lunch. Most of the cooks we employed were not able to cater properly for these sort of numbers so I would stop my outside jobs and come in to cook for the groups.

Each time we had guests Mother was exceedingly charming to all of us, guests included, in marked contrast to the way she behaved towards us once they had gone. It was as if someone turned a switch. Everyone noticed the change in her. Some of our staff had been with us for several years now; they had all got along with her in the past but now started to give her a wide berth for fear of being scolded or given the cold shoulder. She still hadn't told me what the problem was and try as I did I could not think of a reason. She was past menopause so I couldn't lay the blame there; I had no conclusions.

Franz and I decided to try to have another child before I got too long in the tooth; I was 38 now. I had always wanted two little boys for some reason. And I thought it would be nice for Ben to have a brother, or sister for that matter, so that when Franz and I were gone they'd have each other.

By July I was pregnant and overjoyed about it. I said nothing to anyone but Franz because anything can happen in the first three months. Anything did happen – I miscarried in my second month. I was very, very down. I knew it was nature's way of sorting out any abnormalities, but I was still so sad.

We were in the process of restocking the Bull Creek area with better quality cattle from our main herd. We had planned for the men to walk the cattle out, with me driving the support vehicle because I didn't want to ride in my condition. Now it didn't matter. I saddled up my horse, gathered up the 600 cows and heifers and walked the cattle out to Bull Creek with Franz and the men. Franz was very supportive; he let me work through my feelings. We would try again for another baby.

Earlier in the year I had bought a second-hand truck to replace our old one, which was on its last legs. I had negotiated to take delivery of the truck immediately and pay $1,000 a month for four months and then $2,000 in the last month. Both the price and the terms of the deal were very good and my mother had approved the deal; she was to pay the instalments on behalf of the business. According to the agreement the truck should have been paid off in full by now.

When Franz went to buy spare parts from a wrecker in Darwin, who was a friend of the man we had bought the truck from, he was surprised to cop a good blasting from him. It turned out that my mother hadn't paid the last $4,000. Franz called from the wrecker's yard to tell me. Mother was away in Sydney; I tried to call her immediately to find out what was going on. I couldn't contact her, so I called Franz back and told him to pay out what we owed. I knew we had just put money in the bank from a cattle sale, and didn't think any more of it.

My mother returned a few days later. When she saw that the cheque had been drawn she became wild with fury. She screamed at Franz and I hysterically, saying that she had already put the cheque in the mail and that Franz was throwing money around and not being careful. We stood there in disbelief. I had seen my mother angry and frustrated and hurt before but this was something else entirely – quite frightening to witness.

My mother had not long before received the results of her most recent mammogram. A very small abnormality had been detected and her doctor wanted to check further. I decided to put her outburst over the truck payment down to a fear of possibly having cancer.

She had to go up to Darwin hospital that day and told me she didn't want me anywhere near her; she would rather be alone. Despite what she said, I was not going to leave her alone. I had been frightened about cancer myself and I knew how hard it was. I was in tears when I climbed into the plane to fly with her to Darwin. I was still rather fragile myself from having just miscarried. To be fair, Mother didn't know about the miscarriage. I hadn't thought it appropriate to tell her – she had her own problems to deal with and I had Franz to lean on.

I spent a chilly week by her bedside in hospital after the doctor cut a lump about the size of a rice grain from her breast. The doctor came back to her with the news that it was cancer – but that if you had to have cancer this was the sort to have. It was a slow-growing, non-invasive sort.

I only left mother's side to buy her some things to make her stay in hospital a little more comfortable. She didn't like the pillows – they were too hard. The teacups were too small. The food was awful. I bought her a pillow, a large cup and all her favourite fruit and other goodies, as well as a few books that I thought might interest her and a large selection of the most current magazines.

One day I was reading a book and Mother was flipping through one of the magazines when she came across an article that was titled 'I lost both my breasts and my husband because of cancer'. She held it up and said 'Nice!' before slamming the magazine down.

'Mum, I just took all the latest magazines and I didn't even look at what articles were in them,' I said, which was, of course, the truth.

Everything I did that week was cast in a negative light. I was on tenterhooks the whole time.

At the end of Mother's hospital stay Franz came to pick us up and take us home. Mother spent several weeks at Bullo recuperating before going to Brisbane to have six weeks of radiation therapy. The doctors were confident it was not an invasive cancer but thought it wise to have the radiation therapy as an extra precaution. Rather than stay in an apartment alone Mother stayed in Caloundra with Aunty Sue and Uncle Ralph, who drove her to Brisbane and back for her treatments. I called her every week but she remained just as distant as ever.

While my mother was away Franz and I finished off the

mustering. By the end of 1999 the cattle markets were just starting to recover, which was good news for next year. All the staff left for the wet, and Bullo was momentarily peaceful. Franz, Ben and I had a trip to Darwin and I went to the doctor, who told me that I was expecting again. That night I called my mother and told her the news. I wanted her to know because despite all the strangeness she was still my mother and we were, as far as I was concerned, still close.

There was a long pause before she responded: 'When did you know?'

It sounded more like an accusation than a question. I ignored her tone and said 'I just went to the doctor today.'

'I see,' she said.

That was the only thing Mother said to me about the pregnancy, ever. She didn't congratulate me or ask how I was or say that she was excited. Nothing. I hung up the phone in tears.

On Christmas Day it might as well have been −30 degrees my mother was so cool towards Franz and I. Normally, my mother was generous to a fault with gifts but this year she made it clear she was not at all impressed with Franz and me. Ben, however, did well and was spoilt by all of us. I am pleased that he was still young enough that most of the odd behaviour in our family went over his head. I had bought my mother gifts as I always had; she opened them and thanked me very formally and then left the room. My mother was one angry woman and I didn't know why.

For New Year some of our friends – Jeff, Kylie, Leon and Aaron – flew down to Bullo from Darwin. Mother chatted to everyone and was a gracious hostess. But she did not speak to Franz and me unless we directly addressed her. It was, if nothing else, a remarkable feat of willpower.

Franz and Jeff made some New Year bombs and let off fireworks, which Ben loved. We brought the millennium in with a bang. Little did we know just how appropriate bombs were – during the coming year we were to be at war.

Everyone left the next day except Aaron, who planned to stay on for a few days to help Franz in the workshop. Gone was the gracious hostess. Now Mother would turn up at meals, serve herself and leave to eat alone. At no time would she speak to us unless we addressed her and then her answer was curt.

After Aaron had gone Franz and I went to Mother who was in the kitchen to try to sort out the escalating mess we were in. We told her that we couldn't keep going on like this and asked if we could talk about what had upset her so much and try to sort it out.

'I'm not putting up with your crap any more,' she said.

'What crap?' I was bewildered. Just a year earlier we'd toured happily together.

She ignored my question and said, 'I've had it. No more. I'm finished. Either you buy the place or I'm selling.'

'What?' I was in shock. 'You can't. We don't have the money. And we had an agreement.'

Mother glared at me. 'This is my asset and I'll do what I like with it,' she hissed.

'How could you do this Mum,' I implored.

'Don't you call me that ever again. I'm no longer your mother.'

'What? What do you want me to call you – Mrs Henderson?'

My mother turned her back, strode into her office and slammed the door. I ran off to our bedroom and Franz, who had remained amazingly calm, came to comfort me.

Mother and I had spoken many times about the future and I had always understood that I would eventually take over the station, and she would retire to the coast and travel between the station and the coast as she pleased. She would always be part of Bullo and we would always be mother and daughter. I had trusted her implicitly. I had nothing in writing but I didn't think for a minute that I would ever need to.

I had spent the last 20 years of my life putting everything into Bullo. I had worked hard, as had both of my husbands, because we were investing in our future and were also looking after my mother's asset.

———•••———

I was 4 months' pregnant and having trouble with my blood pressure again. I made an appointment with my doctor in Darwin on the 4th of January, and told my mother that we would be flying out on the 3rd. Early on the morning of our departure we packed up the plane and waited for my mother to rise.

When she appeared at 8.30 am and saw the plane all packed up she shouted: 'You said the appointment was in February.'

'No I didn't,' I said, 'and what does it matter anyway? I need to go.'

She was furious and made it clear in no uncertain terms that she didn't believe me. I was in tears by the time I climbed into the plane. Never in my life had she spoken to me, or anyone else, in such a manner. She just didn't speak like that.

Franz, Ben and I flew to Darwin through heavy weather and only just touched down as a storm hit. The plane had given Franz trouble during the flight and on inspecting it, after we had landed, he discovered that a part needed to be replaced. The part had to come from down south so we would be returning a day later than planned. Franz called Mother to explain. She was very cold and clearly didn't believe him; there wasn't much we could do about it.

We resolved to make the best of our delay. After all, we did have an innocent little boy with us who was increasingly caught in the crossfire between adults. *Toy Story* was showing at the cinema so that night Franz took Ben for

Me and Blazing Boots our thoroughbred stallion.

Hardy Kruger, a documentary filmmaker from Germany, and me on a dozer.

Me in the bull catcher.

A bull I caught, tied up and ready to load onto a 6 × 6 pickup truck.

My mother and me with a film crew from the ABC.

Dragging a reluctant cow into the pen.

Franz fishing at Bullo River.

Franz on Denver as a broken
stock horse.

Franz and me on our wedding day.

Flying home from Darwin with Franz, Mother and Ben one week after he was born.

Robert (Franz's younger brother), Ben and a big barra.

Mother appearing on
This is Your Life. Front row
from left: me, Ben,
Mother, Danielle and
Natalie. Back row from
left: my mother's
brothers, Uncles Blue,
Warren, Brian and Todd.

Mother signing books for
visitors to Bullo.

Me in the grader with baby Ben next to me safely strapped into the baby car seat Franz fitted especially for him.

Getting up some flying time for my private helicopter licence with my instructor, Graham Hillsmith.

Mustering with horses and helicopters.

The Six Mile Yards where we muster the majority of our breeders (up to 3,500 head).

We're used to battling the elements in the north. This is Bullo homestead after a wild storm blew the roof off.

Homestead Creek flooding right to the back door.

Franz and stockmen throwing a horse onto the ground for branding and castrating.

Cattle in portable yards waiting to be drafted. Bob Thornton, a stockman, and I are sitting on the rails.

Ben playing in a bucket of water.

Ben caught this 38lb barra on his 5lb line. Franz had to land it for him, of course.

Left: Rachel, Franzie and Ben.

Below: The boys and me swimming in Homestead Creek.

An aerial shot of a bend in the Bullo Gorge.

Above and opposite: Some of the wildlife on Bullo.

Misty paddock on a Bullo morning.

A typically beautiful sunrise over the Bullo stock yards.

his first cinema experience. I stayed back at the apartment we had rented because I was feeling so ill due to my blood pressure. Franz said that Ben was awestruck and stood up and yelled, 'Go Woody, go' in one of the more dramatic scenes. Everyone laughed when he did this, but Ben was oblivious, totally involved in the story. Ben came back full of excitement, his eyes wide as saucers, and recounted the whole film to me with barely a breath between his words.

The part we needed for the plane arrived the next morning and Franz had installed it by lunch time. The weather was closing in fast so we left straight away through a gap in the clouds. It was heavy weather all the way home to Bullo; we weaved our way determinedly through storms. Ben was pleased to get home, although I couldn't stop thinking that this may not be home for much longer. This was now Mother's asset, not our home at all.

The next morning, the ever calm and logical Franz said, 'Okay, let's get some figures and try to see if we can make this plan work.' That same day we asked my mother for the current account figures, which I was entitled to see as a director of the company. My mother laughed at us. We were not to be given any access to the figures.

I went again to the office to try and speak to her. She was on the phone and as I came to the open door I heard her saying that it was Franz who had turned me against her.

I was frozen to the spot, amazed by how easily the words rolled off her tongue. In the eight years of our marriage Franz had never said a thing against my mother to me. I had not turned against her at all, let alone allowed someone else to turn me against her. I wanted more than anything for everything to go back to normal. And I certainly wasn't blinded and besotted with Franz to the point that he controlled me. It felt as though I was in a dream. I was too upset to speak to her and walked away reeling.

While all of this craziness was going on Franz and I continued to work; there was some comfort in the familiar tasks.
We took turns watching Ben. When I was repairing ruts in
the airstrip Franz had Ben in the workshop. He would come
back black with grease and dirt, but he did have lots of fun,
as all little boys do in workshops.

My Mother's behaviour seemed to be increasingly erratic.
One day she would not be speaking to Franz – another day
she would be extremely cordial to him. She wouldn't utter
his name – and then out of the blue she would seek him out.
For weeks she would not speak to me, would not even look
in my direction, then suddenly one day she sat down next to
me and started speaking in a most civil manner. I thought,
with a flood of relief, that finally we could sort things out.

As soon as I let my guard down my mother told me that
Franz had only married me for money. He was a gold-digger
and that's why she wasn't leaving the property to me. I
looked at her dumbstruck. She had obviously forgotten that
when Franz and I had married she wasn't a best-selling
author and Bullo was struggling to stay afloat. There was
no money to speak of back then; just a lot of hard work
as we climbed slowly out of debt. No one had worked as
hard and conscientiously as Franz had over the past eight
years. I managed to keep my cool instead of doing what I
really wanted to do – scream at my mother in frustration.

'Okay, I'll have Franz sign all his rights of claim away.
I know he will do that if I ask him to,' I said.

My mother didn't say anything to that; it wasn't what
she had been expecting. Franz walked in and joined the
conversation at that point. He and I put a counter offer
to my mother. We put forward a buy out plan of several
million dollars, without all her stipulations, and said that
we would buy a certain number of shares in the company
each year until eventually we would own Bullo one day.
She responded by saying she would want not only full
control of the property until we had made our final
payment but also to be able to change her mind and sell

the property out from under us without notice, until we had paid the last cent.

'We can't agree to terms like this,' said Franz. 'What if we're three quarters of the way through payment and you decide to sell? What would you then pay Marlee?'

'I'll pay her something' she answered flippantly.

'Would you put in writing what you would agree to pay her?' Franz asked very reasonably.

'I'm not putting *anything* in writing. You will just have to trust me,' my mother said, grinning.

'I already trusted you and look where it's got me,' I said solemnly.

Mother flashed me a look.

'Could you draw up an agreement as to how we should conduct business in the short term?' Franz asked.

'No. I'm not putting anything in writing and if you leave now before I have sorted out my affairs you'll get nothing,' Mother replied.

It seemed that my mother still needed us to run the property until she'd got what she wanted – her money and an escape plan. She knew she had us between a rock and a hard place, and we knew it too.

I left this unpleasant exchange deep in shock, which seemed to be almost my permanent state now. My mother had tried to put grave doubt in my mind about Franz. She was trying to break us up.

I was beginning to believe that Mother didn't want to sell Bullo to us. She knew that if she sold to us she wouldn't get as high a price as she wanted, and it would take longer to get her money. If she sold to someone else she'd receive full market price straight away and wouldn't have to wait for her money. She would be off to the coast and her new life, and wouldn't have to take our lives and many, many years of hard work into consideration.

When I had lost Charlie some 14 years before I had put all the cash and assets we'd shared in marriage into Bullo. One of the assets I brought to Bullo was a small herd of stud cows and bulls that I used to breed bulls for our commercial herd. I knew that the value of the herd as it stood today, plus the revenue from cattle sales that had resulted from the stud cattle, which had all gone into the station's coffers, must have come to millions. I pointed this out to my mother one day.

'You never paid me for agistment!' she shot back.

'The station made all the money from them; I didn't make a cent,' I said. She couldn't really answer, and she stormed off.

Up until this point none of our discussions had seemed all that real to me. I kept thinking that everything would come right. Now, I finally started to realise that this was happening to me – and what else would happen to me if I didn't get organised. I sat down and made a list of the main contributions to Bullo I had made in the last 15 years. The value and past revenue from the herd, even after subtracting agistment fees, came to $2.5 million. I had also put in $100,000 in cash from Charlie's life insurance, and his tools and machinery. On top of that I was owed who knows how much in unpaid wages for well over ten years' work. My mother had started paying Franz and I a joint wage of $40,000 once her books had become successful, but she had ceased to pay us anything several months ago, in September 1999. If we asked for our wages one of her more frequent responses was 'we don't have any money'.

Franz and I tried several more times to come to some sort of resolution. I even called family members and friends and asked them to speak to Mother. I called trusted friends to mediate. It was clear to me that she didn't want to settle anything with us. She wanted to sell for full market price as soon as possible and have us out of the picture. At one stage she made us an offer should she sell, but didn't put anything in writing, and told us on more than one occasion that if we displeased her in any way we wouldn't see a cent. Regardless, money was never the issue for Franz and I; what we wanted was to make our future on Bullo.

At this point our options seemed rather thin on the ground. I thought about whether we should just pack up and walk away, but decided that I would never be at peace with myself if we did that. The first thing I needed to do was investigate if we had any legal recourse. I had no idea if I had any legal rights to Bullo as there was nothing in writing between my mother and I. I also didn't have a lawyer. Apart from my mother's lawyer the only person I could think of who was in law was Sue, who had visited our property briefly on holidays. I didn't know her well but called and asked for advice. Sue put me onto John who told me that he was in criminal law and that I needed a commercial lawyer. He gave me the names of two lawyers he recommended, who were in Darwin. I called one of them, made an appointment and Franz and I flew up on the day.

Patrick Loftas was very good to us. He listened patiently to my lengthy, tearful explanation of the awful situation we were in. He then put us in contact with one of the best commercial lawyers in Darwin, David De L'Winter, whom we made an appointment to see a few days later. In the meantime our plane would have its 100-hour maintenance check, which usually takes a few days, and I would fly to Brisbane for a day to see Monty Roberts, the horse-whispering guru. Franz had organised the trip, hoping it would get me back on track.

The plane had only been in the air about 20 minutes when the cabin began to fill with smoke. One of the engines was on fire. I was gripped with fear that I might never see my beloved husband and son again, or give birth to my baby. That fear reminded me that I had something to fight for. It galvanised me into action.

The pilot turned the plane around and brought us down safely at Darwin airport. I avoided the waiting media who had come to cover the near-accident and headed off to collect my luggage and call Franz. What my rather dramatic flight had done was give me some direction again. Knowing clearly what I now had to do – fight to stay on Bullo for the sake of my husband and children – gave me strength. As my mother had taught me, there's a strength in us all.

When Franz came to the airport to pick me up he immediately saw the change in me. He smiled. He was glad to have the old Marlee back. The trip away – all 40 minutes of it – had worked its magic! On the off chance that David De L'Winter might have an appointment free that day I called, and he did. I liked David straight away; he was astute and gave us clear advice on the logical steps we needed to take to secure our future without procrastinating. Franz and I flew home with a lot to think about. Homecomings had now become full of dread and sadness.

Franz went and spoke to my mother again, in the hope of working out an amicable arrangement with her. He was giving it one last shot. I wasn't surprised when he came back shaking his head. We were to continue running the station and doing as we were told until the time when she would let us know if she would consider selling to us.

17

MY MOTHER WAS UP TO SOMETHING. She was defensive – more so than usual – and almost unapproachable, even on matters of importance for the running of the station.

I puzzled over what was going on – until it occurred to me that Danielle and Martin had the financial capacity to buy Bullo, and that if Mother sold it to them, publicly it would look all right, as they were family.

I called Danielle early one day and asked her outright if she had spoken to Mother behind our backs about buying the station. She answered that she had indeed spoken to Mother about buying Bullo. I told Danielle that she might at least have spoken to me about it. She responded that she didn't see what business it was of mine. I said goodbye and hung up before we had an argument. I felt betrayed by Danielle – I never thought she would do such a thing. Everything seemed to suggest that my mother was just stringing Franz and I along while she sorted out her affairs.

That afternoon I was cleaning Ben's bedroom, Ben babbling away happily, when my mother burst through the doorway dramatically. She was furious and took me to task about calling Danielle to find out what was going on. Ben stood looking at her with wide eyes. I told Mother that financially and ethically Bullo was not hers to dispose of without consideration of me because I had spent the last 20 years of my life, most of it unpaid, working by her side. I had invested my whole life into the property. We had had a deal. She had told me she intended to leave the property to me for all my hard work and support.

She had no answer; she glared at me, stomped out of the room, and slammed the door so hard I thought the walls would fall down. I cried softly to myself. Ben came over and gave me a hug.

'Why are you crying?' he asked with deep concern on his four-year-old face.

'Nana upset me a bit. It's okay,' I said to him smiling.

'No it's not!' he piped up emphatically.

He left his room with purpose in his stride. From what I understand he told Nana she wasn't allowed to yell at his mama and upset her, and that if she did it again he would shoot her and put her down a black hole. It did sound very bad, I must admit, but anyone who's known a four-year-old knows that they have wild imaginations. Ben had gone with his father to catch several killers over the past few months and afterwards had witnessed all the bones and offal being put in the death pit, where we buried dead cattle. Ever since, he had been telling anyone who displeased him that this would be their fate if he didn't get his way. My mother was one of a long line that included Franz and myself for various infringements on Ben's freedom, but my mother decided that Franz and I must have been talking about killing her in front of Ben.

Franz and I continued with our work despite the grim position we were in. Our goal was to settle an arrangement with my mother that allowed her to escape to the coast for her well-deserved retirement, and us to continue working and living on Bullo. We considered Bullo to be our future; and like all parents on the land we hoped it would also be the future of our children.

Franz had been trying to establish a website for Bullo for several years to help the tourist side of the business.

Under a government-funded scheme we were eligible to have a satellite dish installed and to get Internet access. All we had to provide was a computer, but there was no way my mother would agree to buying one; she hated them. I had tried to talk her into getting one to write her books on but she was adamantly opposed. She did eventually work on a typewriter that could be corrected a page at a time – a great improvement on writing by hand. Franz and I thought the government assistance was too good to pass up so we paid for the computer out of our own pockets.

I was six months' pregnant and busy answering all the tourist inquiries, mowing the lawns, maintaining the airstrip, cleaning the house and looking after Ben. Franz was servicing and fixing equipment, fences and flood gates, doing maintenance on buildings and checking the stock.

Once the cattle season started I knew the only way I would be able to cope with my workload was with the support of Ben's nanny, Rachel, a tough, warm-hearted and loyal young woman whom Ben adored. She had gone home for the wet season – and if my mother had her way, would not be coming back. Mother informed us that she would not allow Rachel back that year because she was guilty of theft. That was absolute baloney. Mother simply didn't like Rachel because she was close to Franz and I. At the same time Mother told me she expected me to continue working, which would be impossible if I was looking after Ben and our new baby unassisted. I called Rachel and told her of my mother's decision. Rachel was devastated. She loved Ben; she cared for him as if he were her own.

My mother had always let her two big rottweilers come into the house, but now she let them come in covered in mud and sand when I had just cleaned. When I said something to her about it she replied that it was her house and she'd do what she wanted. I stopped cleaning in a silent protest against this, and our unpaid wages. I continued to cook and clean the kitchen, do the lawns and slash the airstrip, though. It was important to keep doing all of that in light of the many tourist bookings we were receiving.

Bookings were becoming more and more difficult to deal with now because my mother wouldn't pass on messages or call Franz or me to the phone when someone rang for us. Every time we needed to make a call we had to ask her for the phone and then return it to her immediately afterwards.

She also now refused to eat with us. She would serve herself the food I had prepared for everyone and then eat in front of the television in the living room.

Franz took Ben out most evenings after work to catch a fish and get him away from the house, something I was very glad of. Ben caught a good-sized barramundi himself one evening and later on the phone described it to our friend, Jeff, as 'the biggest barra in the whole world'. That made Franz and I laugh. Amazingly this little four-year-old was keeping us sane.

Ben came to me one day and said, 'Nana's office smells, Mama' and presumably it did because it hadn't been cleaned since I stopped cleaning that part of the house that Mother and her dogs inhabited. I was so sad to hear him say this, and I was bewildered too.

Now that the wet was coming to a close we hired our first employee for the year, Lyndon, a man from Katherine. My mother wouldn't come out to meet him. When she did eventually meet him, she was charming with him as she was with all visitors. Still, she refused to talk to me unless absolutely necessary, and then very curtly. She wouldn't even stay in the same room as me. I first became aware of this new tactic one day when I was in the kitchen cooking. Mother came striding around the corner and as soon as she saw me she turned on her heel and left. She would only come out of her wing of the house after I had left the common area for the night.

A rather predictable pattern was now establishing itself; Mother would get herself more and more wound up over a period of days and then explode at Franz and I.

On the 5th of March I wrote in my diary that our mother–daughter relationship 'will never be the same again'. On that day she'd confronted Franz and I in the living room, accusing us of trying to kill her. She said that Franz had on more than one occasion tried to shoot her while she was walking on the airstrip. She said she had heard the bullets whistle past her ears they were so close. (I didn't say anything, but bullets don't whistle; that's purely for the movies.) She accused both of us of having plotted to do away with her for years. Clearly we weren't terribly competent in this role, as she was still alive and well – despite our obvious abilities with guns and other potential murder weapons you find on a cattle station.

I could tell by the look in her eyes my mother knew she was being foolish, but for some reason she continued to behave in this erratic manner. I don't think she truly believed some of the things she said about Franz and I, but unfortunately a lot of other people did and still do.

No one could possibly blame her for selling Bullo out from under us and fleeing with her life if her evil son-in-law and blindly besotted daughter had been plotting against her. Our situation would have been hysterically funny, except it was real.

In mid-March, Joy, our cook for the cattle season, arrived. You could cut the air in the house with a knife the tension was so bad. I apologised and told Joy that we were having family problems but that I would try to make sure they didn't affect her, and left it at that. My mother was immediately all over Joy and running Franz and I down to her. Mother worked overtime to have Joy on her team. Joy listened and went along with Mother, but she was a lot more switched on than my mother ever suspected. I guess my mother had been lulled into a false sense of security by a long line of muddle-headed cooks. Joy was the first of many misjudgements my mother made that year.

Franz and I had always used the company accountant

in the past, but that was no longer an option. We appointed a new one, Karen Green, who originally came from a Western Australian farm so understood our situation. She offered to call my mother and try to mediate. Franz and I were willing to try anything. I didn't think my mother wanted to settle with us and my gut feeling was right. She told Karen there wasn't anything to talk about and ended the conversation right there.

In late March Lisa, who ran the household, and Dan, who worked for us as a stockman and flew tourists in the helicopter, arrived for the season. Mother wouldn't let Franz fly into Darwin to pick them up. She told them to get a bus to Kununurra. They made it as far as Katherine and couldn't get any further because the roads were impassable due to flooding. Mother called the local police to check if this really was the case. Finally she sent Franz to Katherine to pick them up.

I believe that Mother thought Lisa was her ally and that was why she allowed her to come back, unlike Rachel. I was closer to Rachel because she was looking after Ben, but had always gotten on well with Lisa too. But Lisa mostly worked inside while I worked outside so I think Mother had assumed that Lisa was more aligned with her. Lisa was my mother's second misjudgement.

Most afternoons I went down to Homestead Creek to take Ben for a swim, to get him out of the house, and also because he loved it. When Dan and Lisa arrived they walked down to the creek with Franz to see me. They didn't quite have a handle on what was going on but knew it was serious. Lisa came up and gave me a big hug and I burst into tears. It didn't take much at all to set me off these days. I was about seven months' pregnant.

My mother went straight to work on Lisa, running down Franz and I. Lisa told her that she was here to do a job and that she didn't want to get involved in family politics. She said she hoped that everything could be kept professional. My mother just redoubled her efforts to enlist

Lisa to her cause. Lisa took it all in, but had already made up her own mind.

At the end of March my mother had to fly to Sydney on business and the calm that settled over the house when she had left was utterly blissful. She chartered a plane from Kununurra at great cost because she didn't want Franz to fly her. We had been happily and willingly flying Mother in and out of the nearby towns for the last eight years on her own aircraft, but now she announced it wasn't safe. Before my Mother had left Lisa had approached her about getting another girl to help her look after the homestead and tourist accommodation. Mother told her that I was in charge of employing people. That was certainly news to me. I told Lisa I had been stripped of all authority – except when it suited Mother it now seemed.

'Well,' Lisa said with a mischievous smile, 'if you're in charge, I would like to have Rachel back to help. Apart from everything else, she's been here for three years and knows the system and we work well together. It makes sense.'

I agreed completely with all that Lisa had said but knew that Mother would be furious if I re-employed Rachel. However, she had said to a third party that I was in charge. I called Rachel and offered her a position looking after the house with Lisa. Rachel was free, and keen to come back and help.

Several days later I received a fax from my mother's accountant notifying me that I was to be removed as a director of the company at a board meeting being held in Sydney that day. My mother and I were the only directors of our family company, Bullo River Pty Ltd. Mother held all the shares bar one, which I only held in trust for her, so it was easy for her to remove me. With the recent changes to company laws she didn't even need to appoint another director; it was legal for her to be the sole direc- tor now. She had always had a very firm control of the business side of things. In recent years I had spoken to her about taking more responsibility for the finances but while she agreed that I needed to learn she never did show me.

There was little I could do about my removal, but while I was still a director I did make a formal request to have the financial records handed over. Neither my mother nor her accountant answered my request.

In early April Franz and I went to Darwin for my regular check-up. I was about seven-and-a-half months' pregnant and feeling awful. I had had regular blood tests and for the first time my results showed that my blood sugar was too high. I probably had gestational diabetes, though I had to wait for further tests to confirm this. If I did have it, I would have to follow a strict diet and check my blood sugar level twice a day until our baby was born.

My mother returned to Bullo in the second week of April. Her face permanently bore the look of someone who had just eaten a box of lemons. With her return a dark cloud descended over the household.

On my 39th birthday Franz made me a beautiful birthday breakfast and Lisa and Joy made me a cake. Mother came out, glared at everyone menacingly and disappeared into the office. Apart from the by now familiar cold shoulder from Mother I had a nice day and went fishing with Franz and Ben in the evening.

Franz took me up to Darwin again, where I spent all day at the hospital having blood sugar tests that confirmed I had gestational diabetes. I got blood-testing equipment to use at home and was given strict instructions on the types of food I would need to eat for the remainder of my pregnancy. I was to eat high-fibre, slow-energy-release food; and cut out refined or sweet foods, most fats, coffee and alcohol, although I was already avoiding the latter. Uncontrolled diabetes can mean death; it affects all major organs. And in pregnancy it can lead to the baby becoming abnormally large and needing to be delivered prematurely.

We flew home to Bullo in the late afternoon with our by now customary feeling of dread. Franz told my mother about my health problems and she flatly refused to acknowledge them.

Rachel arrived in the last week of April with a late cyclone. I had mixed feelings about her arrival. While I was glad to see her, I also knew that life at Bullo had became unpleasant for the staff as well as Franz and I. They were happy to go about their work and not get involved in our personal life, but that was now unavoidable.

Before I had been removed as a director of the company, Franz and I had managed to get hold of an old cash-book that showed the running costs of the station. They were several years old, and it was not the whole picture, but they were all we had to go on. Mother was furious and demanded back the cash-book; we gave it to her, but not before entering the information on our computer. I asked Karen, our accountant, to do some number crunching based on these old figures. I hoped we could make my mother a realistic offer for Bullo.

While Karen was looking at the figures I set about finding us a lawyer. I had been very upfront about our financial circumstances with David De L'Winter; basically we didn't have a cent. In one of our phone conversations he told me that some large legal firms took cases on a speculative basis. David recommended his friend Cory, who was a partner in the law firm Minter Ellison and who occasionally took on speculative or pro bono cases. Before any legal firm will consider taking on such a case they require a face-to-face meeting to see whether you are credible, and have a legal leg to stand on.

I made an appointment and, nearly eight months' pregnant, set off to find out if we had a case and if a legal firm would represent us on a speculative basis. Franz, God bless him, never doubted me. He patted me on the head and told me that if anyone could do it I could.

I took the station car, as Mother had banned us from using the plane without her specific permission, and drove the 850 kilometres to Darwin. With very nearly the last of our money I bought a ticket to Brisbane, where I was to meet Cory. The flight was agony; the baby was sitting low and causing pain like an electric shock in the area of my cervix. When we landed I had real fears that I may go into labour there and then. I took my time and eventually made it to the luggage carousel and took a taxi to my hotel, where I gratefully lay down flat. I was exhausted and over-wrought.

The next day was Mother's Day. Franz and Ben rang, which cheered me up, but I felt terribly lonely. I took a walk along the beautiful Brisbane River and found the building where Minter Ellison had their offices. Rising black and sleek well above all the other buildings was number 1 Eagle Street. Tomorrow I would find out which direction our future would take; the anticipation was enormous and the responsibility weighed heavily on me as I walked slowly back to the hotel.

The next morning I was up early as my little baby was very active; I suspect it could feel my tension. I walked back to number 1 Eagle Street in the vain hope that the walk would calm me down. I found an elevator that took me to the very top of the building, where I waited in a plush lounge area with possibly one of the best views of Brisbane. I was feeling as one must feel when about to be sentenced. This could be our only chance to save Bullo.

The interview lasted several hours. I gave an abridged version of my life, concluding with the most recent events. It was harrowing and emotional to talk about the ordeal. Cory was highly professional and cut right to the core of the matter: he thought I was credible and that I had a case. He said that their company could represent me on a specu-lative basis, but they had no office in Darwin and they would need to have someone based there to do the leg-work. He said he would be happy to work with David De

L'Winter, if he was agreeable. I left with a feeling of hope coursing through my body for the first time in ages. It felt good.

I called Franz straight away and told him how everything had gone. He too sounded hopeful. Then I called David and asked him if he would be willing to work with Minter Ellison; he said yes. My heart was bursting with joy. He went on to say that he was about to become a consultant with another large national firm, Hunt and Hunt, which had offices in Darwin. Now that I knew I had a case they might be agreeable to taking it on, which would be more practical than being represented by Minter Ellison in Brisbane. David said he would put the plan to them that very afternoon.

Hunt and Hunt said they were interested in taking on our case, subject to an interview with them. I was full of apprehension as I went to Darwin to meet one of their partners.

The first time I met Meredith Day I thought she had the saddest eyes I had ever seen. I felt she must have suffered some terrible tragedy not long ago because of what can only be described as the heavy aura she carried. I liked and trusted her immediately. Meredith had grown up on a sheep property in South Australia and understood everything I was talking about with regard to working on the land. She drew no rosy pictures of what the future held but agreed that we did have a case and that she would take it on. I sat in her office with tears of relief streaming down my face.

'My mother has never had a good thing to say about lawyers. She thinks they're the scum of the earth,' I said. 'I've always believed that there are a great many good people on this earth who will help you if they can. Fortunately for me I've found rather lot of them lately.'

Meredith laughed. She was well used to the 'bad lawyer' tag; it went with the job.

I did discover why she was so sad. Only a few months before, she had carried her own child to term and it had been stillborn. My heart went out to her; I could only imagine the pain she was in. She was burying herself in work to deal with her grief, which was just what I had always done. She was concerned for the welfare of my unborn child as it was obvious that I was emotionally stretched as far as possible.

Franz and I were still waiting to hear from my mother about how her book had gone in America. Though I believed Mother was stalling for time while making other plans, Meredith recommended, and I agreed, that we wait until we heard from my mother before we acted.

At the end of May the company phone in the office was ringing nonstop all day with calls for Mother. Franz and I had given up using the company phone because asking Mother for permission wasn't worth the trouble. We had a separate phone line for the staff to use, and Franz and I had started using that. I made a number of calls to find out what was going on. It appeared my mother had been contacted at least one businessman to try and sell the property to them; she was also trying to sell the helicopter. I was shell-shocked and distressed that Bullo could have been sold off without us even knowing about it. But I was in for another shock.

Joy, our cook, took me aside and said she needed to talk to me alone.

'I've tried to stay out of it but I have to tell you. Your mother just came and told me that, with the exception of me, she intends to fire all the staff, including you and Franz, once this lot of tourists have left on Thursday.'

Today was Sunday. We had five days. My blood had frozen and my mind was racing.

I went to my mother for one last try. This time I was alone. Just Mother and me. I made another offer to purchase, based on what Karen, our accountant, had come up with after going through our finances and the figures from the old cash-book.

I proposed that we pay Mother $1 million – which Karen thought we could get from a bank without too much difficulty – and a further $1 million in instalments over a number of years. The money she would receive would all be tax free because the company had been formed before the introduction of capital gains tax laws, which meant there was no tax on the sale of the company's shares. Taking into account what Mother owed me for unpaid wages and the assets and cash I had invested in Bullo, and the debts the company carried via mortgages, bank loans and hire purchase, my offer equated to Bullo's realistic value of $4.5–5 million.

'I'm not taking that pittance,' she said before leaving the room.

The battle lines were now clear. I called Meredith at home and told her of the most recent events. She advised that I try to get an injunction to stop my mother from selling the property and firing Franz and me and the staff. I would have to go to Darwin to prepare for court. I needed to go and have my diabetes monitored anyway, so Franz asked my mother for use of the plane the next day to fly me into Kununurra, where I could catch a jet to Darwin. I knew she would say yes this time.

Meredith had warned me it would be hard to get the court to agree to an injunction, but had also said that once in place it would be equally hard to remove. Whether we could prepare for court in four days was doubtful – it was a race against time to save our home. In Kununurra Franz gave me a big hug and told me he knew I could pull it off. I flew to Darwin with my heart in my mouth, where it remained firmly lodged my entire stay.

Over the next four days Meredith, her assistant, Danielle, and I worked on a Statement of Claim all day and well into some nights. That statement set out why I believed I had some legal claim to Bullo; I knew our future rested on how well this document was presented.

We ran it past David, who made some sound points and suggested a few changes. Then, I went through it again with Judith Kelly, my barrister, who was to represent me in court. She went through it quite brutally, to prepare me for how I might be questioned in court. She had me in tears in no time. She softened her manner for a moment and explained that this was what I had to expect and needed to be able to deal with.

'Right,' I said, taking a deep breath, 'ignore my blubbering and keep at it.'

Judith was a tiger and I'm glad she was on my side. Underneath her professional demeanour was a gentle, loving mother and yet another person willing to help me in my distress.

I asked the lawyers to try for a closed court to keep the media at bay. I knew how image conscious Mother was and hoped that, if successful with the injunction, we could come to a quiet and confidential agreement.

Our lawyers managed to get court time on the Thursday afternoon we were all to be fired. I was terrified that Mother would fire everyone before we had the injunction in place so on Wednesday night I called Franz and asked him to take everyone except Joy out to Twenty-two Mile early in the morning to fix the floodgates, and not to come back until evening. By then I would have our answer one way or another.

I went with Meredith to the courts, taking the back entrance in case there were any media out the front. We went into the courtroom but I was so overwrought that I couldn't bear to stay there and left to wait in the hall outside. It felt like an eternity, but was only 40 minutes or so before Judith and Meredith came out with smiles on their faces. The judge had granted the injunction; Mother couldn't fire any of us for now, or sell Bullo until we either settled between ourselves or appeared before a full court where they would decide. The only point he had disagreed with was our request for a closed court. Apparently the law grants such a request only if it is in the interest of the public, which he did not deem saving my mother's reputation to be. The media had not yet got wind of our dispute, but I didn't think this would be the case for long.

We had done it. We had bought some time. For the moment at least Bullo was safe and we had been spared getting kicked off the station penniless. Meredith typed up the court orders and late that afternoon faxed them down to Bullo.

At 5.30 pm Franz saw the court papers come through on the fax and gave them to my mother. She went absolutely crazy according to Franz; she was so red in the face he thought she would explode. She screamed at him that he was fired, the staff were all fired, and it was too late for an injunction because the property had already been sold. (Meredith had checked and there had not been any transfer of shares that day. The company was still intact.) Mother demanded of Franz that we remove the injunction immediately or be prepared to suffer her wrath. Frankly, we had already suffered so much of her wrath in the preceding months that this was not a particularly distressing threat. The only thing that had changed was that finally we had a card to play of our own.

Mother was in shock. She hadn't seen our move coming. At about 6.00 pm on the same day four people turned up at the station in a 4WD. Bonnie, one of her female friends, two backpackers and a biker came to Bullo, presumably to start work. Mother was now in an embarrassing situation. It might have been funny if it wasn't so serious.

The four extra people moved into our guest rooms and spent the next days eating, drinking beer and generally hovering around doing nothing while my mother attempted to remove the injunction. Mother contacted her lawyer and told Franz she was confident that the injunction was only a temporary hitch and she would have it cleared up in a few days. She didn't realise the seriousness of an injunction and that one could not simply remove it. Franz, holding the fort while I was in Darwin, never lost his calm. I think it drove her crazy.

Following the granting of the injunction, I flew to Kununurra and then called everyone I knew there in the hope of finding someone who could give me a lift to Bullo.

My friends John and Pauline were driving to Darwin and would be passing by Bullo. They dropped me off at the front gate, where Franz picked me up. It was another painful trip with the baby sitting low. Every time we hit a bump – there are an uncountable number on our road – it felt like an electric shock.

On the drive home Franz recounted the drama of the last week. It had been difficult to remain professional with the tourists because of the way Mother had been acting. She had gone out of her way to be rude to Lisa and Rachel while they had simply been trying to do their jobs. Some days she drove them to tears, but they were both committed to seeing it through with us to the bitter end.

When I arrived home I served the original court documents on Mother and asked if I could speak to her in the morning. She was extremely curt. She had to control herself because some of our supposed replacements were around the house. I was so tired as I walked to my bedroom.

In the morning I had my talk with Mother outside the office. She had a new employee by her side, Jeanette. She had bare feet, her shirt had the sleeves cut off, and she was wearing a black Akubra hat. She stood right behind my mother, arms crossed, scowling at me like a bodyguard.

Mother was smug. She repeated confidently that the injunction was only a temporary setback, she would have it lifted, and that the property had already been sold. I told her that I knew no sale had taken place. She replied that verbal agreements were binding. I reminded her that we had had one of those for a long time and it didn't seem to be worth much. She flushed red and threatened that if I didn't take the injunction off, Franz and I wouldn't see a cent. I replied that I didn't think we would ever see a cent anyway, and that I had no intention of lifting the injunction until we had reached some form of agreement. I told her that I didn't want to go to court again.

I believe in hindsight that Mother thought that she could have this sorted out in her favour in no time. She was to discover that it wasn't going to be that easy on the 1st of June, the date of the next court hearing, which would determine the guidelines of the business while the injunction was in force, and at which a date to test the injunction would be set.

Mother clearly felt she needed a lot of protection because over the next few days she made one of the replacements into a second bodyguard. He was a small, thin man called Weed. He had a long, long beard and tattoos all over his body. Knowing my mother, I knew he was about her worst nightmare. He had taken to calling her Mum and I saw her cringe on more than one occasion when he sidled up and put his arm around her shoulder.

Bonnie's defacto partner, Paul, had turned up a few days after our supposed replacements arrived. I had met him briefly at the birthday party that Martin had organised for Danielle in Darwin. I had instantly disliked him and my opinion was to worsen over the coming months.

Leaving the replacement people hanging, but with the assurance she'd sort everything out smartly and her plan would proceed as before, Mother chartered a plane and flew out to Darwin to see her lawyers. By now she had come to the realisation that it was not a matter of simply lifting that irritating injunction. She left Jeanette in charge of the phone and fax that were locked in her office. At night Paul slept on the floor in front of the locked office door as an extra precaution against us. God knows what Mother had told Bonnie and Paul, and why they had come to her rescue after many years of hostility and estrangement. Whatever she'd told them it had worked.

The house and business were past dysfunctional. Complete strangers were in charge of the office phone and fax. We had no say whatsoever in any money matters. We couldn't even buy a sink plug. But Franz and I tried to

continue with the daily work of cattle mustering and catering for the guests. We had a group of tourists come to fish
for barramundi. They were a nice group of people and
seemed to have a good time. The atmosphere was much
improved with Mother gone, even with her personal
employees hanging around watching our every move.

There was a spare seat on the plane that had delivered
the fishing group and it was going back to Darwin so I
caught a ride on it to attend the court hearing on the 1st of
June. I had become friends with the mother and daughter
who ran the apartments where we generally stayed on our
trips to Darwin. Berace Taylor had done a lot of model-
ling in the past, which didn't surprise me. She and her
daughter Marlow were stunners – tall and blonde with the
most enviable figures. They were beautiful people on the
outside, and I was to find that their interiors were even more
stunning.

When I arrived Marlow made me a sandwich and then
I waddled down to the Hunt and Hunt offices. Meredith
and her assistant, Danielle, had been working tirelessly
taking statements from a list of people who had agreed to
testify in court for us if needed. I think my mother would
have been shocked by the number of people who were
willing to go in to bat for us.

On the day of the hearing I went to the courts with
Meredith and Danielle, and Judith and David met us
there as well. I drew great strength from these people. I
didn't have a single doubt that I could have been better
represented.

My mother was there. She gave me her by now standard
withering look and turned her back on me. I hate to sound
unfeeling but by this stage a sort of black humour was
important for keeping myself going.

Bonnie, of all people, was by my mother's side in court.
I felt a little sorry for Mother's lawyer; he was looking very
harassed. In court, Mother and her lawyers tried to make
an arrangement whereby Bonnie would be in charge of

Franz and I at Bullo, a proposal I completely refused to entertain for obvious reasons. I did agree that Mother could have Bonnie and Paul, her partner, as observers on Bullo. It was not something I really wanted to agree to but it was the lesser of the evils and the court expects both sides to give and take. Bonnie and Paul would be allowed to observe our activities and report back to my mother but in no way were they to interfere. They were to be my mother's eyes, watching us daily as we worked outside, something she had never done. Having agreed to the arrangement I knew that the coming months were going to be particularly unpleasant; I could feel it in my bones.

I could also feel our baby engaging right there in court. I was sure the birth was not far off. I was feeling unwell and overwhelmingly tired. I went to the hospital after the court hearing to see my doctor. It turned out I was two centimetres dilated – the baby could come any time now. Franz and I agreed that the welfare of our child came first. I had had high blood pressure for several months, and that, plus the diabetes, made the decision for us. I would stay in Darwin. Franz called our friend Jeff and asked if we could hire a plane from him so that Franz could fly up when the baby came. As we had very little money Jeff said we could pay him back at a later date.

Our friend Aaron, like a lot of other people, thought the situation on Bullo was more than bizarre and wanted to see for himself, so he dropped in to spend a day with Franz. My mother was charming to him. He told me later that she said that he was welcome at Bullo and should come back and meet the new owners, who would be there the following month. The new owners were, apparently, to be none other than Danielle and Martin. This was the perfect solution for Mother. Danielle and Martin could afford to buy outright without owing my mother anything – and my mother didn't owe them anything for unpaid wages and investments, so she'd walk away with the full sale price. Just the small matter of my having worked the property for most of my life, along with two husbands, seemed to have escaped their notice.

Bonnie's attendance at the court hearing now made more sense. Perhaps Danielle was planning to have Bonnie run the station for her. I actually felt sorry for Bonnie; it seemed to me she was caught up in something she didn't fully understand.

I realised now, with blinding clarity, the dynamics of my family that I'd never really understood. The latest situation with Bonnie as observer, Danielle as new owner and me as villainous outcast was just more of the same; roles that seemed contrived to suit the circumstances – only now the stakes were higher and the circumstances more bizarre.

Shortly after this we heard the news that Martin was busy in Arnhem land trying to sell hunting safaris on Bullo. That's how sure my mother was of having her way.

Franz, Ben and Aaron caught a lift up to Darwin on one of Jeff's planes returning from a charter flight. It was good to see Franz and Ben away from the unpleasantness of Bullo. We decided it was best that Ben stay with me in Darwin as the situation at home was getting worse by the day. Marlow and Berace came to our rescue, offering to take Ben and me into their own home in Darwin. I gratefully accepted as we had nowhere else to go. Berace told me that they would look after Ben when I went into labour. My gratitude to these people, who had up until recently been complete strangers, has no bounds; once again my utter faith that there are good people everywhere had been rewarded.

Franz took Jeff's plane home, ready for when I went into labour, but Jeff needed it back sooner than he had thought so I started ringing around to try and find another plane to hire. In the course of my phone calls I found out that my old flying instructor, Ron, was flying a cattle consultant down to Bullo. Mother had hired the consultant to prepare a report on the health of the cattle in our main homestead yards. A complaint had come to us via her lawyers that these cattle were dying of thirst and dust inhalation. I have always been obsessive about watering down the cattle yards – after all, I don't particularly like working in dusty conditions either. We took a variety of measures to keep the dust at bay. At the end of the day one can only do so much in our part of the world – to say there shouldn't be any dust in a yard is like saying there shouldn't be any paper in an office.

Nonetheless I put my mind to the task of countering this claim. I called Dean, a well-regarded cattle buyer I had dealt with for over 15 years, and asked him to be out at the yard at the same time that the cattle consultant was. If necessary, he would be able to say he had been there too and that the cattle were not dying of thirst and dust inhalation. We heard no more about that complaint, however others now started to come to us via Mother's lawyers on a daily basis. All of these complaints had to be answered in one way or another and they were to occupy a great deal of our time and energy.

For part of each day while I was in Darwin waiting for the birth of our second child I helped Meredith and her assistant, Danielle, in any way I could to compile the huge amount of material needed to uphold our injunction and answer the unending complaints and demands of my mother's lawyers. They wanted to know exact future muster dates, numbers of sale cattle, and how much money each sale would make. It wasn't possible to give exact numbers, as my mother well knew. Nevertheless we had to give them an answer, so I drew up a muster plan with estimates based on previous musters.

Mother paid Franz some of the money due to both of us for outstanding wages. I wondered if she had done this because it would look good in court. However, she refused to let Franz use the company phone at all. She wouldn't even let him call up cattle buyers. No one could call him either. She refused to pass on any messages, and if I called asking to speak to him she just hung up. And she had changed the staff phone number and wouldn't tell anyone the new number, which meant no one could call him – or anyone for that matter – on that line either. I had no way of calling Franz when I went into labour. Franz couldn't wait with me in Darwin because he was working solidly and had to keep an eye on things for us. One day Ben looked at me and asked why I was crying; I told him that I was just a little sad.

As always there was a solution. I had the Telstra technician's direct number in Kununurra and I knew him a little from his past visits to repair the phone. I called him and explained my dilemma, and he gave me the new number without hesitation. My mother heard the staff phone ring, worked out that I had the number and immediately had it changed again. I got the new number and dialled. I imagine Mother was furious, but I really didn't care one bit. I resolved to have our own phone put in as soon as I got home; this phone business was petty and I didn't like being drawn into my mother's games.

Franz kept in touch as much as he could and brought me up to date with what was going on at Bullo. My mother obviously had Danielle and Martin completely convinced that it was all go ahead for them to become the new owners because Martin chartered a plane from Cloncurry, along with three other men, and turned up to inspect 'his' property. Franz had a long talk to Martin who I doubt listened to a word; he was in it strictly as a business deal and wasn't interested in family fighting or ethics.

Next Bonnie and her five children turned up to join Paul, Bonnie's partner, and two of his children from a previous relationship who were already at Bullo. With Mr Weed of the Hell's Angels, plus Martin and the three men he brought with him, and Mother's other personal staff, there were an extra 12 people to feed. Martin and the men that came with him stayed for several days looking over the station and making plans for the takeover.

I went for another check-up. My blood pressure was

high and still rising which didn't surprise me, all things considered. I was overdue and the doctor didn't like the way my pregnancy was progressing; he wanted to induce my labour if I still hadn't had the baby in a few days' time. Each day I waddled up to the Hunt and Hunt offices, which were starting to feel almost like home. Little Ben was so good. He would play by himself in the corner of the office while we worked through all the statements and affidavits.

On the morning of the 15th of June I went again for a check-up. I felt like I was about to go into labour. The midwife checked me and said I was a little more dilated but it didn't look like I was ready yet. It certainly didn't feel that way to me but I went back to Berace and Marlow's flat to wait. That afternoon, at about 5.00 pm, the contractions started. I called home and Joy answered the phone. I asked her to get a message to Franz, although I knew he couldn't make it to Darwin that night as it would soon be sundown. Berace took Ben and Marlow drove me to the hospital. Marlow patted me on the hand.

'Don't worry, I'll stay with you,' she said, smiling her beautiful smile.

By the time we had reached the hospital my contractions were quite close and regular, and it looked as though I would have our baby in the next few hours. Franz called and we agreed that he should come in the morning. Franz stayed by the phone with several of the other staff at Bullo all through the night. They called regularly, and talked to Marlow as I became less and less able to speak.

The midwives were wonderful but as the night drew on it became clear that things were not progressing as they should. I felt like I was getting nowhere. I had pushed our baby nearly all the way; the midwives could see his head but he would go no further. I was in intense pain and my contractions were hard and fast. My doctor came to see what he could do; he tried the suction with no luck. Forceps were not an option – he said that even if he could get them in he would have to pull with force that he was not comfortable with; he might hurt our child. I was writhing in pain as I signed a consent form with something like a big X for a Caesarean section. Marlow, bless her, was with me through it all, holding my hand and keeping Franz up to date on the phone.

I was wheeled into surgery in the early hours of the morning of the 16th of June. The anaesthetist was almost up there with God in my mind when he put in a spinal block and stopped the pain. One moment I was almost fainting in agony, the next I felt a blissful nothing. From then on it was all quite quick. The doctor and the nurses went to work on the other side of the raised sheet and not long after, I had our second, not so little, son on my chest. He was a whopping nine pounds with a 38 centimetre head. The doctor said that with his head measurement there was no way I could have had a natural birth. I believed him.

I was feeling rather worse for wear but our little boy was in perfect order, and that was what mattered. Marlow gave me a kiss and went home to get some sleep while the doctor stitched me up. When he had finished a nurse brought Franzie to me. He was the cutest little guy ever and for a while at least I was lost in the pleasure of nursing him. I forgot about all our troubles.

The next morning, before he left the station, Franz went to Mother's locked office door to tell her that she had another grandson. He felt, despite all that was going on, it was the right thing to do. She opened the door a crack, glowered at him as he told her the news, and without a word she slammed the door in his face.

18

FRANZIE WAS DOING BRILLIANTLY and started putting on weight straight away. He was a good eater and sleeper and never cried. He had to be one of the happiest, most contented babies ever. I like to think he was sent to save our sanity.

Franz flew up from Bullo, picked up Ben from Marlow and Berace's apartment and came to the hospital. I was so glad to have them with me. I knew that this peaceful, joyous time would not last long as there were so many problems for us to return to at home.

The Caesarean had knocked me around badly. I had all sorts of drips and tubes sticking out of me. I couldn't walk at all. The doctor wanted me to stay in hospital for at least a week.

Franz returned almost immediately to Bullo. Shortly after he arrived home, one of the guests we had staying, Tim, a farmer from England, had an accident while helping with the drafting. He had his hand under the gate chain when a steer hit it with full force and the chain severed half of his finger. The men had retrieved the finger and put it in an esky to keep it cool and clean. Tim needed to be flown straight to the hospital. Franz wasn't allowed to fly the plane so he asked Bonnie, who was there observing, to do it.

'I'm not flying him into town,' she said.

Franz took Tim up to the homestead and went to the office. Mother was horrified by Tim's injury.

'Take him in!' she ordered Franz. That was all she said before slamming the door in his face again.

Lisa put a dressing on Tim's hand and Franz and Tim left for Kununurra. The Kununurra hospital said that they couldn't do anything for him and he would need to go to Darwin hospital the next day.

I was in the private section of Darwin Hospital, and received a call from a forlorn Tim in the public wing. In all the chaos no one had thought to bring any clean clothes for him, or his wallet, or anything for that matter. He had travel insurance, which would allow him to transfer to a private ward, but the hospital required him to pay a bond of $900 first. He had called Bullo, wanting to ask Franz to get his credit card number from his wallet so he could pay the bond. Mother refused to get Franz and hung up on Tim. I paid the bond on my credit card and got him a toothbrush and a hair comb – which made me laugh when we finally met because he was all but bald.

Tim kept me company over the next few days. He looked longingly at little Franzie; later I learnt that it was his greatest wish to have a family of his own. The doctors were not able to save his finger but made a neat job of sewing up the skin; Tim now has nine-and-a-half fingers.

Tim and I were discharged from the hospital, and he decided he wanted to come back to the station while his finger healed. My mother reluctantly agreed. After their incident on the phone, Tim, who had been totally uninvolved with the Henderson family drama, willingly got involved because he was so mad. He made a statement for my lawyers to use in court. She was not pleased by Tim's now obvious support for Franz and me.

I bought the appropriate dressings for his finger and got instructions on when to take the stitches out. Tim chartered a plane from Darwin to fly back to the station and let

Franzie and I come as his passengers, which was a great relief. I hadn't known how I was going to get home. Because of my difficult labour and the Caesarean I could still barely walk. I was doing more of a shuffle. Little baby Franzie was a joy, however.

We had a good flight home. Franzie slept the whole way and on arrival we were greeted by a huge banner that said 'WELCOME HOME MARLEE, FRANZIE AND THE POM'. On one side we had a fabulous welcome from Lisa, Rachel, Joy, Ben, Franz and all the other staff – and on the other we had my mother, her large entourage, my sister and her family glaring at us.

After I had unpacked and settled Franzie down I went to speak to Mother to sort out the phone matter. I kept calm and spoke reasonably. Franz and I saw no reason to match Mother's behaviour. I pointed out that since she had locked up the company phone there hadn't been any more tourist bookings, which normally came in all year. This was, I believe, a way of making Franz and I look like incompetent businesspeople in court. Restricting our use of the phone stopped us from being productive; meanwhile she sent complaints daily through her lawyers about our lack of productivity.

She was defensive when I raised the tourist issue and refused to give me the phone to use. She told me that it was broken and Telstra were fixing it. I shook my head. It was a cordless phone that we had bought ourselves.

'Telstra don't fix private phones,' I said. 'And if it is broken I can get Franz to look at it.'

Franz really can fix just about anything. Mother flatly refused. Then she told me that she had no intention of speaking to me until the next court hearing which was a couple of weeks away. Until then all communication would be through her observer, she said. I assumed she meant Bonnie. She slammed the office door in my face yet again. As it turned out, the court case was cancelled because Mother's lawyers wanted more time.

In the time I had been away giving birth to Franzie, Bullo had degenerated into chaos. The car we used for transporting the tourists was now filthy, and my mother had seen fit to install a steering lock so that Franz and I couldn't use it – even when our replacements weren't using it recreationally.

It was not uncommon to see pannikins of rum being drunk from mid-afternoon onwards. Breakfast was the only peaceful time, because early in the morning the replacements were nowhere to be seen as they were getting over their hangovers. They scared Joy, Rachel and Lisa but they neither frightened nor intimidated me; rather, I thought they were a pathetic lot who had nothing better to do than get involved in someone else's family feud.

One night we were all sitting at the kitchen table eating dinner when Bonnie swaggered up to Lisa, put her face close to hers and demanded clean sheets, right now. I told her firmly that in future she was to ask me if she wanted something and at no time was she to direct the staff as it was not her place. Bonnie backed off but became very sarcastic; she proceeded to ask me in a theatrically simpering voice if she could have some sheets. Lisa went and got some and gave them to her. Bonnie left with the sheets, and a few minutes later returned with some of them, unfolded, and dumped them in the kitchen sink with all the dinner dishes. 'I don't need these,' she said before walking away smirking.

On that evening we also found out from the police that someone had lodged complaints with them about Franz and I threatening my mother's life, and digging up and sabotaging the road. Mother's 'guests' told the police that they wanted to take possession of the key to the gun safe because of the threat of us shooting Mother.

Franz and I could see things were getting well out of hand so we decided to send every gun on the property to the

Timber Creek police station with one of the helicopter mustering pilots who offered to drop them off on his way past there until all of this was settled. Franz bundled them up straight away and handed them over. I watched as the chopper disappeared over the horizon – it was the first time in my memory there were no guns on Bullo. Not having any guns would be a serious handicap for us, but we resolved to work around the problem. At least there was one accusation that would have to cease: if we didn't have guns we couldn't shoot Mother.

I desperately wanted to install our own phone line, so I went and raised the issue with Mother. She wouldn't hear of it.

'We have nothing more to talk about. The property is sold and if you wish to speak to me do so through my lawyers.'

I kept calm. It was bloody hard but I did.

'This is ridiculous. We still have to run the business. I do need to be able to talk to you and I do need the use of a phone,' I said.

Bonnie was standing by to throw in her two cents' worth on everything. This was my sister who had sued my mother after my father's death, who had not spoken to us for years, and who my mother had said on many occasions was no longer her daughter.

I called Testra on the staff phone and asked to have the staff line transferred into Franz's and my name; this I managed to do. I had Franz move the phone into our bedroom, which was also our office and nursery. We finally had a phone that people could call us on, and which the staff could use. My mother was unhappy about it but couldn't do a thing to stop me.

That night at dinner Bonnie marched up while we were eating and slammed down a piece of paper on the table in front of me. It was a long list of questions about management issues, which she wanted answered immediately.

'I will speak to you after I have finished dinner,' I replied calmly.

She stood behind me all through dinner heckling me and the others at the table. She had her pannikin of rum in her hand. We ignored her completely, which I am sure drove her up the wall. My mother, who was sitting just around the corner, was well aware of what was happening and did nothing.

Before I had eaten my last mouthful Bonnie was yelling 'So have you finished?'

I turned and looked at her calmly, and looked at the list.

'These are ridiculous questions. Are these your questions or Mother's questions?' I said.

After I had asked her this question several times Bonnie finally conceded they were not hers.

'I told Mother that I would speak directly to her about all management issues,' I said. 'I told her I would not communicate through her lawyers or through anyone else for that matter.' I added that as an observer Bonnie was not supposed to interfere in any way.

She yelled at me, but I didn't respond. I had discovered the power of passive resistance.

I waited while Ben finished dinner, throughout which all of us could hear Bonnie and Mother debating loudly in the living room. I gathered up Ben and Franzie and walked towards their bedrooms. Out of the darkness Mother and Bonnie suddenly appeared, yelling at me. Rachel whisked the children away for me. Mother and Bonnie were both yelling at me at once, accusing me of refusing to speak about management issues. Strangely enough I felt rather detached from the whole scene and rather sorry for the pair of them. They truly struck me as pathetic. I let them yell and carry on until they had run out of steam momentarily. Then I reminded Mother that that was exactly what I had tried to do with her only that morning and she had refused to talk to me at all. Off they went again. I waited until they drew breath and reiterated what I had said earlier to Bonnie – that I would very much like to speak to Mother in the morning but not now.

They continued to yell as I walked away. I can't bring myself to repeat the names they called me, and believe me, I have heard some colourful language in my life. I closed our bedroom door behind me and breathed deeply. I was shaking. Rachel was so sweet.

'You were great. You stood right up to them. They're scared of you,' she said.

I smiled but didn't feel nearly so confident. I had a troubled feeling about the escalating tensions on Bullo. The atmosphere was already boiling over without Mother turning up the heat. Franz and I had to make sure we didn't react, giving Mother something to use against us in court. Still, I had fears about where it would all end, even if Franz and I did manage to keep our cool.

———•••••———

Ten days after Franzie's birth I went down to the yards to draft the cattle, leaving Franzie and Ben in Rachel's care. I had heard complaints from the staff that Bonnie and Paul had been getting in the way while I was gone and I intended to put a stop to that right now. I made it clear they were to only speak to me about work and business and not to interfere with the drafting. I said that if they didn't abide by their roles as observers I would have them back in court so fast they would be blinded.

Franz was the only one who realised how unwell I still felt at this point. He did and didn't want me down in the yards. I told him I would be careful and that if it was too much I would go home. It was worth all the pain in the end. Bonnie and Paul stayed out of the way of the work in the yards from then on.

After the draft I went to speak to Mother about the management issues that needed to be discussed but she screamed that she wasn't speaking to me. 'Great, here we go again!' I thought.

At lunch Bonnie turned up in the kitchen, where I was eating with the staff. She had another list of questions in one hand and her pannikin in the other. I told her again as calmly as possible that I would talk to Mother directly about management issues, but would not communicate via her or via memos or via lawyers. She shoved the list under Franz's and my faces repeatedly while we ate. Each time we would take the list out of her hand and put it down on the table and ignore her.

After lunch I returned to speak to my mother and she again slammed the door in my face.

Another thing that made life incredibly difficult on Bullo during this period was not knowing who would and wouldn't be eating each meal time. Martin and his men had since departed but other people turned up unannounced and left on a regular basis. Joy would cater for anything up to 12 extra and then they wouldn't turn up at all. They would have a barbecue out on Mother's veranda instead. Mother's veranda, which had once been a pleasant retreat, now looked like hillbilly lane.

Joy came to me exasperated. I told her to ask them if they required a meal, and if they turned up to eat after saying they weren't going to then it was their problem. That's what happened that very night. They told Joy they were having a barbecue and then at dinner time all 12 of them lined up in the dining room to be fed. Of course there wasn't enough food. The pannikins of rum had been on the go for some time, and the hungry crowd weren't happy. My mother, who had arrived with them in the dining room, stormed up to me screaming that I couldn't tell her that she couldn't eat in her own house. I said I thought it was reasonable that Joy be informed whether or not they'd be eating. I pointed out that Joy had asked if she would need to cater for everyone and had been told not to do so.

My mother swore at me, spun around and stomped off with all the crowd in tow, with the exception of Bonnie, who stayed to heckle the staff at the dinner table.

'Why does the baby have black hair? All mine look like the father,' she said, pointing to little Franzie. 'Why aren't you sitting next to Franz now Rachel? Have you gone all shy now that Marlee's back? Aren't you getting much now that Marlee's back, or are you screwing someone else?' she slurred.

I was embarrassed. After all, she was my sister. I got up to put the children to bed and get them away from the ugly scene that had become our regular dinner accompaniment. While I was in my room feeding Franzie, Paul cornered poor Rachel. He was eyeball to eyeball with her.

'I know you've been fucking Franz and I have proof,' he said.

Rachel burst into tears and came into our room. I knew that everything Bonnie and Paul were saying was untrue. I know such things do happen, but on my life, I knew it was not the case here. I was sure of Rachel's loyalty and I was sure of my husband. I calmed Rachel down and told her to hang in there. I vowed I was going to have these people removed.

I lay down after another long day, hoping I could put an end to all the madness soon.

Unfortunately there were new trials in store for us. Each night the replacements turned the television up to full volume and watched videos and drank until 2.00 am or later. I closed all our bedroom windows and put a blanket along the bottom of the door to stop some of the noise. After all, we did have a new baby. Franzie, bless him, slept through it all. Franz and I found it a lot harder to switch off. It was okay for them to stay up late as they never got up early, often sleeping until 9.00 or 10.00.

Meredith had arranged through the courts to have a mediation meeting in Darwin with a professional court mediator to try and work out a deal for the sale of Bullo that Mother would accept, and that was actually possible for us to achieve. Mother's lawyers probably would have made it clear to her how unfavourable it would be if she didn't participate in the mediation. For my part I really wanted the mediation to work.

I made a request through Mother's lawyers to use the station's plane for transport up to Darwin for the meeting. I said we would pay the cost of the flight as soon as Mother saw fit to pay all of our outstanding wages. Mother's lawyers must have told her to let us use the plane and to pay everyone immediately. Franz and I were given the plane to use and everyone except me received their wages. Mother chartered her own plane, even though there was room in the station plane and we were more than willing to fly her.

I had resolved that at the mediation I would press for the eviction of the bulk of the replacements, whose numbers had again swollen to 15. To have a couple of bodyguards and observers was one thing, but 15 extra mouths to feed seemed a bit much, and I doubted that anyone could make a reasonable case for their continued presence. It had now reached the point where Lisa and Rachel would clean the guest accommodation and homestead in anticipation of paying guests and the replacements would trash them just before the guests arrived. They ate the food that we had prepared for the guests and seemed to be doing anything they could to make our work impossible.

The mediation took one long day. Mother and her lawyers (her accountant had missed his plane), Franz and I, our lawyers and accountant, and the court mediator sat around a huge round table. Mother refused to look at me or speak to me directly. She worked hard to gain the sympathy of the court mediator, who I noted was well and truly on to her game. We did get her to agree to the terms of a sale, but it was like extracting teeth. We knew we would have a hard job ahead of us to sort out the financing, but in the meantime, we were to be allowed to use the company phone for business calls and the good car for tourist work, and were to have access to the company chequebook to purchase essential parts. Further, there were to be no more than two observers or bodyguards, and the people had to be nominated by my mother and mutually agreed upon with us. My mother agreed to the cast of extra troublemakers departing without a word of protest. I know she was thoroughly sick of them too and was glad to have an excuse to be rid of them. My mother, for all her outlandish behaviour of late, did have her standards and did know what it was to live in a civilised manner. At the end of the mediation I felt exhausted, and depressed that we had to go to such lengths just to get a reasonable agreement.

The next court hearing to test the injunction was set down for the 5th of October in Alice Springs. There was always the risk that the injunction could be lifted at that hearing, allowing Mother to sell to whomever she liked, so now that we'd got Mother to agree to terms of sale, we were desperate to get financing in place before the court date fell. We had 90 days to get an up-to-date valuation done on the property, make a business plan, submit these to the banks and get approval for a loan.

Mother flew back a few days later. Joy left on the next plane out – she'd had enough, and I didn't blame her. Lisa and Rachel agreed to cook if I would come in and cook for the large tourist groups.

The replacements all had to leave within a week according to the agreement we'd reached in the mediation. In the meantime they were drinking from morning to late at night, and had the television blaring around the clock.

The day before they had to leave, the tension on Bullo was bad indeed. They had said that they didn't want to be catered for that evening, and once again turned up at the dining room at the last minute demanding to be fed. I had

Rachel get Ben and Franzie out of the kitchen as trouble was clearly on the way. Bonnie was very, very drunk. She swaggered over to Franz, who was sitting at the kitchen table eating dinner, picked up one of the serving dishes and tipped the entire contents onto his dinner plate and all over the table. She yelled in his face: Had he had enough? Did he want more? Paul yelled at me. They were both drunk and slurring. As hard as it was, we had turned the other cheek until this point and did not intend to start engaging with them now. I have no doubt it made them madder.

Meredith had given me some wise advice. She had worked in the family court and knew how terrible things could become between family members.

'Marlee,' she said, 'no matter how bad things get don't do anything in retaliation. You won't regret following this advice in the end.'

It was to be very good advice but without a doubt the hardest I have ever had to follow. I have a feisty nature and at times I could barely control my temper. I do believe, however, that I have emerged a better person for having done so.

Later that night Paul bailed Tim up against the wall and kept him there for an hour. Tim fled down to the staff quarters too afraid to go back to his own room. Paul took off into the home paddock on the four-wheel-drive motorbike, brandishing a rifle he had brought down from Darwin before parking at the back gate. By now the staff justifiably feared for their lives. One of our stockmen crept past Paul, who was sitting at the back gate with the gun, and tapped very quietly on our window to tell us what had happened. He was clearly frightened so Franz crept back to the staff quarters with him to see if Tim was okay. He was all right, but shaken. Franz told everyone to stay there for the rest of the night and that he would keep an eye on Paul to make sure he didn't go down to the staff quarters. In the meantime I called the police; we all had real fears that someone would get shot that night. The police took note and said they would come out to take statements. It had all gone too far. If they didn't leave in the morning I fully intended to use those statements in court if need be.

The next morning, despite the fact that the staff were still shaken and hadn't slept, Franz and I decided that he should go ahead with the muster he'd planned and get everyone out of the house. Franz was not at all happy about leaving me alone but I promised to keep the door locked until he returned. Tim was upset and had spent most of the night writing a damning statement.

The muster went well and they were finished by lunch time. As they returned, the replacements left in the station's good car as well as one of their own cars. Only Mr Weed remained as an observer, which we were all okay with. Of all the strange and difficult people my mother had brought to Bullo, Mr Weed was the most reasonable and polite. With 14 people departing at once, a blissful peace descended over the house, despite the fact that Mother turned up the television so loud no one could talk in the kitchen.

While my mother evicted the replacements, she did not honour all of the terms she'd agreed to at our mediation. We finally got the station's good car back, but she kept it locked. Nor were we able to use the business phone or fax. To make her comply with the signed agreement we would have to go to court again; after talking to Meredith we decided to instead concentrate our efforts on bringing a final settlement to fruition.

We got on with the work of mustering, drafting and branding while trying to get the evaluation done and prepare a business plan. We still had no current figures for the company so in the end we made our best guesstimates based on the old figures.

The whole affair was well and truly in the media now. Current affairs shows, newspapers and magazines were calling Hunt and Hunt wanting interviews. I put them all on hold until after the hearing in Alice Springs. Neither Franz nor I thought it was a good idea to say anything at this point.

In mid-July we had our first busload of 60 tourists for lunch. I spent several days preparing the food; little Franzie slept in his stroller while I cooked and Rachel helped me juggle the children and the cooking. On the day they arrived we also did a muster of the majority of our breeders, up to 3,500 cows, calves and weaners. It was a busy day with the girls and I catering for the tourists and Franz and the men assisting the helicopter from the ground. Mother breezed in and entertained the guests as if she didn't have a care in the world. She had truly missed her calling; she should have been an actress.

Michael, one of the policemen from Timber Creek, came out to take statements about Paul and Bonnie assaulting Tim, and Paul's threats to Lisa and Rachel. My mother started on Michael as soon as the busload of tourists had departed, bringing up an old allegation that she had made that I had assaulted Bonnie. She had called Michael at 10.30 one Sunday night and told him that I had assaulted Bonnie and she wanted me charged. The incident was supposed to have taken place one week after I'd left hospital following Franzie's birth. (I could barely walk for weeks after the Caesarean.) She had wanted Michael to drive out that night and arrest me, but he had called Franz, and once he'd found out the circumstances had told my mother he didn't think there was any ground to take the matter further. His wife had had a Caesarean so he knew exactly how ridiculous the allegation was.

That afternoon all hands were on deck to start the big draft. Michael called in on the way past to say goodbye; he told us to do our best to keep our hands clean and wished us luck. I thought grimly that we would need it. He dropped off Tim at the yards; he was supposed to leave with Michael but had decided to stay on and help us. I was thinking we may have to adopt him. His help was well appreciated as we had a huge number of cows to draft. We were drafting until late the next day and ended up with a total of 3,200 head, not a bad effort for a skeleton crew. Normally we would have had at least four other stockmen

in addition to Franz and myself in the yards – now we
had two. Dan had sprained his ankle which meant Franz
and one other stockman had to cope with most of the work.
I still couldn't run or climb at this stage so we had struggled to get through the draft. I worked the drafting gate,
Lisa, who ran the house, and Tim, a guest, worked the eight
round yard gates and Rachel watched the children for me.
At the end of each long day we had to cook for ourselves
as my mother refused to hire another cook to replace Joy.
We spent the next week taking turns cooking, and trucking and branding the cattle.

We continually received faxes from Mother's lawyers
complaining that not enough work was being done and
that we were hiding cattle and selling them on the side.
Basically, Mother spent every day faxing her lawyers, who
faxed our lawyers, who faxed us. Each night after work
I answered all the questions and allegations and faxed our
lawyers, who faxed her lawyers, who faxed her. Meredith told me we had to answer everything even though it
drove me up the wall. I trusted her advice and did what
she asked. So far everything Meredith had told me had
been spot on.

—•◦•—

By the first week of August we had completed our business
plan and had had an evaluation of the property done. We
were finally ready to submit everything to the banks. I
made an official request to Mother's lawyers to use the
station car to drive to Darwin, and Mother was told to
let us. Franz, the children, Rachel and I drove the 850 kilometres to Darwin through the night so that we could make
our first appointment in the morning. Rachel had a week's
worth of time off owing to her and she said she would
use it to watch the children for us while we met the lawyers
and submitted our plan to the banks. We had tourists
staying that night and Lisa said she could handle the next

morning's breakfast for them. I don't know what we would have done without Rachel and Lisa.

Over the next few days we submitted our business plan to every major bank, then attended another mediation meeting.

We were told that Mother wanted to increase the sale price of Bullo from what we'd all previously agreed upon. In the end Meredith thought that we should largely ignore this and do everything we could to raise the finance for the original agreed-upon sale price. She thought that if we got the money on the table, it may make Mother see things in a different light.

I knew in my heart that Mother would not settle with us if she could get the injunction lifted. Our impending court date – only two months away – weighed heavily on my mind. We were relying on the banks now.

Back in Bullo, we got everything ready for our next muster at Bull Creek. One by one the banks called back declining to provide the finance we needed. My heart sank lower with each call.

Mother sent another of her letters through her lawyers; now she wanted to sell the cattle, the plane and the helicopter. If she did this there would be no way we would ever get finance because the station's assets, and our means of earning money to make our repayments, would be diminished. My mother argued that the selling of these assets was to cover Bullo's debts. We asked for proof of these debts but she declined to provide any. Fortunately, it turned out that the injunction prevented her selling anything other than our normal cattle sales. This did not improve Mother's mood but it was a great relief to us.

We did the Bull Creek muster and then the next day drafted the cattle. We weren't the most able-bodied of drafting teams. I still wasn't back to my pre-pregnancy mobility and Dan was still barely able to walk on his sprained ankle. It never rains but it pours. A very large bull hit one of the yard gates, the chain snapped and the gate came back with the full force on Franz's leg. He fell to the ground in the cleanskin pen, one of the most dangerous as it houses bulls that have never been mustered before. He was doubled up in agony. We got him out of there fast before he had several holes in him as well. I was sure, seeing how hard the gate had hit his leg, that it was fractured. Franz struggled on all day but in much pain.

Over the next week and a bit Franz's leg got worse; he couldn't sleep from the pain. Finally, he went into Kununurra on his day off to have his leg x-rayed. It was fractured. He came home with his leg in a splint, limping on crutches. The daily fax of complaints from Mother's lawyers – that none of us were working and that we were hiding cattle – got to me that night. I called Meredith, who had given me her home phone number, in tears. 'Is there no end to this woman? Franz has been working on a fractured leg, Dan shouldn't even be walking on his ankle, I'm still recovering from a Caesarean and looking after our new baby,' I blurted. I was sobbing out of frustration and sheer tiredness. Anyone who has been sleep deprived will know where I was coming from. 'We can't do more than we are!'

Meredith calmed me down and told me to hang in there. It was getting harder and harder to turn the other cheek and keep going but that's what Meredith once again advised me to do.

Ten days before our court hearing, another one of our prospective financiers had dropped out. We were fast running out of time and banks. Things were not looking good – then Bonnie turned up out of the blue in a Kombi van, with seven children inside. Mother's former bodyguard, Jeanette, had also reappeared. We were back to ten extra people, including Weed. The new arrivals immediately dirtied the just-cleaned guest rooms, pulled out all the linen that had been packed away in mothballs for the wet season, took over the house and ate all the food I had prepared for the guests. The guests we had with us at the time, who were very nice people from New Zealand, were shocked. I kept the kitchen and one corner of the homestead clean, apologised profusely and gave them a discount for having to put up with the disturbance. After a few days, Bonnie and the children piled into the van and yelled as they drove past me in the yards, 'We'll be back!' Jeanette and Weed remained at Bullo.

The guest rooms were in an appalling state. There was a whole box of soiled nappies with maggots crawling out of them; rotten food in corners; and the children had wet the sheets. It was beyond me that someone I was related to and had grown up with could behave this way. I told Rachel not to touch a thing. None of us were cleaning up after those filthy people again. I came out the next morning to find all the dirty dishes neatly stacked in with the clean plates. The same had been done with the dirty cutlery; it was all mixed up with the clean. God, I so wanted for all this to end soon.

My mother hadn't paid wages to any of the staff for over two months. When Rachel went to my mother and asked for her wages Mother told her that she had to say 'Please, Mrs Henderson, could I have my wages?' or she wouldn't get them. Rachel thought this was quite funny, and did ask Mother in the required way. Mother wrote a cheque, but spelt both Rachel's Christian and family names incorrectly and screwed up the cheque like you would before throwing rubbish in the bin.

We were down to two possible financiers: the Elders Bank and the National Australia Bank. After that we were finished. I was constantly feeling sick in the stomach with nerves. What a mess our lives had become. They were barely recognisable.

The date for our showdown in court in Alice Springs approached. We made an official request to use the car to drive to Darwin, from where we would fly to Alice. It was granted. I left Ben with Rachel and took little Franzie with us because I was still feeding him. I left Bullo with a very heavy heart. If the judge lifted the injunction we would be returning only to pack our belongings and leave for good. Franz and I had already made inquiries about renting a container to store our things in and were looking for a job for Franz to tide us over until we could find our feet. It was a devastating thought that I could be leaving my home and losing my entire life's work in a matter of days.

Franz was supportive, understanding and encouraging: 'We will be all right no matter what happens. We have each other; we have our boys.'

He was so right. Still, I was terribly down and depressed that our lives had come to this. My mother was rather more cheerful, and quite smug, as she flew out on her chartered flight for Alice Springs.

The Elders Bank called us in Darwin and rejected our application. Franz collapsed with a terrible flu at about the same time. He couldn't even sit up he was so weak.

Our only chance now was the National Australia Bank. And it was only two days before the court hearing.

The day before our flight to Alice Springs, the National called and said that they could do a deal. Our plan would need a little work to fit their guidelines, but they would agree to the finance. I cannot begin to describe how I felt. Elation! I had our lawyers contact my mother's lawyers to inform them that we had finance approved and that we should avoid the cost of another court hearing. In short, we should all now settle and get on with our lives.

My mother had other ideas. She wanted her day in court.

Franz and I, along with little Franzie and our lawyers, were booked on a 5.00 am flight to Alice Springs, which would give us plenty of time to get to our afternoon court hearing. We had settled into our seats when it was announced that the plane had a fuel leak and that we all had to disembark. The flight was pushed forward an hour, every hour for the next nine hours. Finally they got us seats on another plane. The catch was that we couldn't take our luggage; it would follow the next day. The lawyers unpacked their numerous bags full of books and documents and took only what they knew they would definitely need. I grabbed the bare minimum I needed to keep Franzie clothed and off we went. Little Franzie was so good through all this. Meredith's assistant, Danielle, said, 'When I have a baby I want one just like Franzie.'

We made it into Alice at 5.00 pm and rushed to the court – we were late for our hearing. My mother's lawyers accused us of engineering the whole thing. Our lawyers were not at all pleased and replied that if they would like a letter from Qantas to confirm the reasons for our delay it could be arranged. I found it almost comical. Did they really think Qantas would hold up a jet for nine hours for us? Wow, if we had such power we wouldn't be in the predicament that had brought us to Alice in the first place. The judge was not impressed and told my mother's lawyers to pull their heads in. Outside the courtroom, Mother's lawyers told Meredith's assistant, Danielle, with great confidence that the whole case would be over in half a day's time; they would have the injunction lifted and that would be that. The media was waiting for us outside the court. We walked straight past and went wearily to our hotel.

In court the next day, the discussion centred on the most significant point of law to be decided, the 'balance of convenience', or basically, who would be the most inconvenienced by the injunction remaining in place until we came to either an out-of-court settlement or a full-blown court case?

On the second day, to our surprise, the judge said that he had already made his decision in regard to the balance of convenience issue. We were all caught off guard, as judges can take weeks or months to come to such a decision. I sat on the edge of the hard court bench not even able to breath I was so tense.

'With regard to the issue of balance of convenience, if I lift the injunction, Mrs Ranacher will be inconvenienced for the rest of her life; if I leave it on, Mrs Henderson will be temporarily inconvenienced.'

I had tears streaming down my face; the relief was indescribable. I looked at our lawyers, who both had watery eyes as well. On the other side of the court, if looks could have killed Mother's lawyers would have been dead.

The judge set down a date in May the next year for a court case in the event that we didn't settle matters before then. The story made the evening news and was in the papers the next day.

19

WE SLEPT WELL THAT NIGHT FOR THE first time in a long time, knowing we still had a home to go back to. We wanted to get everything settled as quickly as possible so while we drove home to Bullo. Meredith, her assistant, Danielle, and David got busy doing due diligence checks on the company and checking out tax implications and stamp duty.

Though the Darwin branch of the National Australia Bank had approved our loan, it now had to be approved by their head office. On the 27th of October we got the phone call we had been waiting for. The head office had approved the finance as well. My mother was still away at the time but the bank called her and told her the news. She returned to Bullo the same afternoon. She wouldn't speak to us.

On the 31st of October our lawyers put an official offer of purchase to my mother, making it clear we couldn't offer more because the bank wouldn't approve any more. It was a fair price, the price we had all agreed upon. I thought that Mother would find some way to make life difficult. Unfortunately I was right.

Out of the blue, Bonnie, Paul (Bonnie's partner), a friend of Weed's and eight children arrived and moved straight into the guest rooms I had cleaned and made up for two businessmen from New Zealand who were coming to discuss bringing in groups of 30 people at a time the following year. I had to make up two more rooms for the New Zealanders. Bonnie and the others were as unpleasant as ever and my mother became particularly difficult once they arrived. Franz and I apologised to the New Zealanders and asked them to look past these people and the current atmosphere as it wouldn't be like this if the sale went through. They stayed for one day while Franz showed them around. I am happy to say that they had faith in us and have since sent three tour groups from Stanford University in the US.

Paul, our second stockman, and Rachel – convinced that they would never see their wages – had finally resigned. Franz didn't want to drive them into town because he didn't want to leave me alone with Bonnie and the others, so Paul and Rachel drove the station Toyota into Kununurra themselves, and left it with a friend of ours so that we could pick it up later when we went in to pick up a food order.

The day after the New Zealand businessmen left Bonnie and her partner, Weed, his friend and Jeanette packed up. As well as their own possessions, they also loaded up the pool furniture, lounge chairs from the house, some statues and tables. My mother said that they were 'gifts'. I had suspected that something like this might happen so had locked the guest bedding away, and locked all the guest rooms so they couldn't take the furniture out of them. Personally I didn't care as long as they left for good.

At the last court hearing it had been agreed that Franz and I would submit a daily work report to Mother. Initially Franz had just been giving it to Mother but we had received a fax from her lawyers accusing Franz of not doing the daily report and hence being in breach of a court order. Now, we gave daily reports to everyone: Mother, her lawyers and our lawyers. I could only wonder at what would be thrown at me next. I really wished Mother would direct her energies to settling the sale.

In late November, an article that Sara and Bonnie had participated in together came out in *New Idea* magazine. It said ridiculous things, such as that my mother lived alone with only the company of her dogs for two years, and that she was doing everything in her power to help us. 'If she's been helping us so far I'd hate to see what she'd do if she ended up in opposition to us,' I thought after reading the article.

On the 20th of December we were still waiting for my mother to settle. The bank's original offer had expired by this stage so we had to get an extension. I had so wanted to have everything settled before Christmas. I wanted to enjoy some quiet time with my husband and sons, as sad as it would have been given all that had happened between me and my mother. I was feeling very depressed. All the energy that I'd managed to summon to get this far was gone, and still there was no resolution in sight. For the life of me I couldn't understand why mother was dragging it out. She had her offer. She could take her payment and go, just as she'd wanted.

I called David and asked that he speak to her lawyers about the settlement, and I also suggested to them that Mother go to Aunty Sue's in Queensland for Christmas. She didn't really need to be here to do the settlement and it would be better for everyone if she went to join her sister, not least of all for her. David agreed. Her lawyers agreed. My mother refused.

Christmas came and went. Little Franzie didn't really know what was going on. We made the best of it for Ben. Franz took him out onto the airstrip first thing on Christmas Day to look for reindeer tracks. The sight of them peering intently at the ground, Franz with such a serious look on his face, warmed my heart. Ben came back with eyes as wide as saucers. Yep, he and Pa had definitely found some, just as children everywhere had found evidence of reindeers and Santa. It was this sort of special moment that gave me the strength and will to push on.

The offer we had put to Mother relied partly on vendor finance, upon which she had placed a number of conditions. We would borrow part from the bank and owe Mother for part. We sifted through the many, many items, agreed to what was reasonable and declined what was, in our opinion, unreasonable.

By mid-January we were still trying to settle with my mother. Our lawyers and accountants would do their part in a matter of days; we would hand over the contract to her side for weeks. She would not speak to us, stayed in the office all day with her dogs and most of the time she only came out at night. She had her own fridge with all her own food and she cooked for herself now. She hadn't eaten anything I cooked in months. I was concerned about her state of mind but it seemed that I had to accept there was nothing I could do but save ourselves.

We kept working and waiting. Franz serviced the equipment in the workshop and I mowed the lawns, slashed the airstrip and started to teach Ben as he was now enrolled with the Katherine school of the air.

It was the wet season. The road had been closed to all vehicles since December; by late January food was getting a bit low. We still had beef and barramundi and some tinned food – I had run out of flour so we had no fresh bread or any fresh fruit or vegetables. Mother had been ordering in food on the mail plane weekly and keeping it in her personal fridge. Franz hadn't had any wages for nearly six months now, and I hadn't had any for a year. We were flat broke. There was no way we could afford to have food flown in on the mail plane. We asked her to let us use the plane to fly to Kununurra to pick up some food. She refused.

Regardless of the situation we still did whatever we could to promote tourism later in the year in the event that we had settled by then. I was certainly beginning to wonder if our efforts were all a waste of time. Australian Pacific bus tours had been bringing in people for the last two years but they wouldn't renew the contract until the sale was settled, and their brochures had to be printed now. The Australian Pacific contract was worth a great deal to us. If we lost it we wouldn't be able to meet our first year's payment to mother – and of course if we defaulted she could sell us up.

The next thing that came to our attention was that mail we knew was coming never reached us. I called the postmaster, who told me to call the police. They counted and flagged the mail, and indeed, our mail was going astray. I filed this with the police but hoped I would never have to take it further. I didn't want more trouble; I just wanted to get on with our lives.

In late February we got an early morning call from the Timber Creek police and I immediately thought, 'Oh God, what has she accused us of now?' Thankfully my fears were groundless. The Victoria River had flooded and broken its banks. More than 600 people had to be evacuated from stations and communities along the river and they wanted Franz to come and help in the helicopter. There is no way in the world Mother wanted Franz to fly the helicopter but she couldn't refuse a police request. Franz was away for three days evacuating people and flying the police around.

He came home but was still on alert because the police were worried that the town of Timber Creek would go under next. I was so glad to have Franz home. I had missed him dreadfully. He was a lot more his old self having been out of the hellish place we had been locked in for so long. The flood waters peaked at the Victoria River Bridge at 21.3 metres. Everyone held their breath to see if Timber Creek would go under. Luckily the tides turned, the flood waters receded and Timber Creek was spared.

On the 25th of February my mother left Bullo on a charter flight for Darwin. We had finally reached a point where our respective lawyers thought we could settle, so we were all going to Darwin to thrash things out, and hopefully complete the sale. I was so pessimistic by now that I wasn't going to believe it until it happened. Jeanette arrived on the plane that came to pick my mother up. Franz and I despaired. Why would she bring this woman back here if she really intended to settle? We could not with any degree of comfort leave the property like this, so we called a friend, who agreed to watch over Bullo for us while we were in Darwin. We made an official request through the lawyers to use the station plane as the road was closed. When we set off for Darwin we hadn't had any fresh fruit or vegetables for eight weeks.

We spent the next harrowing week arguing about all the stipulations my mother had listed and the fact that she had requested more money. D-day was delayed again and again until finally, on the 2nd of March, we met at the National Australia Bank's conference room to sign the papers. I borrowed a friend's nanny to look after the children and Franz and I went to face the fray.

Because of the complicated structure of the company it took six hours to sign all the papers; at one point there were 17 people in the room. Mother sat through it all sour-faced and silent. At 2.00 pm everyone else sighed in relief as the last document was signed. Mother and her accountant led the way out without a word to Franz or I. As she passed me I looked at her and she gave me a look that chilled me to the core. I believe she thought that we wouldn't last a year.

I heard her say to her accountant as they left the room: 'Oh yes, the media will be waiting.' She drew herself up to her full height to meet the cameras and walked out the door. On that hot March afternoon there was not a soul in the street outside the Darwin National Australia Bank. It was completely deserted. As I watched her through the large glass doors I saw her shoulders slump; I could see she was shocked.

Franz and I stayed and talked to our new bank manager about details such as accounts and credit card facilities so that we could get started in running our business at Bullo.

As we walked out into the street I felt sad, tired and empty. There were no winners. There was no victory in this ugly dispute. The past year of our lives had been full of bitterness, and wasted time and money. None of what had happened needed to have happened. That was what upset me the most. I was now estranged from my sisters and my mother. My father was long gone. This was in some ways the conclusion to that journey Mother had made with Bonnie and me all those years ago when we had first set foot on Bullo and sat in the shed waiting for my father to whisk us away to the homestead that didn't yet exist.

The task ahead was daunting, as it must have been then for my parents. Franz and I owed the bank millions and my mother another seven-figure amount on top of that. All we had really gained was the opportunity to save Bullo. We hadn't actually saved it yet. One slip and I knew my mother would sell us up without hesitation.

'Well, where do we start?' Franz's question brought me back to the present. I looked up at this kind, generous, patient, strong man who had been my rock through all the turmoil. Not once had he swayed in his loyal support. I loved and admired him well beyond words. I smiled.

'I have about 120 things on my list that we need to do in the next couple of days, but first how about lunch? I'm starving!'

Franz took my hand and we walked together, lost in our own thoughts on the first day of the rest of our lives.

ACKNOWLEDGEMENTS

I DO NOT BELIEVE THAT ANYONE gets through life without the help and guidance of others. I have been particularly lucky in this regard.

My first thanks go to our lawyers, David de L Winter, Meredith Day, Danielle Howard, Judith Kelly and Cris Kourakis QC. People rarely have anything good to say about lawyers. I was blessed to find and work with this group of absolute professionals who despite working within the often difficult boundaries of the legal system have not lost compassion and generosity. They helped me in one of my life's most difficult periods and without their wise counsel and patience my family and I would not be here on Bullo today.

My thanks to Karen Green and David Timbrell who lead us through the accounting minefield and with very limited information helped us put together a realistic business plan to present to the banks.

Of all the banks we approached (and we did approach all of them) Will Proft of the National Bank Darwin, was the one who made it happen. He understands that businesses are both money and people. He did the hard work of bringing the financial and bank guidelines in line with the complicated human dynamics of our case and made the deal work, for which I am very grateful.

At Bullo, on the bloody battlefront that was our home, my deepest admiration and thanks to our staff and my friends, Lisa Willmott, Rachel Winspear, Dan Grant, Paul Wrigley and Joy Chappell. They stood by us through some very dark times. I don't know how I would have managed without them.

To Berace and Marlo Taylor both thanks and admiration. They took me into their home when I was alone and pregnant. They are the good people in life that give us all hope when we are down.

My thanks to Tim Arnold who took up our cause and helped us. To Aaron Healey who was such a good friend when we needed one. Jeff and Kylie hunt our good friends of Air Frontier, who let Franz use one of their aircraft to come and see Little Franzie after he was born.

The list of people who helped us in some way is long and I acknowledge them all with special mention to John and Pauline Kirby, George Iro, Bernie O'Kane, Jackie Meyer, Dean Thompson, Arthur Handsbury, Megan and Drew Kluska and Tim Scott.

This book and I definitely owe much to my literary agent Deb Callaghan who I thoroughly enjoyed working with. The whole process was much more cathartic after answering Deb's probing questions. Her queries and comments on the original manuscript left me in fits of laughter at times – City people!

My thanks to the team at Random House who have made the whole very daunting publishing process seem easy. It was a pleasure to work with such a professional, enthusiastic and committed group of people.

I wish to pay special tribute to both my parents, for that matter, all parents. It is the hardest job in the world to get right. I would not be who and where I am today without mine. I believe in their own capacity they did their best as parents and one can ask no more than that. My unconventional upbringing was full of amazing people and places that have indelibly colored my memory in my roller-coaster life. It has given me the courage to follow my convictions, to dare to be different, the strength to get up and keep going when I had been knocked down.

I have had the full keyboard of life, good bad and otherwise. The sweetest key, Franz and our boys. I count myself as truly fortunate.